W9-CYD-016

GOING TO SCHOOL IN SOUTH ASIA

GOING TO SCHOOL IN SOUTH ASIA

EDITED BY AMITA GUPTA

The Global School Room
Alan Sadovnik and Susan Semel, Series Editors

GREENWOOD PRESS
Westport, Connecticut • London

Library of Congress Cataloging-in-Publication Data

Going to school in South Asia / edited by Amita Gupta.
  p. cm.— (The global school room, ISSN 1933–6101)
  Includes bibliographical references and index.
  ISBN 0–313–33553–2 (alk. paper)
  1. Education—South Asia—Cross-cultural studies. 2. Education—History—South Asia—Cross-cultural studies.
  I. Gupta, Amita, 1959–
  LA1144.5.G65   2007
  370.954–dc22   2006038693

British Library Cataloguing in Publication Data is available.

Copyright © 2007 by Amita Gupta

Library of Congress Catalog Card Number: 2006038693
ISBN-10: 0–313–33553–2
ISBN-13: 978–0–313–33553–2
ISSN: 1933–6101

First published in 2007

Greenwood Press, 88 Post Road West, Westport, CT 06881
An imprint of Greenwood Publishing Group, Inc.
www.greenwood.com

Printed in the United States of America

The paper used in this book complies with the
Permanent Paper Standard issued by the National
Information Standards Organization (Z39.48–1984).

10 9 8 7 6 5 4 3 2 1

This book is dedicated to the loving memory of Atul Diesh, who sailed the seven seas and is deeply missed by all who knew him; and to all the South Asian victims of the tsunami and the earthquake.

CONTENTS

SERIES FOREWORD

Over the past three decades, with globalization becoming a dominant force, the world wide emphasis on schooling has accelerated. However, a historical perspective teaches us that global trends in schooling are by no means a recent phenomenon. The work of neo-institutional sociologists such as John Meyer and his colleagues has demonstrated that the development of mass public educational systems became a world wide trend in the 19th century and most nations' schools systems go back significantly further. *The Global School Room* is intended to provide students with an understanding of the similarities and differences among educational systems throughout the world from a historical perspective.

Although comparative and international educational research has provided an understanding of the many similarities in school systems across nations and cultures, it has also indicated the significant differences. Schools reflect societies and their cultures and therefore there are significant differences among different nations' school systems and educational practices. Another purpose of this series is to examine these similarities and differences.

The series is organized into nine volumes, each looking at the history of the school systems in countries on one continent or sub-continent. The series consists of volumes covering schooling in the following regions:

North America
Latin America
Europe
Sub-Saharan Africa
North Africa and the Middle East
South Asia

Central Asia
East Asia
Oceania

As the first volume in the series to be published, *Going to School in South Asia* edited by Amita Gupta provides an important and timely examination of the educational systems in India, Afghanistan, Bangladesh, Bhutan, Maldives, Nepal, Pakistan, and Sri Lanka. Through the history of the educational systems in each country and an analysis of contemporary systems, the authors provide a rich description of how schooling is related to national culture, religion, identity, social, political and economic structures, and economic development. Moreover, the book illustrates the importance of historical, philosophical, and sociological perspectives in understanding the similarities and differences among societies and their schools. Finally, the book provides everyday examples of what schools in each country are like and how curriculum and teaching practices reflect the larger cultural, social, religious, and historical patterns of each society.

Going to School in South Asia is emblematic of the series in that it provides students with an understanding that schooling needs to be understood in the context of each local culture, rather than viewed ethnocentrically from a U.S. or Western perspective. We often tend to make broad generalizations about other continents and assume that culture and schooling are uniform across countries. This book demonstrates the importance of examining national systems to uncover differences, as well as similarities.

In *The Japanese Educational Challenge* (1987), Merry White argued that the purpose of studying another country' educational system is not necessarily to copy it, but rather to learn from the lessons of other societies, and where appropriate to use these lessons to improve our own schools, but only in the context of our own culture and schools. *Going to School in South Asia* provides many important lessons, but it also cautions us to understand these in the contexts of national and cultural differences.

We invite you to explore schooling around the world, beginning in South Asia and then the rest of the world, as subsequent volumes are published.

Alan Sadovnik and Susan Semel

REFERENCE

White, M. (1987). The Japanese Educational Challenge. New York: The Free Press.

ACKNOWLEDGMENTS

First and foremost, I would like to acknowledge the vision of the series editors, Susan Semel and Alan Sadovnik, and the editors at Greenwood Publishing for realizing the importance of a book series that centers around schooling issues on a larger scale such as this. In these times of increasing international partnerships and businesses, as cultural boundaries between nations are becoming less restrictive and more permeable, it is vital to bring to all students, and those of education in particular, a more global perspective which can only lead to a better understanding of the world-views, ways of life and educational values of people who live in different parts of the world.

I would, of course, like to thank all the authors for their valuable contributions. The writing of this book has passed through some turmoil and turbulences in the very regions it was exploring. During the time it took to put this book together South Asia experienced some of the worst natural disasters in world history: the tsunami which devastated Sri Lanka, Maldives and parts of southern India; and the earthquake in Pakistan and northwest India that killed thousands of people and left countless others homeless in remote mountainous regions. South Asia also experienced violent acts of terror during this period: the train bombs in Mumbai; the bomb attacks in New Delhi on the eve of Diwali, the most prominent Hindu festival; a series of bomb attacks in Bangladesh and Pakistan; continuing violence and bombing in Afghanistan; the on-going acts of violence by Maoist insurgents in Nepal and by the Tamil Tigers in Sri Lanka. These are only some of the many such events, but despite it all educational efforts in these countries continue and devoted educators such as the authors in this book have worked relentlessly in their own professional and personal commitment to education and education-related issues in the countries they have written about. I thank them for their commitment and attention to detail and time.

I wish to acknowledge many others: the colleagues and friends who provided valuable help in leading me to those who contributed to this book: Kate Menken, Marina Fernando, Yen Yen Woo, and the late Dr. Pieter Steyn; Debby Adams at Greenwood and my copy editor John Clement; and the much appreciated technical support of Henny Wong and Chi Ng at CCNY's School of Education.

I would like to thank sincerely my parents, my grandfather, extended family and friends who have once more patiently borne with me as I struggled to meet book deadlines for a second year in a row. Finally, I want to acknowledge again the continued support and love of Nihaar and Naman: my sons, my pride and joy, my brightest stars.

Working on putting this book together has increased my own understanding of the complex and multi-layered relationships within each of the South Asian countries, and it has been truly a gratifying and educative process.

Chapter 1

INTRODUCTION: CULTURE, CURRICULUM, AND POINTS OF INTERSECTION

Amita Gupta

South Asia is the term that has been given to the world region comprising of eight countries, the largest of them being India. The other countries starting from the west and going clockwise are Afghanistan, Pakistan, Nepal, Bhutan, Bangladesh, Sri Lanka, and the group of islands known as Maldives. All these countries have an interesting but complex relationship defined by shared historical and geographical influences, as well as by the similarities and differences in cultural values and philosophical worldviews. Although South Asia is considered as one geographical region, each country has been independently influenced by deep-rooted political, socio-cultural, philosophical, and spiritual beliefs that are reflected in the languages, religions, and the general way of life of each country's population. However, despite the religious diversity within each of the countries there are distinct groups that constitute the dominant population and give each country its special characteristics. India and Nepal are predominantly Hindu societies; Pakistan, Afghanistan, Bangladesh, and the Maldives are predominantly Islamic societies; and Sri Lanka and Bhutan are predominantly Buddhist societies. The political structure of the governments in each of these countries is also different. India, Sri Lanka, Maldives and Bangladesh function as democracies with elected prime ministers and presidents; Nepal and Bhutan have essentially been monarchies and each is currently headed by a king; Pakistan is currently headed by a military president; and Afghanistan is in the process of shifting from under the control of local warlords to a democratic government. Political strife and local insurgencies in most of these countries pose major obstacles that the respective governments have had to work to overcome. However, despite these specific historical and political differences, the ancient period in history saw numerous collective and overlapping influences on these nations. The education and school curriculum in most of the individual South Asian countries in the earliest times were mostly informed by the teachings of the *Veda* which were the scriptures of

Ancient India and which form the basis of the Hindu religion. The same caste system that originated in ancient India is also seen to have existed in the historical past of most of the other South Asian countries. Another overlap in many of their histories is the long lasting colonizing impact of the Europeans including the Portuguese, Dutch, French, and the British. One of the legacies of the colonized rule was the spread of the English language in popular education, and this can be seen to have occurred most extensively in India.

South Asia is a world region with a long and continuous history that covers more than 5000 years. Excavations in the early 20th century had revealed ruins of an advanced civilization that was said to date back to about 2500 B.C. But more recent archaeological findings and excavations of artifacts such as scripted tablets have dated this civilization even further back to 3300 B.C. This civilization is known as the Indus Valley Civilization and numerous cities belonging to this ancient society have been excavated and have been determined as being spread across a vast area of land that lies in what is now Pakistan and western India. The two sites that have been studied in greatest detail are Mohenjo Daro and Harappa, and these are considered to be two of the earliest urban developments in the world. These cities were carefully planned with straight streets and houses built in even rows, and a well-designed underground sewage and drainage system. The most fascinating discovery was the Great Bath at Mohenjo Daro, a public bathing and water storage facility built in the center of the city. Other artifacts excavated include a range of beautifully designed jewelry in gold and silver; clay figures of goddesses, humans, birds, and animals; other items of pottery; measuring weights in various denominations; and official seals engraved in an archaic form of the Vedic language which was a precursor of the classical Sanskrit language. With the discovery of these seals and weights it becomes apparent that this must have been a literate society familiar with language and mathematical concepts. This indicates that some form of formal or informal education must have been available to people. The narrative below provides a glimpse of the way of life that might have been possibly lived by the people of Mohenjo Daro.[1]

It was about 2000 B.C. The ancient city of Mohenjo Daro lay on the banks of the river that is now called Indus. The houses were constructed in neat rows and had flat roofs, with the doors opening out on a central courtyard. Each house had a private bath, and there were also public baths in the city. A well-designed sewage system of underground pipes and channels built out of baked bricks carried the waste water away and kept the city clean. In the central courtyard, the women cut vegetables, ground spices, boiled rice, and washed clothes. In the afternoon they gossiped and spun cotton. The men were mostly craftsmen—potters, brick-makers, goldsmiths, coppersmiths, boat builders, stone carvers. The children played actively around them. Hirap and his sister liked to play with the little animal figures carved out of clay and soapstone—the elephant, bull, tiger, rhinoceros and alligator. Their friend Zanzar was a potter's son, and he showed them a clay whistle in the shape of a bird that his father had made for him. Another friend, Zebar, was the son of a prosperous merchant who bought gold necklaces from the goldsmith and traded them to the people of another valley far away by the river Nile. The friends walked together and once out of town they passed fields of barley and wheat cultivated by villagers who lived in mud huts. As they walked they passed Brihadrath who was the priest's son. He could not play and join in their games always because he had to spend a lot of his time learning hymns, and run errands as a messenger telling people of coming festivals. He told them he had just eaten lunch—barley bread and date pickle—and could not yet run with them down to the river where they were headed. By the river was the boat yard where large boats were built. The city had extensive trade connections and heavy traffic by way of sea as well as land. The children sought out their friend Kapardi the shipmaster. He told them of distant places from where came some of the most beautiful items. He said that gold came from the southeast (from modern day Mysore) and a lovely green stone (emerald) came from the south. Caravans traveled to the far north (Afghanistan) to get a brilliant blue stone (lapis). Kapardi also told them that the best dates came from another land of brick-built cities which lay by the banks of the Tigris and Euphrates rivers. The children listened in fascination to all of these stories of travel and trade, of rivers and valleys, and then as dusk began to darken the summer skies, they made their way back home.

SOCIETY AND CULTURAL VALUES

Most research and discussions on education and schooling in South Asia usually center on projects and initiatives that are aimed to develop educational opportunities for the disadvantaged in these "developing and third world countries." International organizations such as the United Nations and the World Bank, as well as several private foundations and non-governmental organizations focus their attempts within rural and low poverty regions of these nations, and work toward making schooling more accessible to those children who are denied schools, and toward improving school facilities and the quality of education where they are currently provided. Many of these educational projects have been designed and managed by experts who have been trained in the educational institutions of Europe and North America. In many instances educational objectives that have been identified for classrooms of the West are taken as the basis or models for those methodologies that are to be implemented in schools across South Asia. Often, these ideas have been rooted in the core concepts of Western educational approaches and developmental and learning theories that emerged in the early years of the 20th century in response to the specific needs and new challenges of America's changing culture and society, and thus these approaches find varying degrees of resistance and/or failure in their implementation in the South Asian contexts. Despite their current levels of poverty, many of the South Asian countries have had long traditions of education and schooling. It would behoove not only Western researchers and organizations but also local agencies in their efforts to expand and sustain educational opportunities to first understand the historical development of schooling in South Asia, and the nature of the social, cultural, philosophical, and spiritual forces that shaped and prioritized educational objectives in this region. Questions to explore would be why and how people clustered and communities developed; why certain cultural characteristics and traits have endured for centuries; what the general public of each society has wanted its children to learn; why certain societies have grown technologically and economically while others have not; and so forth. At the same time, it would be prudent to recognize that any historical examination is ultimately a reconstruction, an attempt to achieve understanding or give meaning, serving to illuminate particular aspects of a phenomenon.

Intimate connections are seen to exist between a culture's philosophical values and its educational values that shape schooling and curriculum in that society. For the purpose of this discussion it becomes necessary to clarify the definitions of culture and values. Culture has been defined most extensively within the field of anthropology which in itself entails the study and examination of a way of life. According to one of the accepted definitions "culture consists in patterned ways of thinking, feeling and reacting, acquired and transmitted mainly by symbols, constituting the distinctive achievements of human groups, including their embodiments in artifacts; the essential core of culture consists of traditional (i.e. historically derived and selected) ideas and especially their attached values."[2] One analogy that might be used to understand the significance of culture is to compare it to personality: if personality determines the identity of an individual, then culture determines the identity of a human group, and this group can be anything from a nation, a region, an organization, or a family. Although there can be many variations within a large group, subcultures within a society do, however, share common traits with other subcultures of that society and it is these common traits that make the members of one society distinct from others. The intra-cultural differences within a society are usually smaller than the inter-cultural differences between different societies. Closely connected to a society's culture are its values and these can be described as people's beliefs or tendencies to prefer one state of affairs over others. Cultural values are thus seen as being manifest in the skills, attitudes, and knowledge held to be important or prioritized by a cultural group; and determine how people interact with each other, solve problems, make decisions, communicate with each other, negotiate, how they view the concept of time, approach task accomplishment, and so forth.

Additionally, it is also helpful to view culture as an iceberg with all the cultural aspects occupying the space within this iceberg both above and below the surface of the water.[3] The exposed tip of the iceberg is the smaller and more superficial part, and symbolizes the more visible and tangible aspects of culture such as food, clothing, art, music, physical appearance, and so forth. The hidden part symbolizes the harder-to-perceive and the deeper underlying values, beliefs, and attitudes of the culture including such aspects as spiritual beliefs; notions of beauty and modesty; child rearing practices; patterns of interaction with superiors, subordinates and peers; work habits; relationship and patterns of interaction with family and friends; attitudes toward interdependence and individualism; implications of specific gestures and body language; speech and conversational patterns in various contexts; definition of personal space; conception of self in relation to others; patterns of demonstrating and handling emotions; notions of leadership; definition of sin; understanding of time; status accorded by gender, age, occupation, educational level, class, caste, kinship; concept of childhood and the image of the child; styles of teaching and learning; styles of eating; meanings given to the idea of guests and hospitality; and so forth. The idea of the iceberg demonstrates clearly that our first and most conscious perceptions of any culture, those perceptions that we most readily construct, comprise only the tip of what is contained in that iceberg. The more important aspects of that cultural iceberg lie hidden from view and need much time, effort, and sensitivity to be discovered and understood.

PHILOSOPHY AND EDUCATION

Educational philosophies are usually expressions of a society's deepest beliefs and values, and a nation's philosophy of life is reflected in its philosophy of education. A system of education is most commonly derived in response to questions such as: What is the aim of education? What are the activities that will achieve that aim? What are the learning theories that will govern the activities? What are the teaching and assessment strategies that will be used? What is the nature of the role of the students, teachers, and administrators? The answers to all of these questions form the educational philosophy of a school or society. In the West, educational philosophy has been variously conceptualized such as a general theory of education, or as a screen for selecting educational objectives, or the application of philosophical ideas to education. In attempting to identify an educational philosophy it is necessary to confront value-laden questions regarding the underlying values and beliefs that a community upholds. These questions arise from greater philosophical issues about the nature and purpose of life, the roles and abilities of human beings, and worldviews that express what is good, what is true, and what is real. Ultimately, it is this overarching philosophy that is reflected in any learning or psychological theory or school curriculum.

Several examples may be provided of educational philosophies within which the most common Western psychological theories of development and learning can be grouped.[4] The educational philosophy of *Perennialism* is based on the idea that the distinguishing characteristic of human beings is their ability to reason, and that the purpose of education should be the development of rationality through the teaching of eternal truths. The teacher's role is to interpret and tell, and subjects are taught through disciplined drill. The educational philosophy of *Idealism* holds that ideas are the only true reality, and reflects the refined wisdom of men and women. The aim of education is to search for true ideas and character development. To achieve this aim the students must be able to sharpen their intellectual processes by learning about ideal behavior which is to be modeled for them by their teachers. *Realism* rejects the notion that ideas are the only reality, and acknowledges rather, that reality exists in the world as it is and that education should teach students the laws of nature and the physical world by developing their skills of observation. The curricular content influenced by this educational philosophy would prioritize facts and knowledge about math and science, and like nature classrooms too would reflect order and discipline. *Experimentalism,* also known as *Pragmatism,* takes into account that the world is in a constant state of flux and change, and reality lies in actual experiences or interactions with physical and social worlds. Such an educational approach would prioritize social studies and physical experiences. Hands-on, practical, inquiry-based problem solving would be the basis of the curriculum and the teachers would be facilitators of the students as learners. *Existentialism* recognizes that goodness, truth, and reality are individually defined and driven by internal impulses. Schools based on this educational belief would allow students to discover themselves and their place in society, and the teaching would focus very strongly on individualization and the individual interpretation of arts, ethics, and philosophy.

In addition to the above philosophies, *Eastern Philosophy* may be considered to be another philosophical paradigm.[5] This includes Indian, Chinese, Japanese, and Middle Eastern schools of thought, among others, that have influenced educational philosophies in those respective regions of the world. Most of the European philosophies had their origins in the ideas of Ancient Greece, by which time philosophy had already reached a high level of development in both India and China. While Western philosophy emphasized science and logic, the senses and materialism, Eastern philosophy emphasized the individual's inner world and intuition; and unlike Greek philosophy that separated philosophy and religion, within the Indian and Chinese schools of thought philosophy and religion were very closely and almost inseparably intertwined. In its practical applications Western educational philosophy is seen to emphasize material goods, social advancement, and changing standards, whereas Eastern educational philosophy places a stronger emphasis on the sense of duty, familial ties, and veneration of elders and ancestors.

CULTURE AND CURRICULUM

The philosophical and cultural values of a society subsequently become the basis for teachers and educators in their making specific decisions about schooling and curriculum: What is the relationship between education and society? In the education of a child what is the role of the school, of the teacher, and of the family? What is the expected nature of the interactions between adults and children? What knowledge, skills, and attitudes should children learn? It will be seen in each of the chapters of this book that these questions found a range of answers during the historical development of schooling in South Asia depending upon whether the decision makers were natives or European colonizers; whether they were Hindu, Muslim or Buddhist priests; whether they were monarchs or democratically elected leaders. This then necessitates the understanding of curriculum from a reconceptualized perspective by illuminating the philosophical, historical, and political dimensions of what was taught and learned in school.

This approach assumes that knowledge is actively and socially constructed by individuals as they try to make sense of their world, and attempt to give meaning to their attitudes and behaviors.

The most popular definition of curriculum is that it is a plan which appears in the textbooks for a particular grade level. Another definition is that curriculum represents the experiences that students have and how these experiences are related to their lives and classrooms. Thus the various sources from which a curriculum may be derived and determined are essentially the student, society, or the subject area. The many different definitions of curriculum represent the different value orientations and priorities held by different people for accomplishing specific political agendas. Curriculum is not value-free nor produced in a vacuum, and decisions regarding curriculum such as what to teach and how to teach are determined ultimately by a culture's beliefs and values which prioritizes that set of knowledge, skills, and attitudes which are to be learnt by its children in order to live a good life in a just society. Additionally, this body of knowledge, skills, and behaviors are taught formally as well as informally to children through educational and social agencies such as schools, colleges, museums, religious institutions, media, and entertainment, and at home by parents, grandparents, extended families, and friends. Further, the underlying values of a society also determine the "hidden curriculum" by which attitudes, beliefs, and norms are communicated implicitly but powerfully to inform children of which specific sets of knowledge, values, and skills are, and will be, positively reinforced and rewarded and which will not. Thus, in countries such as those in South Asia, although formal schooling is still being developed in terms of both quality and public access, informal learning and non-formal education may exist extensively and at a very sophisticated level in a child's family and community life.

This raises the question of what a community is. A community may be defined as a group of people who are socially interdependent, and who share certain practices that not only define the group but also nurture the group. Such a community is formed not overnight, but is developed on a continuum of memory and is a community that usually has a long history. Strong communities cherish their traditions and ensure that their children learn these traditions. Thus in the historical examination of these South Asian countries one is presented with communities that have developed over a few thousand years, each with a strong sense of tradition that became the basis of a set of educational practices and schooling. Few educators in the modern world acknowledge questions that are central to the process of educating children: What kind of life is worth living? How should I live? How do I find meaning in life? The ancient Indian texts such as the *Veda* negotiate these questions, and have provided recommendations on how to live a life of purpose and fulfillment.[6] Perhaps that is why Vedic texts became the basis of education for several centuries in the South Asian region, and the core concepts of Vedic philosophy even now inform people's daily behaviors specifically within Indian society.

It is clear that cultural values determine people's behaviors: how they interact with each other and solve problems. Thus, with various sets of cultural values there is no one right way of managing, organizing, and interpreting the world. People fall somewhere in-between on the lines of continuum when we discuss approaches or ways of communicating, interacting, negotiating, managing, making decisions, and so forth. Depending on their values, or worldviews, people exhibit differences in their:

- communicating styles, which may be direct and explicit or indirect and implicit, with more or less display of emotions depending on what is considered to be appropriate in their worldview; complexities within each language would influence this depending on metaphors, symbols, and vocabulary; non-verbal communication would be influenced by body language, perceptions of personal space and privacy, mannerisms, facial expressions, voice intonations, and so forth;
- styles of interacting with others, which may be egalitarian or hierarchical, depending upon whether or not and how status is respected, whether it is achieved independently or ascribed by birth, age, gender, education, kinship or connections, and in which order; interactions may also be different between members of the same sex as compared to that between members of the opposite sex;
- attitudes to time, which may be linear or cyclical, depending on how much importance is attached to past events and accomplishments; some cultures view time as moving forward in a straight line as a sequence of events, whereas other cultures might view time as moving in a circular manner intimately connecting the past and present with future possibilities; this would also determine people's perceptions on punctuality, lateness, and so forth;
- approach to task completion, which may be product oriented or relationship oriented, depending on whether or not the end product is prioritized more than the relationships developed during the process;
- views of personal success, whether success is measured in terms of independence or interdependence, depending on whether people regard themselves primarily as individuals or as members of a larger group, and if the interest and success of the group is more important than individual and personal accomplishment.

Subsequently, formal and informal educational approaches in each culture reward those desired values and behaviors in children that adults in that particular society exhibit and expect their children to learn and possess. Everyday behaviors and attitudes that come into play in social, educational, and even business interactions are profoundly defined by a culture's underlying values, and there is developed a tradition of behaviors and attitudes characterizing societies over time. However, culture is not all static, and it continues to evolve gradually with time as new influences are introduced into a society.

To further clarify the influence of an evolving culture on educational practices, I will provide an example of a specific curriculum that I observed in schools in urban India during a previous study. Since India has been a colony of the former British Empire, I wish to introduce here the term "post colonialism" as a research paradigm that seeks to situate contemporary educational issues in the context of underlying colonial experiences. From this vantage point, the colonized condition may be variously described as a continuing contest between the dominance of the colonizers and the consequent legacies that were created, or the inter-cultural negotiation between the ideas of the colonizer and the colonized. In many schools in India, this hybridization of and the transactions between ideas, discourses, and pedagogies is clearly evident in the interplay between the teachers' formal preparation and their pedagogical practice, and between their learning to become teachers and their actual work in the classrooms.[7] Within the Indian educational system, there has been an evolution of different pedagogies as a result of the influence of different historical, political, and religious elements and events. Consequently, there are several instances in urban schools where the classroom curriculum reflects these various historical influences and discourses especially at the early childhood level. Education as a systemic phenomenon in India appears to be complex, multi-layered, and confusing and the curricula cannot be named or defined as it does not fit into any one identifiable model or educational philosophy that is familiar in the West. At the early childhood level I observed in some schools a unique kind of early childhood curriculum: the goal of teaching academics and developing academic proficiency in young children was juxtaposed with the goal of teaching values and developing good character, and at the same time there was also the intention for some child-centered practices as defined by the newer tradition of American progressive education. Further, this curriculum was being implemented within a school environment that had large class sizes but a high level of energy and engagement on the part of the students. The concept of cultural hybridization of diverse elements—ancient and modern, traditional, colonial, and progressive—was very apparent in this socio-culturally constructed curriculum, which was seen to comprise of the closely intertwined strands from three distinct discourses. These discourses reflected: (1) the deeper underlying educational purposes that represented values from Indian philosophy; (2) the educational policies that had been put in place by British colonial administrators in colonized India; and (3) traces of some core concepts from progressive education that are commonly seen in many American early childhood classrooms. These findings raised further comments about the relationships between the how, the what, and the why of this curriculum: how had the present curriculum in these early childhood classrooms evolved; what specific early childhood educational objectives did teachers work toward by way of this curriculum; why did practitioners choose to select these particular educational objectives; in what ways did this curriculum differ from one that is held to be "appropriate" as per the definitions provided by the dominant Western early childhood discourse; and how were the boundaries of philosophies and educational theories shaped by culture, history, and politics navigated in the practical implementation of the classroom curriculum?

The discussions on educational challenges in the ensuing chapters reveal remarkable parallels that each South Asian country is facing today. The more striking observation is how each of these traditional societies is faced with the challenge of maintaining some of that culture and tradition in the face of the ever-increasing influence of Western media and commerce on the children and youth of that society. Although trade and commerce with the West is advantageous to economic growth and development, it invariably occurs in juxtaposition with an infiltration of Western values which many times are in conflict with the more traditional Eastern worldviews. This commercial, economic, and cultural influence of the West may be viewed by some as neo-colonialism, as the West makes its colonizing presence felt not just on the land but also in people's minds. Values and attitudes that children in South Asia are learning are now more defined by the values and attitudes reflected in Western media, journalism, and corporations. The other challenge facing many of these countries is the tension between schools that offer an English education and those that offer an education imparted in the local and indigenous languages. More and more, the language of the English-speaking nations is being recognized as *the* language of power, and with increase in globalization comes the increase in the need to be fluent in English. Thus the success and sustainability of local schools themselves depend on whether or not they can teach students the skills to survive in this English-speaking competition, and one can see how each of these countries is struggling to reach a compromise on this issue.

There is thus indeed, a powerful connection between current schooling and teaching practices, and the social-cultural-historical past and present of a society. In the end, educational changes and innovations can only be implemented successfully and be sustained in a community if they make sense within the existing worldviews of the local people. And it is this very exploration that the book tries to achieve as the connections between local worldviews and educational development is historically traced in each of the countries in South Asia.

CHAPTER OVERVIEWS

This book is anchored by the chapter on India in which I provide an examination of the historical development of a continuous system of schooling and education that has changed and evolved, but nevertheless existed, for about 4000 years. Educational goals and objectives have always reflected deeper philosophical and spiritual values, and the nature of education in India was seen to shift to reflect the values of those philosophies that happened to be dominant at any given period in time. The spiritual values primarily reflected the influences of the Vedic, Buddhist, Islamic, and European Christian traditions. Modern India reflects a postcolonial hybridity not only culturally and socially but also in urban education which today combines traditional Indian educational beliefs, colonial European educational beliefs, as well as some American progressive educational ideas. The teacher in India has always been revered and respected and I have tried to illustrate how the image of the teacher has been based on the ancient and traditional notion of the "guru." Historically, India has been through times when her educational institutions were valued and other times when schools, universities, and libraries were destroyed by invaders. India's educational system today exists as a parallel system of private and government schools and colleges, with some institutions barely meeting the basic requirements for hygiene and adequate facilities, while other institutions boasting of graduating some of the best-prepared students at the school and college level. This chapter, with its in-depth description of educational approaches in India's ancient and modern periods serves to contextualize the other chapters because historically, each of the other South Asian countries has been closely linked to and influenced by events that occurred within the political and educational systems of the land that has been known for centuries as India.

Roozbeh Shirazi provides a detailed exploration of the development of schooling within Afghanistan's centuries old and culturally rich social, political, and ethnic fabric. He describes the detrimental and destructive effects that political conflicts over time have had on educational growth and development, in particular the effects of ethnic rivalry, and the struggle for power and control in the region. The Cold War had some of the most damaging impact and resulted in the rise of the Taliban and subsequent Al Qaeda groups under whose influences schooling became a vehicle to train young soldiers in Afghanistan. Today, after U.S. attacks on militant groups in Afghanistan and with the transition into a democratic form of government, the development of schooling and education has been made a priority but only with the aid of foreign help and non-government organizations.

Sajeda Amin writes about the system of schooling that currently exists in Bangladesh, tracing its development under various political and social forces prior to and following the emergence of Bangladesh as an independent country in 1971. This predominantly Muslim country was at first a part of eastern India, the region which felt the early impact and start of European trade and administration through the East India Company. Amin describes the historical importance given to education in this region and the existence of widespread schooling in eastern India, but also points out that despite this the Muslim representation at both the school level and in government employment was extremely low. In present-day Bangladesh schooling has been made almost universal although a recent trend indicates a high increase in the establishment of mosque schools. Snapshot images are provided of a typical school day in both a rural setting as well in an urban private school.

Tenzin Chhoeda introduces us to educational and schooling issues in the tiny Himalayan kingdom of Bhutan. This monarchy is a deeply religious and peaceful one and educational decisions have been profoundly influenced by the concepts of Buddhism. Within the framework of a spiritual philosophy that values spiritual well-being and happiness more than material wealth, this kingdom has been measuring its success and growth in terms of not its G.D.P. but its G.N.H., or gross national happiness. The system of public schooling was started in Bhutan only as recently as the 1960s, and Chhoeda traces the goals and further development of this system of schooling that was started literally from scratch.

A brief overview of the schooling in the islands of Maldives is provided in the chapter co-authored by Mohamed Latheef and myself. This group of islands covers a total land area of 300 square kilometers, and the administration is faced with the challenge of supervising and maintaining a cohesive system of functioning schools across these several hundred islands that are dispersed in the Arabian Sea and that can be accessed only by boat and that too only sometimes when fair weather allows. Another challenge has been to provide and maintain all levels of education from pre-primary to college on each island, in many instances for a bare minimum number of students which makes it difficult to develop and sustain the institutions.

Tara Niraula provides a vivid illustration of the historical development of schooling in Nepal, another Himalayan kingdom. In contrast to the mountain kingdom of Bhutan, one encounters in Nepal a monarchy that has been marked by political strife over the course of its history. Education remained a privilege of the royals and public education was introduced into the country's fabric only over the last 40–50 years. Progress in the educational sector has been severely impeded by conflicts between the monarchy and the democratic government, and in recent years political unrest has been aggravated by the Maoist insurgencies as schools and other educational institutions have been increasingly used as political agencies to promote and nurture particular political agendas.

Sajid Ali and Iffat Farah trace the evolution of schooling and the school system in Pakistan. With the end of the British rule in India in 1947 came the Partition, and what is now the country of Pakistan emerged from the northwestern region of the Indian sub-continent with its dominant Muslim population. Thus, because of this shared ancient history, the early history of education in Pakistan overlaps closely with the background of education in India. Ali and Farah provide a detailed account of the school system in Pakistan, and describe the system of *madressas* and various categories of mosque schools that evolved in this Islamic country, providing details on the teaching practices and curricula that developed in the mosque schools. The authors also describe how the different governments in Pakistan have had various influences on the system of private schools, the public-private partnerships, and the debates on whether English or Urdu should be the language of instruction in all or some schools.

Swarna Jayaweera presents an extensive review of the history of schooling and education in Sri Lanka. She describes the deep influence of Hinduism and Buddhism on the education and lives of Sri Lankans in the ancient and medieval periods, especially with regard to two systems of education, one formal and the other a non-formal guild system of apprenticeships. The early modern period saw the establishment of European colonies in Sri Lanka, starting first with the Portuguese, followed by the Dutch and the British. Each of the colonial powers implemented their own ideas of colonizing education until Sri Lanka's independence in the 1940s. The chapter also provides an in-depth discussion on the power issues between vernacular schools and English education schools; a discussion on the age-old ethnic conflict between the Sinhalese and the Tamils that continues to exist, and a reflection on the relationship between the large numbers of school and college graduates but low employment opportunities.

In conclusion, South Asia is a region of great diversity and the system of schooling in each country is markedly different in terms of scope and vision. India, the largest of the countries in the region, struggles to serve also the largest population of more than 1.1 billion people, and currently has a schooling system that is the second largest in the world. Maldives has the smallest population of about 300,000 people. The other countries are somewhere in-between with regard to the size of their populations: Afghanistan has an estimated 31 million; Bangladesh about 147.3 million; Bhutan has 635,000; Nepal has 28.2 million; Pakistan has 165.8 million; and Sri Lanka about 20.2 million people. But all these different countries have also a shared history and culture, and one of the distinguishing characteristics that is seen to be common to all is the high value that has been traditionally placed on education and learning.

NOTES

1. Adapted from story titled "In the Ancient City of Mohenjo Daro." in *Once Upon a Time...* (Part 1) by M. Choksi and P. M. Joshi (1971) New Delhi, India: National Book Trust.

2. Kluckholm (1951) as cited in Hofstede, G. (1984) *Culture's Consequences: International Differences in the Work-Related Values.* Beverly Hills: Sage.

3. Gary Weaver (1986) in R.M. Paige (ed.) *Cross-Cultural Orientation: New Conceptualizations and Applications.* Lanham, MD: Rowman & Littlefield.

4. Wiles, J. and Bondi, J. (1989) *Curriculum Development: A Guide to Practice.* Columbus, O.H.: Merrill Publishing Company.

5. Ozmon, H. and Craver, S. (1995) *Philosophical Foundations of Education.* New Jersey: Prentice-Hall.

6. The first written accounts of the *Veda* can be traced back to 2000 B.C. Interest in the Sanskrit language began to increase in Europe after Charles Wilkins translated the *Bhagvad Gita* into English in 1784. The German Sanskritist, Friedrich Max Muller (1823–1900), who taught Comparative Theology at Oxford and provided one of the most splendid editions of the *Rig Veda*, the first book of the *Veda*, considered it to be the earliest historical account of world history, and the *Veda* are also considered to be among the oldest religious writings in the world. The language used for the earliest compositions is the archaic Vedic from which Sanskrit was later derived. The *Veda* consist of four books called *Rig Veda, Sama Veda, Yajur Veda,* and *Atharva Veda,* and together the works are six times as long as the Bible. The idea that the *Veda* were composed in northern India is supported by the fact that all the geographical limits mentioned in Vedic literature fall within the confines of India's original boundaries. The first book of the *Veda* is the *Rig Veda* and it contains 1017 hymns divided into ten different books of which seven form the original nucleus. Each of these seven books is ascribed to a different seer and was passed down to his descendants. The books were thus family collections handed down from one generation to the next and were guarded jealously as a family inheritance.

7. Gupta, A. (2006) *Early Childhood Education, Postcolonial Theory, and Teaching Practices in India: Balancing Vygotsky and the Veda.* New York: Palgrave Macmillan.

Chapter 2

SCHOOLING IN AFGHANISTAN

Roozbeh Shirazi

OVERVIEW OF COUNTRY

Afghanistan is a landlocked country situated along the ancient Silk Road which was an important series of trade routes stretching from China to Europe, and it is bordered by Iran, Pakistan, China, Uzbekistan, Tajikistan, and Turkmenistan. Due to its strategically important location at the crossroads of Asia, present-day Afghanistan is an amalgam of ethnicities, languages, and cultures resulting from the rise and fall of various historic empires including the Persian, Seleucid, Parthian, Mauryan, Kushan, Sassanian, Abbasid, Mongol, Safavid, Mughal, and Durrani empires, each contributing to the richness of Afghan history and culture. However, Afghanistan's mountainous terrain and arid climate have, at the same time, also helped to repel many other invaders thus preserving Afghan independence throughout history. Although Afghanistan recognizes its day of independence as August 19, 1919, the country has had a long and dynamic history spanning thousands of years.

The population is ethnically and linguistically diverse, but predominantly Muslim with an estimated 80–85 percent of Sunnis and an estimated 15–19 percent of Shi'a. Pashtuns, who make up the country's largest ethnic group, speak the Pashto language and live primarily in the southern central and eastern regions. The Tajiks who speak Persian (known in Afghanistan as the Dari language) live in Herat and are concentrated in the northeast of the country. The Turkic-language speaking Uzbeks reside in the north of Afghanistan, and the nomadic Turkmen generally live close to the Turkmenistan border. The Hazara, whose name means "thousands," speak Persian and are predominantly Shi'a. The Hazara reside in the central interior of the country and are popularly believed to be descendants of Mongol invaders. Other ethnic groups include the Baluchis and the Pashai, both of which groups, though smaller than the others, speak their own languages.

Politically, the country of Afghanistan came about as a result of the unification of the Pashtun tribes in the 18th century under Ahmad Shah Durrani, who became known as the founder of the Afghan nation. During the 19th century, an intense rivalry dubbed as the "Great Game" developed between Britain and Russia for domination of central Asia. The Russian Empire was expanding southward, while the British continued their colonized rule in India. Afghanistan was seen as a natural boundary, or buffer state between the two European powers. However, Afghanistan's relative autonomy was challenged several times during this period. Under the Durrani dynasty, Afghanistan fought three wars with Britain, the third of which resulted in Afghanistan's official date of independence in 1919. The country enjoyed relative peace and increasing prosperity throughout most of the 20th century, but a new political rivalry between the United States and the former Soviet Union, known as the "Cold War" helped contribute to the deterioration of political and economic conditions in Afghanistan. In 1978 the government was overthrown by Afghan communist factions and shortly thereafter, the country was invaded by the Soviet Union in what became known as the Afghanistan War. The conflict lasted until 1989, and resulted in the death of thousands of people, the destruction of agriculture and industry in Afghanistan, and the displacement of 5–6 million people to neighboring countries.

Afghanistan endured many more years of civil war even after the Soviet withdrawal as different armed groups known as *mujahedeen* vied for control of the country. In 1996, fundamentalist Islamic students known as the Taliban forcibly took control of most of the country and imposed their strict interpretation of Islamic law on Afghan society. The Taliban made little to no attempt to rebuild Afghanistan, and allowed the terrorist organization Al Qaeda to operate within the country. On September 11, 2001 Al Qaeda coordinated massive attacks in the United States, which led to the United States attacking the Taliban government and occupying Afghanistan. The United States and other countries are currently helping to rebuild an Afghanistan devastated by decades of violent conflict.

HISTORICAL DEVELOPMENT OF EDUCATION

Social and political forces, both from inside and beyond Afghanistan, have played an important role on the development of education in Afghan history. The following sections of the chapter will explore Afghan education across different historical periods: ancient times (50,000 B.C.–A.D. 700), classical and early-modern Muslim rule (A.D. 700–1800s), state formation and modernization (1800s–1945), the Cold War and ensuing civil conflicts (1945–2001), and the present (2001–present). Although these periods are important in the development of Afghan education, they do not always indicate clear-cut boundaries between educational developments as often the historical events of one age carry over and have effects on the following period.

ANCIENT TIMES (50,000 B.C.–A.D. 700)

Humans have lived in the territory of what comprises modern-day Afghanistan for many thousands of years. Teams of archaeologists have unearthed Stone Age implements and remains indicating that Afghanistan is among the world's first sites to have domesticated plants and animals. Humans inhabited northern Afghanistan as early as 50,000 B.C., and excavations of prehistoric sites indicate that they were among the world's earliest farmers. In ancient times, Afghanistan was a primary site for many important historical civilizations and religions. In Afghanistan, as with other civilizations in ancient times, religion served as a primary vehicle for learning and cultural transfer between generations. Since most education in the ancient world was religious in nature, Vedic, Zoroastrian, Greco-Bactrian and Buddhist beliefs were reflected in education in pre-Islamic Afghanistan, coexisting and overlapping at various stages.

Vedic Education

Beginning in 2000 B.C., Aryan tribes from central Asia began migrating into the Iranian plateau and into India. Aryan tribes, though leaving no written records, left a major impact on the region stretching from modern-day Iran to India. The Aryan tribes that settled south of the Hindu Kush Mountains in India divided their society into castes, or hereditary social classes, and are thought to have compiled the main books of Vedic literature, the *Rigveda, Samaveda, Yajurveda,* and *Atharvaveda*. It is believed that during the later Vedic stages the caste system became very prominent in Indian society and of the Vedic books, only the *Atharvaveda* could be known by the lower castes, or common people, while the first three were studied by the *Brahman* priests (the high religious caste) to guide religious affairs of the community. The priesthood was hereditary, and early Vedic religious learning was transmitted orally from one generation to the next. Due to the oral nature of learning, the proper chanting of religious hymns during ceremonies was stressed, and Vedic education emphasized correct pronunciation and memorization. Later Vedic education saw the rise of organized schools led by teachers known as *gurus* to teach the literature that included the *Veda* as well as other texts that were based on Vedic philosophy. Each *guru* had to master the four *Vedas* before being able to teach. *Gurus* set the standards for admission to a school and generally specialized in teaching one of the *Vedas*. While education for common people was limited to the *Atharvaveda* and vocational training, learning opportunities for the higher castes were extensively available. In order to better understand the *Vedas*, students were taught subjects including phonetics, meter, grammar, etymology, astronomy, geometry and algebra (to aid in the construction of altars), as well as philosophy and logic. Promotion to higher levels was not standardized and was instead based on the teacher's evaluation of a student's progress. Thus Vedic education in Afghanistan during the ancient times was advanced, but it was primarily religious and excluded most social tiers of society.

Zoroastrian Education

The Aryan tribes which had settled toward the north and west of the Hindu Kush Mountains held religious beliefs related to their Vedic counterparts, and the monotheistic Zoroastrian religion emerged from these western Aryan beliefs. Although historical records do not provide conclusive evidence on the date and location of his birth, the prophet Zarathustra, known in the English language as Zoroaster, is believed by most scholarly estimates to have been born in Balkh in modern-day Afghanistan and lived sometime around 1700 B.C. However, some ancient writers place his birth date as far back as 6000 B.C., suggesting that Zoroastrianism is the world's oldest monotheistic religion.[1]

The religion is premised on the struggle between the forces of good and evil, and teaches that the road to salvation was through a life of good thoughts, good words, and good deeds. In departing from making memorization and religious literature the base of its curriculum, ancient Zoroastrian education contrasted with traditional religious education in other societies. By 500 B.C., Zoroastrianism was adopted by the kings of the vast Achaemenid Persian Empire, which spanned three continents and extended from Egypt to the Indus valley. The Achaemenid kings, though Zoroastrian, did not impose their faith or culture on their subjects. Greek accounts of Achaemenid Persian cities describe a city square reserved for schooling for males, from young boys to men past the age of military service. The teachers in a Zoroastrian school were the elders, who led a dynamic process of debates on practical issues and Zoroastrian principles. Although records about female Zoroastrian education are sparse, Zoroastrian beliefs viewed teaching as an act of piety and learning as a religious duty for all people young and old, men and women.

Greco-Bactrian Education

The military successes of Alexander (known as Alexander the Great in the West) against the declining Achaemenid Persian Empire changed the topography and culture of Afghanistan. While admiring the culture and customs of the Persians and even adopting Persian dress, Alexander also did much to bring Hellenic culture to the East. Greek colonist cities were built throughout Afghanistan by Alexander and his army near modern-day Herat, Qandahar, Balkh, and Sistan. Alexander's death in 323 B.C. prompted the division of the newly conquered territories amongst his generals. The general Seleucus established the Seleucid Empire, which at its peak stretched from Syria to the Indus Valley. The conquering Macedonian army hired philosophers and historians, retired officers, and married inter-racial couples to spread Greek ideas, and the citizens of many cities adopted Hellenic philosophy, religious sentiments, and politics. The synthesis of Greek and the local knowledge was best exhibited in the art, coins, and architecture produced during this period, but few records remain that describe the educational activities. Realistic artistic representations of the human form in these media indicate that Greek contribution was strong in medical and physical education. Greek influence was perhaps strongest in the region of Bactria, which in 250 B.C., seceded from the Seleucid Empire and remained a center for Indo-Greek culture for nearly two centuries before it was overrun and conquered by nomadic tribes in central Asia. Although politically and militarily vanquished toward the end of the first century B.C., the Greeks left a lasting impact on the culture of the region which would be seen in the art and education of powers that later emerged in the region. During the 3rd century B.C., the Persian Parthian Empire began to grow in strength to the west of Afghanistan, and the Buddhist Mauryan Empire in India began to expand northwards into Afghanistan.

Buddhist Education

The Mauryan Empire was also born as a result of the political chaos that arose from Alexander's death in 323 B.C. The founder of the Mauryan dynasty in India, Chandragupta Maurya, defeated Seleucus the Greek in battle and established the Mauryan Empire. At its height, the western boundaries of the Mauryan Empire extended from central India into what is currently Pakistan and southern Afghanistan. After several bloody campaigns early in his reign, the Mauryan king Ashoka, the grandson of Chandragupta Maurya, converted to Buddhism and renounced conquest and violence. Ashoka declared Buddhism as the state religion of his kingdom and was instrumental in spreading Buddhism from Afghanistan to as far east as Japan. In Afghanistan, the main relics of the Buddhist era were two massive statues of Buddha carved into cliffs located at Bamiyan. Unfortunately, these statues were destroyed in March 2001 by explosives and tank shelling by the Taliban government and no records remain to elaborate on Buddhist educational activities at Bamiyan. It is known that Buddhism was most practiced in the central and southeastern regions of present-day Afghanistan, while the north and the west were predominantly Zoroastrian.

Historical accounts indicate that Buddhist education was conducted in monasteries and was open to all members of society, regardless of caste. In addition, Buddhism highlighted the importance of early childhood education, and parents were encouraged to instill daily habits and an affinity for nature during the ages of three to five. These practices helped expand the demand for basic education. Education was primarily religious in content, conducted orally in vernacular language, and emphasized memorization. Buddhist schools also stressed humility and asceticism, and to this end promoted public confession of faults and sanctioned corporal punishment of students. Although primarily offering a religious curriculum, Buddhist schools provided secular subjects as well. Children began their education by learning the alphabet, followed by grammar. Secondary schools taught arts and crafts, and higher education offered medicine, logic, and philosophy. Pupils who completed a high degree of education would go on to become teachers and monks themselves, either in their own or other monasteries. The period from A.D. 200–600 witnessed the rise of new powers in the

Afghanistan area, such as the Kushans and the Zoroastrian Sassanian Persians, but none decisively controlled the region. Smaller kingdoms fought for supremacy among themselves, and religious beliefs of the Zoroastrian, Buddhist, and Brahmanic (also known as Vedic or Hindu) systems were all practiced and transmitted by means of their own education systems.

EDUCATION DURING CLASSICAL MUSLIM RULE (A.D. 700–1300)

In the 7th century A.D., the land that would one day be called Afghanistan was a mosaic of distinct peoples and religions speaking various Indo-Iranian languages that alternatively coexisted peacefully and fought among themselves under the suzerainty of the Sassanian Persian Empire. Simultaneously in the Arabian Peninsula, a new religion preached by a prophet named Mohammad was rapidly winning converts who would soon permanently change the world. This new religion was called Islam, which in Arabic means "submission to the will of God" and its followers were known as Muslims. After Mohammad's death in A.D. 632, Muslims led their armies into battle against the Byzantine and Sassanian Empires. Muslim armies captured Syria and the Levant from the Byzantines, and in A.D. 636, Arab Muslim armies decisively defeated Sassanian forces. The Sassanian Empire, already weakened by decades of conflict, had tenuous control over its territories in Mesopotamia as well as in eastern Persia, which is present-day Afghanistan. By A.D. 674, Muslim armies had conquered eastern Persia and extended as far east as Sind on the west bank of the Indus River in what is now Pakistan.

The victorious Arab armies brought their religion with them, and Islam eventually displaced Buddhism and Hinduism from eastern Persia. Zoroastrian conversion to Islam was gradual, but complete. Still there was an overlapping relationship between the Arab culture and the cultures of eastern and western Persia. The scholarly traditions of Persia were largely incorporated into Islamic scholarship, and Persian artistic and administrative traditions were admired and adopted by Arab rulers, as had been done by Alexander earlier in history.

Nevertheless, the impact of Islam on the region and the rest of the world was immense. The Islamic Empire eventually extended from Spain to India, and for several centuries, Arabic became the language of scholarship and administration across much of the world, although it did not supplant the Indo-Iranian languages used among the people of the former Persian Empire. The use of Arabic as a common language allowed for an explosion of scholarship, and universities and centers of higher learning emerged in Persian cities such as Nishapur, Balkh, Ghazni, and Herat, as well as other metropolises such as Baghdad (in modern-day Iraq), Bukhara (in modern-day Uzbekistan), Cairo (in modern-day Egypt), Agra and Delhi (both in modern-day India), Damascus (in modern-day Syria), and Cordoba (in modern-day Spain). Throughout the Abbasid Caliphate (A.D. 750–1258) Persian, Indian, Egyptian, and classical Greek texts were translated into Arabic and used by Islamic scholars from across the Muslim world to pursue new mathematical and scientific discoveries. Many of these texts had been lost in Europe and the West due in part to the Roman destruction of the Great Library of Alexandria in Egypt that had been founded by Alexander. During the Abbasid Caliphate, Afghanistan was known as *Khorasan*, or simply, "the East" in Arabic, and was controlled by different rulers including the Arab-Persian Abbasids (750–1151), the Turkic Ghaznavid Dynasty (962–1151 C.E.), and the Persian Samanid (875–999) and Ghori (1151–1219) Dynasties.

Elementary Islamic Education

In Islam, education has traditionally been held in high esteem in accordance to the Qur'an and a Muslim child's education began at home the moment he/she was able to speak the holy words "There is no God but Allah." Similar to other periods in Afghan history, religious instruction was the basis for education during the Muslim rule, and most learning took place in mosques. Girls were usually provided with a rudimentary education at home that would be sufficient to read the Qur'an and pray. Mosque schools, known as *maktabs*, were widespread and were primarily attended by males for primary education. At these schools were taught reading, writing, and religious rituals. Boys usually began schooling at the age of six years, and learned the curriculum and Islamic rituals with the help of easy-to-remember poetry. By the end of the 8th century, a fairly uniform elementary curriculum had been developed for mosque schools, and was centered on reading the Qur'an and memorizing prayers.

Male students would copy a passage of the Qur'an onto their writing tablet, memorize it, and then erase it. They would then continue on to the next passage, and so on until the entire Qur'an was completed. In addition to the basic tenets of Islam, basic arithmetic, penmanship, prayer movements, and rules for ablution were also taught at mosque schools. Lessons were conducted at the convenience of the teacher and of the students, and there was no requirement or expectation for students to complete their studies by a certain age or within a particular period of time. Students varied in age from six year old boys to young men. Teachers were preferred to be well-educated married men who were neither too old nor too young. Teachers were highly respected, and in Khorasan and Persia, the words "teacher" and "*caliph*" were often used interchangeably.

Higher Islamic Education

Islamic secondary schools were known as *madrassahs*. Higher education was not as clearly defined during the Umayyad Caliphate which existed during the early stages of Islam, and there was no standard curriculum nor formal sites or class schedules. Advanced study was open to anyone who wished it and was free of charge. Elementary education was considered to be terminal, with most students learning a trade via apprenticeship afterward. However, that said, relatively few of the elementary students would continue on to secondary education.

During the Abbasid Caliphate, also referred to as the Golden Age of Islam, higher education was expanded dramatically. Muslim intellectuals such as the Persian scholars Avicenna, Omar Khayyam, and Khwarizmi, drew on culturally diverse sources of knowledge and made important discoveries in the fields of medicine, astronomy, and mathematics. The curriculum of Abbasid *madrassahs* was religious and secular and included subjects such as jurisprudence, exegesis and tradition, literary studies, philology, composition, reading, syntax, rhetoric, history, geometry, astronomy, arithmetic, algebra, music, politics, logic, theology, metaphysics, natural science, medicine, chemistry, surveying, agriculture, phrenology, dream interpretation, astrology, and magic. Students who continued on to secondary education usually desired to become mosque leaders or teachers of specialized subjects such as Arabic language, poetry, logic, mathematics, astronomy, and medicine. Advanced classes for students were usually held in the mosque or private home of the teacher. Larger cities such as Herat, Damascus, Cairo, and Baghdad had universities with lectures and discussion classes. Students of higher education could also pursue a specific area of study by becoming disciples of a scholar. Some students committed themselves to the tutelage of one scholar, while others studied under several master teachers. Scholarship was carried out in the Arabic language until the invasion of the Mongols in 13th century A.D.

PRE-MODERN ISLAMIC EDUCATION AND EDUCATIONAL DECLINE (A.D. 1300s–1700s)

From the 8th through 12th centuries A.D., the Islamic world was arguably unrivalled in the arts, sciences, medicine, commerce, and power. Although education in the Muslim world was vibrant and widespread, political power in the Muslim world was becoming decentralized. As previously discussed, Afghanistan then known as Khorasan, witnessed different rules including those of the Turkic Ghaznavid and Khwarezmid Empires, as well as the Persian Samanid and Ghori dynasties.

In A.D. 1219, Mongol armies led by Genghis Khan invaded the region and eventually established the Ilkhanate Empire which covered Khorasan, Persia, and parts of central Asia. The initial effects of the Mongol invasion were devastating not only in Khorasan, but throughout China, central Asia, and Persia. Mongol armies massacred many of their captives on a genocidal scale and razed the cities of Herat, Nishapur, and Balkh in Khorasan. In addition, the brutality of the Mongol conquest resulted in millions of deaths (the exact number remains contested) that radically and permanently altered the demographics and linguistic make-up of Central and western Asia. Many of the Persian-speaking urban centers were destroyed and most regions of central Asia gradually became Turkic-speaking. Some of the cities, such as Samarqand and Balkh, were rebuilt but failed to attain their previous greatness and importance. The Islamic world was further fragmented as a result of the Mongol conquests and as Arabic ceased to be used as the primary scholarly language. Arabic was replaced by Persian as the sole literary medium in the eastern parts of the Muslim world.

However, the Mongol rule also paved the way for broader cultural and educational revitalization and exchanges within the vast territory under Mongol control. The Silk Road, a network of trade routes extending from China to Europe, played a seminal role in this process. Goods and technologies passed from China to the West for centuries until the Mongol rulers gradually lost control of the routes, and Chinese and European merchants discovered sea routes as an alternative in the 15th century, dramatically shortening the time to receive goods and lessening their cost. During this time, the once-powerful central Asian cities declined in prominence, and the decentralized territory of Afghanistan made up of Persian, Pashtun, Uzbek, Turkmen, and other ethnicities and distinct languages, was contested by the Safavid Persian Empire and the Mughal Indian Empire. Education in the region became increasingly religious at this time, and the study of sciences, mathematics, and astronomy decayed while memorization continued to be equated with learning in traditional Islamic education. The emphasis was on absorbing word for word what was written or said and little attention was given to developing concepts, making inferences, or generalizations. The narrowing of the scope of education during this time would later emerge as a source of contention during Afghanistan's development to statehood in the 19th century.

STATE FORMATION AND MODERNIZATION OF EDUCATION (1700s–1945)

Following a *loya jirga* (council meeting) of Pashtun tribal elders in 1747, Ahmad Shah Durrani, a Pashtun leader of the Barakzai tribe (also known as the Durrani tribe), was elected king of the land known as "Afghanistan" in the Pashto language. Although the boundaries of Afghanistan changed as the Afghans fought with their neighbors, the Mughals and the Safavids, they managed to hold a level of relative autonomy from their cities of Qandahar and Kabul. In the 19th century, Persian and Indian power in the region gave way to the power of the Russians in the north, and the British in colonized India. The kingdom of Afghanistan was threatened by the encroaching European powers, and sought to protect itself militarily and culturally from their advances.

However, to do so required modern weapons, new institutions, and a central bureaucracy that was capable of centrally administering the kingdom. Afghanistan's existing educational system did not have the capacity to spearhead such change. The Islamic curriculum and faith taught by mosque schools, while giving Afghans a sense of identity as Muslims and providing them with the fundamentals of the Islamic culture and tradition, remained as remnants of the formal Islamic learning of centuries ago, and did not teach secular and scientific subjects needed for modernization of the Afghan state.

In the early 19th century, most of the population and ruling leaders of Afghanistan were illiterate, and prior to the reign of Amir Sher Ali (1870–1879) there was no government-supported education in the country. Education being entirely in the hands of the Muslim clergy, the Durrani kings were dependent on the goodwill and support of the Afghan tribes for armed defense. The attempts to change these dynamics provoked a social and political upheaval that has reverberated down to the present.

Laying the Foundations

Due to the First Anglo-Afghan War of 1840, the government treasury was severely depleted. Consequently, the beginning of government education in Afghanistan was somewhat inauspicious. Amir Sher Ali founded the first public school in Afghanistan, the *Bala Hissar* in Kabul. The school recruited young male graduates of the *maktabs* and trained them either in military or civilian affairs for service in the government. Amir Sher Ali's reign was followed by Amir Abdur Rahman (1880–1901) who continued to expand the authority of the central government. Prior to Rahman's reign, loyalties were directed at clans and tribes rather than the monarchy, and traditionally the religious establishment had an extensive say in political and social affairs, often playing the role of king-makers and king-breakers. Rahman was a cruel and calculating ruler who managed to execute his tribal rivals and control the clergy by making them state employees. He was succeeded by his son, Habibullah, who ruled from 1901 to 1919.

Habibullah was able to capitalize on the unity, peace, and stability inherited from his father's reign which allowed him to focus on education and other socio-economic needs of the country. Habibullah was able to further consolidate the power of the monarchy by bringing education under the control of the government and away from the *mullahs* (clergy). In addition, he initiated a government program of inspecting mosque schools between the years of 1904 and 1910. In 1912, Habibullah's government declared its responsibility to promote free "modern" education and implemented the Council of Public Instruction in the following year. The primary duties of the Council were to approve curriculum and textbooks, control hygiene and finances in educational institutions, control and oversight of examinations, and supervision of school administration. Habibullah saw the need for an organized bureaucracy to administer the emergent Afghan state. To this effect, he founded many different schools over the course of his reign, including the Habibia College (1904), the Royal Military College (1906), a primary school in Kabul (1909), a teacher training school (1912), and a secretarial and clerical school (1919). Habibia College was designed to train bureaucrats needed to administer the state, and Habibullah actively promoted its rapid expansion.

Primary Education

The first government primary school, established in Kabul in 1909, taught fundamentals of Islamic religion, Qur'an, theology, *tafseer* (commentary on the Qur'an), reading, writing, arithmetic, civics, calligraphy, geometry, and Persian. Arithmetic was taught using two textbooks compiled by the Council of Public Instruction. Habibullah's program of education was not as radical as might be suggested. King Habibullah strongly believed that modern education was not incompatible with Islam, and religion continued to occupy a preeminent place in the curriculum. This was not enough to appease the *mullahs* who opposed the introduction of modern subjects in to the curriculum and other educational innovations.

Habibullah faced a difficult dilemma in that, to transform the state the educational institutions had to change and evolve, but they were necessarily reliant on the *mullahs* who composed the majority of the literate population in Afghanistan. Thus the process of educational development under Habibullah was necessarily slow and forced. However, Habibullah laid the foundation for secular education in Afghanistan which was to develop parallel to, rather than totally supplant, the traditional Islamic education system.

Higher Education and the Religious Backlash

Amanullah succeeded Habibullah in 1919 and ruled until 1929. It was during Amanullah's reign that the Third Anglo-Afghan War was fought, which resulted in Afghanistan's independence and recognition by the British. He greatly broadened the scope and reach of Afghan education, and he founded many new schools and expanded secondary education with the help of British, Turkish, French, German, and Russian teachers and assistance. However, most of his schools were poorly equipped and organized, and his reliance on foreign resources and assistance proved in some ways to be a liability and resulted in a tug-of-war between himself and the religious establishment. He made plans for a Western-style university in Kabul, but was unable to realize this plan due to strict opposition by religious leaders who insisted that such an institution would have to be devoted entirely to the study of religious subjects. Amanullah circumvented this obstacle by sending many Afghan students abroad, primarily to France and Germany but also to Turkey, Iran, England, and Switzerland, marking the first time Afghan students were sent beyond Afghanistan for further educational training. The clergy responded by protesting the study abroad programs. As a result, students going abroad were placed under a large number of strict restrictions including promising to fast during the holy Islamic month of *Ramazan* (also known as *Ramadan*), reading the Qur'an to strengthen their faith, and observing the restrictions of Islam placed upon food and drink. In turn, Amanullah attempted to create government-administered mosque schools to infuse the curriculum with so-called modern subjects, but few historical records exist detailing the number of such schools created and the impact they had on religious studies.

Social Change, Gender, and Education During and After Amanullah's Reign

Though Amanullah's focus was the expansion of secondary education, he did not neglect primary education. During his reign 200 primary schools were started and he made school attendance mandatory for children of government employees in order to promote a good example for Afghan citizens. All education was free, but estimates of total primary school enrollment were 40,000 for the entire country in 1928, with less than 800 of those students being girls. Girls' attendance was limited by several factors including parental resistance to sending their daughters to schools unsupervised, the long distances they would have to walk between their homes and the school, as well as the dependence of many families on their daughters' contributions to the household. In addition, the introduction of secular subjects in schools was vehemently resisted by the *mullahs* and viewed with suspicion by the Afghan population.

Amanullah's most controversial reform program was his advocacy of women's rights. He revised laws relating to marriage and inheritance, pressed for an end to the practice of *purdah*,[2] and sought compulsory education for girls as well as boys. These changes, seen as an affront to traditions and long-held customs, helped his opposition coalesce and force Amanullah's ouster. Mohammad Nadir Shah, who came to power after Amanullah's overthrow and a brief usurpation of the throne, ruled from 1929 to 1933 and rolled back many of Amanullah's reforms. Nadir took a more calculated, conservative, and gradual approach to educational development and modernization. He believed education to be premised on the good will traditions and institutions of the country, meaning that religious instruction was recognized as the most important part of education. Local control of the mosque schools was returned to the *mullahs*, and the mosque school curriculum continued virtually unaltered. This did not preclude the introduction of modern subjects and did not cause the level of resistance encountered by his predecessors. Nadir opened public libraries in Herat, Qandahar, and Mazar-i-Sharif and reopened the schools, but renamed all those named after Amanullah. The teaching of foreign languages in government schools was postponed to allay fears of foreign influence, but students were again sent abroad. A girls' school was opened as a specialty school for those who wished to study nursing and midwifery 2 years after Nadir took the throne, but academic secondary girls' education did not reappear until 20 years later.

The Afghan Constitution of 1931 made primary education in Afghanistan compulsory and placed all government schools under government supervision. It also removed the constraints on the *mullahs* imposed by Amanullah and Habibullah and made it illegal for foreigners to teach in Afghan schools unless hired by the government. Primary schools under Nadir had two functions—to teach literacy and certain elementary knowledge about daily life, and also to prepare pupils for secondary schools. However the lack of continuity and qualified teachers, particularly in the provinces, made the realization of the latter function difficult. The ascension of Nadir's son, Zahir Shah (1933–1973), to the throne marked the beginning of another period of educational expansion and reorganization.

Zahir adhered to the education framework established by his father, but concentrated on increasing the quantity of schools and the quality of instruction. Zahir turned toward the international community for financial and technical support to realize his education plans. Following the Russian revolution, the newly created Soviet Union (U.S.S.R.) was the first country to recognize Afghanistan as a sovereign state. Soviet-Afghan contacts increased with the Soviet training of the Afghan air force, development aid and infrastructure projects, and the creation of the Polytechnic Institute of Kabul University in 1958.

Educational expansion occurred rapidly as a result of a national budget augmented by private donations and foreign aid, with the total number of primary school students enrolled rising from 60,000 in 1940 to 93,000 in 1945, and the number of teachers rising from 1990 in 1940 to 2564 in 1945. Instruction was provided in both Persian and Pashto languages, and in addition, schools around the country operated on different academic calendars. The schools in the northern, cooler regions held their academic recess during the cold winter months to eliminate the need to heat the classrooms. Schools in the warmer southern regions held their recess during the summer months due to the extremely hot summer temperatures. These practices also helped boost enrollment. However, the student figures represented less than 5 percent of the total primary school-age population, indicating that the vast majority of school-age children were not being serviced. Therefore, in the second and third decades of Zahir's reign, emphasis was laid on building schools in the provinces as well as in Kabul, in addition to more libraries and other educational facilities. The third decade of Zahir's reign also prompted a study of the educational development needs of Afghanistan undertaken in 1949 by the United Nations Educational, Scientific, and Cultural Organization (UNESCO) at the invitation of the Afghan government. The UNESCO study was to set the stage for the preliminary exchanges between the Afghan and U.S. governments which culminated in the long-term U.S. involvement in Afghan educational development.

AFGHAN EDUCATION DURING THE COLD WAR AND ENSUING CIVIL CONFLICTS

As during other periods in Afghan history, external political actors played a major role in shaping the development of Afghan education after World War II. Prior to World War II, the United States had a limited relationship with Afghanistan. In the 1930s, a small number of American educators were hired by the government of Mohammad Nadir Shah to teach at the English-language school, Habibia High School. The number of American educators in Afghanistan would greatly increase during the 1940s and after, especially following the signing of the Technical Cooperation Agreement between the two countries in 1959.

British-drawn boundaries between Afghanistan and colonial India came to play a major role in attracting Soviet and American attention to Afghanistan. The Durand Line, used as a dividing line between the Pashtun and Baluchi populations, ran through lands that had been traditionally inhabited by the Pashtun. In 1947, when colonial India was partitioned into Pakistan and India, Afghan requests for a Pushtunistan state, opposed by Pakistan, went unheeded. The United States, eager for allies and influence in the region, formed an alliance with Pakistan, and consequently did not show much interest in the Afghan claims for a Pashtun state. The Soviets capitalized upon the Pushtunistan issue and were able to expand and exert their influence in Afghanistan, leading to the construction of infrastructure and the Polytechnic Institute.

The team from Columbia University was perhaps the most important of the American education advisors in Afghanistan before the Soviet invasion in 1979. The Teachers College, Columbia University team worked closely with the Afghan Ministry of Education for 25 years to reform and "modernize" education in Afghanistan by concentrating its efforts on teacher training and curriculum development. However, Columbia University's efforts were primarily directed toward boys' schools and male teacher education. Changes that occurred during the 25-year period of Columbia University assistance included the establishment of a primary teacher education program which was established as an academic track in the secondary schools. This program promoted a departure from a strict adherence to the subject material toward a focus on providing an education more aligned with the everyday concerns and realities of people, and to the social and economic needs of the country.

While education was expanding during the second half of the 20th century, there were indicators that economic development, modernization, and foreign aid were not improving the country's economy or standard of living; Afghanistan became further indebted to its foreign creditors. The aim of the Afghan education system was to prepare Afghan youth for state jobs; it did not give its graduates alternate career paths or survival skills. Nearly all the jobs for an Afghan college graduate were to be found in the state bureaucratic apparatus, as there was virtually no private employment. The investment in a centralized state infrastructure had not encouraged the development of the private sector in Afghanistan, and that ultimately helped seal the fate of the monarchy. As in other "Third World" countries, the state expanded the public sector to absorb its graduates; by the 1960s, foreign financing and aid was declining and by the 1970s, unemployment among the university graduates was visible. Jobs were increasingly allocated through family connections rather than merit or achievement, which contributed to social tensions and the division of political elites. This socio-economic crisis, coupled with the Soviet invasion, helped bring about the collapse of the centrally administered Afghan state.

EDUCATION DURING THE AFGHAN WAR

The aftermath of World War II saw the decline of European colonialism and the beginning of a geopolitical contest known as the Cold War between the emerging superpowers, the United States and the Soviet Union, in the industrializing nations of Africa, South America, and Asia. Though never conquering or formally colonizing these nations, it was in the countries of the "Third World" that the United States and the Soviet Union waged their numerous ideological and real battles with often disastrous consequences. The case of Afghanistan is a particularly powerful example of how nations became little more than arenas for the Cold War rivalry, and demonstrates the pivotal role that education played in both Soviet and American ambitions.

In April of 1978, a coup resulted in the overthrow and death of Mohammad Daoud and the establishment of the Democratic Republic of Afghanistan. The new government, headed by Noor Mohammad Taraki, authorized the deployment of Soviet troops into Afghanistan to safeguard the regime against threats. This prompted a drastic shift in U.S. policy toward Afghanistan, dramatically restructuring humanitarian and educational assistance to the country and underscoring the preeminence of the Cold War rivalry in policy making.

Militant Islamist Afghan refugees, also known as *mujahedeen*, concentrated along the Afghanistan-Pakistan border, were armed and financed by the United States and Saudi Arabia to combat the Soviet forces and their Afghan proxies. During this conflict, education outside of Kabul was minimally under the control of the Soviet-controlled Ministry of Education, and schooling was often conducted by international non-governmental organizations (NGOs) throughout different regions of the country.

Many of the educational materials and practices of this period reflected the bitter divisions and ideological rivalries of the conflict. In June 1978, the Faculty of Letters at Kabul University underwent a dramatic curriculum and departmental revision. Russian advisors abolished Islamic courses, such as History of Islamic Civilization and History of Islamic Art. The Faculty of Theology was largely liquidated or dispersed among other faculties and what remained was greatly modified. The new curriculum of Theology omitted those *suras* (chapters) from the Qur'an dealing with the concept of *jihad* and stressed the compatibility of Islam and socialism. It also emphasized those *suras* which mainly deal with human equality and denounce racial segregation.

Changes in the academic calendar and length of schooling were also made to accommodate the Soviet war effort in Afghanistan. Traditionally, schools in northern Afghanistan were closed in the winter, due to the high cost of heating buildings in cold weather. The Soviets changed the vacation to the summer so that students could be recruited to fight against the *mujahedeen* in the winter. Schooling was changed from a 12-year track to a 10-year track, to conform to the Soviet model of education.

American educational support in Afghanistan during the war was also directed toward complementing U.S. foreign policy goals. From 1986 to 1992, the United States Agency for International Development (USAID) underwrote the printing of explicitly violent Islamist textbooks for elementary school children that were primarily used by children attending religious schools in refugee camps and in *mujahedeen* controlled areas. USAID helped to produce textbooks that promoted Islam through violence and promoted resistance to the Soviet invasion. These textbooks instructed children about the letters of the alphabet, emphasizing that "*alef* is for Allah, *jim* is for *jihad*, and *shin* is for *Shakir*, who conducts *jihad* with his sword. God becomes happy with the defeat of the Russians" (Coulson, 2004, p. 17). The third and fifth grade textbooks depicted Kalashnikov rifles, rocket-propelled grenades, and tanks. A fourth grade math textbook states that the speed of a round fired from a Kalashnikov rifle is 800 meters per second and then asks, "If a Russian is at a distance of 3200 meters from a *mujahid*, and that *mujahid* aims at the Russian's head, calculate how many seconds it will take for the bullet to strike the Russian's forehead?" (Coulson, 2004, p. 17).

The use of these textbooks continued long after the withdrawal of the Soviet troops, helping to establish militant Islamist beliefs in Afghanistan. After the Soviets withdrew, there were several years of civil war in Afghanistan, as competing groups struggled to assert control over the state. The destruction the war caused to Afghan infrastructure was immense. Between 70 and 80 percent of schools were destroyed, and many children did not receive schooling during the extended years of conflict or schooling on a consistent basis. The conflict also produced a massive exodus of 3 million Afghans displaced by conflict into neighboring Iran and Pakistan. Afghan children in Pakistan received education in refugee camps while Afghan children in Iran attended state-run schools, albeit with some difficulty in gaining admission to the Iranian schools. Stability would come to Afghanistan in the latter part of the 1990s with the rise of the Taliban, but at tremendous social costs.

EDUCATION UNDER THE TALIBAN

The Taliban, a group of Islamic students trained primarily in the religious schools set up by the *mujahedeen* during the Afghan War, assumed power in southern Afghanistan in 1994 and gradually took over most of the country. Resistance to the Taliban continued throughout their rule, especially within the non-Pashtun ethnicities of the country. The Taliban implemented the *Shariah*, their harsh interpretation of Islamic law throughout the country. The Taliban did little to contribute to the rebuilding of the country in general and to the education system in particular. Boys' education was limited to religious studies, while girls were banned from attending schools and women were not allowed to work. The Taliban destroyed non-Islamic artistic sites, such as the twin statues of Buddha in Bamiyan. During their rule, the Taliban also harbored Islamic militant groups such as Al Qaeda. On September 11, 2001, Al Qaeda coordinated terrorist attacks in the U.S. cities of Washington D.C. and New York. The Taliban's refusal to extradite the suspected ringleader, Osama bin Laden, resulted in the U.S.-led invasion of Afghanistan which toppled the Taliban regime.

PRESENT-DAY EDUCATION[3]

The current situation of education in Afghanistan is one of formidable challenges but also encouraging progress. Most schools have been destroyed, there is a shortage of trained teachers, many children still do not have access to education, and the government is constrained by a severe shortage of resources. The rebuilding process is helping to improve conditions throughout the country, but progress is still slow and hampered by security issues. The new government of Afghanistan has made education a top priority. Article 43 of the Constitution of Afghanistan that has been in effect since 2004, states that education is the right of all Afghans and will be provided by the state, free of charge, up to the Bachelor of Arts (B.A.) level. It also promises that the state will provide instruction in local languages. International organizations are playing a constructive role in providing accelerated learning classes for older students, training for teachers, and providing school supplies. Nevertheless, there are many obstacles that impede children, particularly girls, from attending school.[4]

Types of Schools

There are currently three types of schools in Afghanistan—government schools, which include primary, secondary, and tertiary education, schools run by NGOs which primarily provide community-based accelerated learning classes in regions where the government cannot provide education, and religious schools, of which there are two types, the *dar-ul-ulum* (religious schools with government curriculum) and *dar-ul-hafiz* (traditional religious schools which emphasize the study of the Qur'an and Islamic subjects).[5] All schools, with the exception of the traditional religious schools, follow the national curriculum designed by the Afghan Ministry of Education. Higher education and vocational education programs are being revitalized, but the current government emphasis is on enhancing primary education and considers Grades 1–9 as compulsory education.

Primary Education

Enrollment in primary education in Afghanistan is growing. In 2003, enrollment in primary education was 3.9 million students, or approximately 57.4 percent of children aged 7 to 12 years. Schools in Afghanistan are separated by gender and currently more boys are enrolled in school than girls. The quality of instruction in schools varies. Most teachers have at most a secondary school education. Although teacher training is a priority for both international organizations and the government of Afghanistan, not all teachers receive ongoing or consistent professional development and support in their schools. A teaching hour is 45 minutes in duration and teachers teach 26 hours of instruction per week.

Although the Afghan Ministry of Education supports student-centered learning, overcrowding in classrooms and lack of teacher support can translate into situations where teachers rely on rote learning and memorization of texts as their primary pedagogical methods. Many schools hold classes outdoors in the absence of a school building. First grade curriculum includes the study of Art, Calligraphy, Dari Language, Islamic Studies, Life Skills, Mathematics, and Pashto Language. At the national level, the curriculum and content of education are designed to strengthen social cohesion on cultural and religious levels. The Afghan Ministry of Education desires to foster an educational system built on concepts of peace, rebuilding the nation, forgiveness, and brotherhood.[6] Religion will play a significant role in achieving these goals. The 2004 Afghan Constitution declares that the state will develop a unified curriculum in accordance with Islamic principles and with respect to the branches of Islam followed in Afghanistan.[7] This spirit of inclusion is evident in the textbooks as well, as the Ministry of Education is providing primary education textbooks written in Dari, Pashto, as well as in Uzbek and Turkmen.

Secondary and Higher Education

While the majority of students in Afghanistan are enrolled in primary education, the Ministry of Education plans to have all school-aged children enrolled in schools by 2015. Currently, many Afghan students drop out due to financial need and obligations to help provide for their families.[8] Secondary school consists of Grades 10–12 but is not compulsory in Afghanistan.[9] With regard to secondary education, general education divides into two tracks, the social sciences and the natural sciences. In terms of higher education, Afghanistan is served by 13 universities and 5 pedagogic institutes, a total of 18 institutions of higher learning with 37,000 students enrolled in 2004 (MoHE). Many of the facilities are being renovated and expanded in anticipation of a growing demand for higher education in the coming years.

Reform and the Roles of International Assistance and NGOs in Afghan Education

The destruction wrought by decades of conflict largely destroyed Afghanistan's infrastructure, economy, and central government control. The government of Afghanistan has little power to generate the revenue needed to rebuild the country and has turned to the international community for assistance.[10] Since the fall of the Taliban, there has been a dramatic increase in the number of national and international NGOs as well as international assistance organizations operating in Afghanistan. The roles of these organizations are varied. International donor organizations such as the World Bank and UNICEF operate on a national level and work in tandem with the Afghan Government to set policy or undertake reconstruction and rehabilitation projects. Many NGOs are based in both urban and rural settings, and often provide non-formal education programs to target communities throughout a region or province. The Afghan government, constrained by a lack of financial resources, has been almost entirely dependent on international aid to rebuild the country and expand social services such as education throughout Afghanistan.

Consequently, although the Afghan Ministry of Education sets education policy in the country, the influence of international donor organizations and NGOs operating in Afghanistan on determining educational policy is quite strong. This dynamic, as in other developing countries, has worked to the benefit and detriment of Afghanistan. While international assistance can provide the much needed resources for development, the great number of international organizations can also produce and diffuse competing visions of education policy; this may lead to overlap of and the inefficient use of limited resources. Also, the short-term funding and nature of NGO projects mitigates any gains such programs make, as they are sometimes unsustainable without external support.

Policies that are currently shaping the educational landscape in Afghanistan include support for community-based education and the expansion of Parent-Teacher Associations in schools around the country.[11] Other policy priorities include expanding access to education for Afghan children. Although more children are enrolled in schools in Afghanistan than ever before, girls' enrollment continues to lag behind boys, particularly in the rural and southern regions of the country. The Ministry of Education has implemented a 12-year program designed to have all children enrolled in school by 2015.[12] Afghanistan is also concerned with improving the quality of its education system. To that end, the Afghan Government and the NGO community are working to design a standardized system of assessment, as well as providing teacher training in learner-centered pedagogies. Long-term education policy goals include the decentralization of education, the gradual establishment of private schools, as well as education policy-borrowing from nations to help improve schooling in Afghanistan.

SUMMARY

This chapter provides an overview of the long and rich history of schooling in Afghanistan. Education in Afghanistan, like the land itself, has been shaped by diverse ideas, religions, cultures, and civilizations spanning thousands of years—a tradition that continues on to this very day. Of these social forces, Islam has perhaps been the most enduring and serves as a touchstone of Afghan identity in addition to other existing linguistic or ethnic heritages. From ancient times, religion has played a prominent role in Afghan society and schooling. Since the 19th century, the preeminence of religious education has been challenged by secular mass education, which was seen as necessary for the survival and long-term success of the nation by the central government, and as a threat by the religious establishment.

The tension between religious and secular education continued through much of the 19th and 20th centuries and was often seen as reflective of Afghanistan's own struggles with its colonial European neighbors. Afghanistan's strategic location at the center of Asia and its relative weakness in developing a strong centralized state attracted the attention of the United States and Soviet Union, and each side used development assistance and education to promote its ideological goals rather than the development of the Afghan state. The escalating rivalry between the superpowers helped lead to an extended and destructive period of conflict in Afghanistan that destroyed much of the country's schools and infrastructure, and produced the world's largest refugee population. During the conflict, education was largely disrupted throughout the country, or was laden with violent religious imagery and used as a recruitment tool by forces fighting the Soviet Union. The war-time education materials created with U.S. support were used in radicalized Islamic schools which helped educate members of the Taliban, who imposed strict Islamic rule and banned girls from attending schools. The overthrow of the Taliban regime has witnessed an internationally led effort to rebuild Afghanistan. Education has played a prominent role in these efforts, but schooling in Afghanistan is limited by ongoing security issues, lack of access (particularly to girls and students in rural areas), and poor quality. The Afghan Government is heavily dependent on international resources, but plans to expand education across all levels and achieve full enrollment by 2015.

A SNAPSHOT OF A STUDENT'S LIFE IN AFGHANISTAN[13]

The fall in Afghanistan is sunny and not too cold. The narrow road is bumpy and dusty, flanked by two mud-brick walls on either side. It leads to the main road going into Char-e-Kar, the capital of the province of Parwan. It is also the main road that runs through several small villages just outside of the capital, linking them together. Many people walk on this road everyday to get to their fields, the bazaar, get water for their houses, or return home at the end of the day. They share the road with merchants who ride atop horse-drawn carts, motorcycles and bicycles, and occasionally a truck or a car. This is also the road on which children walk to get to their schools. Some children have a relatively short distance to walk, while others have to walk 45 minutes to get to school. Boys and girls go to school separately, so where there is only one school or one extra room in someone's home to use as a classroom, sometimes boys have classes in the mornings, while girls have classes in the afternoon. Some classes are conducted outdoors, and the children must sit on the ground as they have no chairs or desks. In Dulana Village, the school is a home donated by a villager for use as a school. It is a government school for girls, named Motavaset Dulana (Dulana Primary School) from the first grade up to sixth grade. Classes are conducted in different rooms as well as under a canvas UNICEF tent in the courtyard. Children often bring their younger siblings with them to class, and these children usually sit in the front of the class quietly while their older sisters pay attention to their teacher. In Dulana, as in many other parts in Afghanistan, there is a shortage of female teachers. The teachers in this school are older males, usually a trusted community man or religious figure known as a *mullah* (a Persian word meaning cleric). Many of the girls wear a scarf over their head, in accordance with traditional Islamic dress codes which call for female modesty. Kobra is a fourth-grader at this school and a good student. When the teacher calls on her, she reads a passage from her textbook for the rest of her classmates, and then sits down at her desk. She says that she enjoys coming to school, but she is also very busy at home just like many of her classmates and friends at school. Kobra wakes up early to pray, helps her mother with household chores such as cooking, cleaning, and taking care of her siblings. She walks the twenty minute walk to school with her mother, where she has class for three hours on Saturdays through Thursdays, which is the school week in Afghanistan. Girls in Afghanistan are generally not encouraged to move about outdoors unaccompanied by an adult. When Kobra and her mother return home, she helps her mother with her work and helps prepare dinner for her family. She studies at home, but her mother and father are unable to help her with her schoolwork because they cannot read or write. In the winter, schools will close for the season and will reopen once the weather is warm and the buildings do not have to be heated.

NOTES

1. Accounts of when Zarathustra lived greatly vary; some ancient scholars place him in the fifth millennium B.C.E., predating Judaism as the world's oldest monotheistic religion. See Sahraie and Sahraie (1974) Educational Development in Afghanistan: History of the Teachers College, Columbia University Educational Assistance Program, 1954–1971. Doctoral dissertation, Teachers College Columbia University.

2. Purdah is the practice of using a material to cover a Muslim woman's face and head. In addition, rules of purdah stress that uncovered women remain unseen by males who are not husbands or relatives or cover themselves in the company of strangers.

3. Observations for this section were enhanced and supported by D. Burde (2005). Research Project: Protecting Children from War and Ensuring their Prospects for the Future: Education in the Context of Crisis and Transition, Columbia University. The project was funded by grants from Columbia University's Institute for Social and Economic Research and Policy, the Spencer Foundation, the US Institute of Peace, and the Weikart Foundation.

4. According to HRRAC, girls' enrollment varies greatly from province to province, with the lowest rates found in the southern provinces and rural regions of the country.

5. D. Burde (2006). Protecting children from war and ensuring their prospects for the future: Education in the context of crisis and transition. Paper for annual Comparative International Education Society conference at University of Hawaii, Honolulu, H.I.

6. TISA, 2004 National Report on the Development of education in Afghanistan.

7. Ibid.

8. Human Rights Research and Advocacy Consortium 2004. Report Card: Progress on Compulsory Education (Grades 1–9).

9. TISA, 2004 National Report on the Development of education in Afghanistan.

10. Bloomberg (2005). Karzai's Afghanistan, poisoned by heroin habit, seeks investors.

11. D. Burde (2006). Protecting children from war and ensuring their prospects for the future: Education in the context of crisis and transition. Paper for annual Comparative International Education Society conference at University of Hawaii, Honolulu, H.I.

12. TISA, 2004 National Report on the Development of education in Afghanistan.

13. This vignette is taken from data collected for Burde, D. Research Project: "Protecting Children from War and Ensuring their Prospects for the Future: Education in the Context of Crisis and Transition," Columbia University. Funders noted above.

BIBLIOGRAPHY

Afghanistan Constitution (2004) http://www.oefre.unibe.ch/law/icl/af00000_.html accessed on January 17, 2006.

Barez, A. (1988) "A Brief Look at Soviet Brainwashing in Afghanistan," in Elmi, S. M. Yusuf (Ed.) *Afghanistan: A Decade of Sovietization*. Peshawar, Pakistan: Afghan Jehad Works Translation Centre. 83–110.

Burde, D. (2006) Protecting Children from War and Ensuring their Prospects for the Future: Education in the Context of Crisis and Transition. Paper for Annual Comparative International Education Society Conference at University of Hawaii, Honolulu, H.I.

Coulson, A. (March 11, 2004) Education and Indoctrination in the Muslim World: Is There a Problem? What Can We Do about It? In *Policy Analysis* 511. The Cato Institute. http://www.cato.org/pubs/pas/pa511.pdf

Education in Afghanistan (1998) Encyclopedia Iranica, VIII, 3, Mazda Publishers. http://www.ed.uiuc.edu/eps/people/Shorish-Education_in_Afghanistan.htm

Elmi, S. M. Yusuf (1987) *A Brief Look at the Sovietization of Afghan Education*. Peshawar, Pakistan: Afghan Jehad Works Translation Centre. 1–26.

Library of Congress Country Profile: Afghanistan. February 2005. http://lcweb2.loc.gov/frd/cs/profiles/Afghanistan.pdf

Masani, Rustom (1968) *Zoroastrianism: The Religion of the Good Life*. New York: The MacMillan Co. p 78.

PBS Newshour Extra. Afghanistan Rebuilds its Education System. 2003. http://www.pbs.org/newshour/extra/features/july-dec03/afghan_8-06.html

Poullada, L. & Poullada, L. (1995) *The Kingdom of Afghanistan and the United States 1828–1973*. Lincoln, Nebraska: The Center for Afghanistan Studies at the University of Nebraska at Omaha and Dageforde Publishing. 23–32; 160–190.

Rubin, B. (2002) *The fragmentation of Afghanistan. State Formation and Collapse in the International System*. New Haven, CT: Yale University Press; 2nd edition 2002.

Sahraie Hashem and Sahraie Janet (1974) Educational Development in Afghanistan: History of the Teachers College, Columbia University Educational Assistance Program, 1954–1971. Doctoral dissertation, Teachers College Columbia University, 1974.

Teachers College Columbia University Team (1959) Teacher Education in Afghanistan. (Report no. 11). Kabul, Afghanistan.

Teachers College, Columbia University (2005) Afghanistan Education Projects. Textbooks: New Afghan Textbooks for Primary School Children. http://www.c.edu/centers/afghanproject/index.html?cat=textbooks&id=New+Afghan+Textbooks+for+Primary+School+Children accessed on January 17, 2006.

Transitional Islamic State of Afghanistan (2004) National Report on the Development
     of education in Afghanistan. http://www.ibe.unesco.org/International/ICE47/
     English/Natreps/reports/afghanistan.pdf
University of Washington. Walter Chapin Simpson Center for Humanities. Cities and
     Architecture along the Silk Road. Samarkand. http://depts.washington.edu/
     uwch/silkroad/index.html

Chapter 3

SCHOOLING IN BANGLADESH

Sajeda Amin

OVERVIEW OF COUNTRY

Bangladesh is a small country covering an area of 55,126 square miles with a population of about 147 million.[1] Bangladesh is located at the confluence of three major rivers, Jamuna, Meghna, and Brahmaputra. Most of the country is topographically defined as flood plains, and 80 percent of the Bangladeshi population lives in rural areas. The capital city, Dhaka, is a rapidly growing metropolis of about 14 million inhabitants. The People's Republic of Bangladesh came into being after a nine-month long struggle for independence in 1971. It was previously the eastern province of the Islamic Republic of Pakistan which in turn had been created in 1947 following the cessation of the British colonial rule in India.

Approximately 90 percent of Bangladeshis are adherents of Islam. The rest are mostly Hindus, Christians, and Buddhists. Bangladesh is ethnically and linguistically homogenous and Bangla, or Bengali, is the language spoken by the majority. However, there are also some 75 small ethnic minority groups together constituting less than 1 percent of the population and speaking as many languages. After independence, Bangladesh emerged as a war ravaged economy that had to rely heavily on external aid. A series of disasters in the early 1970s made Bangladesh a symbol of desperate poverty and Henry Kissinger labeled Bangladesh an international basket case. Since then, the country can certainly list some significant achievements: life expectancy for men and women increased from 56 years to over 65 years, infant mortality was halved from over 130 per 1000 live births at the time of independence to 65 per 1000 live births in 2004, and the average number of births declined from over 6.5 birth per woman to less than 3 births per woman over the same time period.

With regard to education, there is a primary school in every village in Bangladesh. Schooling is nearly universal with almost all children beginning primary school and one in every two secondary school-aged children attending school. Universal schooling is a relatively recent phenomenon, however. Bangladesh achieved near universal schooling at the end of the 20th century after intensive investments in early education that began during the 1980s. Prior to these efforts to promote overall schooling, educational achievement was low in the country and schooling was a preserve of the elite. A series of policy measures was designed to overcome barriers that prevented access to schools, and these measures were based on the premise that endemic poverty in Bangladesh was the primary determinant of low levels of schooling. Not only did the poor lack the ability to afford extra resources needed for their children's education, but demands for child labor also competed for the time that children could spend in school.

HISTORICAL DEVELOPMENT OF EDUCATION

Present-day Bangladesh was formerly a part of greater Bengal in northeast India. From ancient times to the 20th century the region was governed by a succession of rulers as part of India. Beginning with the medieval times, the growth and decline of schooling was strongly affected by the decisions made at the highest levels of the state, with such decision-making bodies often located thousands of miles away from where policies were implemented. This historical pattern of governance from a distance continues in present-day Bangladesh with external donor assistance playing an important role in formulating and implementing education policy in Bangladesh. A brief historical overview of the development of education and schooling in Bangladesh is provided below.

Education in the Ancient Times

Very little is known about systems of schooling during the ancient times. It is likely that schooling was primarily connected to religious practice. Writings of scholars traveling through Bengal suggest that there were centers of learning called *viharas* where Buddhist and Brahmanic (Hindu) scripture was taught. Although these were centers of learning for Buddhist and Vedic knowledge they also taught grammar, philosophy, dialectics, medicine, astronomy, music, art, *chaturveda* (four holy scriptures in Hinduism), *sankhya* (counting), *Mahayana shastras* (Buddhist scriptures), and yoga. According to a Chinese scholar Fa-Hien who came to live in Tamralipti (Midnapur in West Bengal) for two years to study and copy Buddhist scripts, there were 300 Bhuddhist *shramanas* (ascetics) studying and living in 6–7 *viharas* in Kajangalga (southwest Bengal), more than 3000 *shramanas* in 20 *viharas* in Pundravardhana (Mahasthangahr in North Bengal), 2000 *shramanas* in 30 *viharas* in Samatata, and more than 2000 *shramanas* in 10 *viharas* in Tamralipti and Karnasuvarna (Murshidabad in West Bengal). Although there is no documentation of the system of learning, it has been suggested that scholars established small tutorial centers in their homes or temples to give tutelage and students moved from teacher to teacher after mastering specific subjects. The evidence suggests that Sanskrit was the language of education but not of everyday communication and education was a privilege for the elite. Given that women were not involved in religious leadership it is likely that any learning related to religion was also limited to boys and men.

Education in the Medieval and Early Modern Period (1400s–1600s)

Education received widespread state support from the Muslim rulers of Bengal during medieval times. It is likely that the Muslim rulers who came from central Asia and elsewhere were influenced by the strong tradition of promoting education in Islam as part of their religious obligation. State patronage and support was available for building mosques and *madrashas* (Muslim schools). Teaching was encouraged by giving land free of rent to scholars who would offer instruction as a part of their duty. Schools were closely associated with religion so different systems evolved for Hindu and Muslim children. Muslim schools were called *maktabs* and *madrashas* and Hindu schools were called *pathshalas*. While Muslim education focused primarily on teaching the Quran and the Arabic language, some Muslim schools also taught grammar, literature, and law. *Pathshalas* taught the Sanskrit and Bangla languages along with religious studies. Persian or Farsi was the state language so both Hindus and Muslims studied Persian. It is likely that girls did not attend these schools since the subject matter taught was oriented toward religion and government, both being areas in which women were not active participants.

Education in the 18th Century

By most accounts, education in Bengal suffered from relative neglect during the struggle for power between Muslim and British rulers and the ascendance of the East India Company. In the early part of the 18th century, education received some limited support from the Company through their support to various European Christian missionaries in Bengal. For example in the early days of the East India Company, Danish missionaries received the support of the East India Company. Although the activities of the missionaries were localized in Serampore, it is likely that they contributed to bringing about several systematic changes in education in the entire region. First and foremost, they introduced regular and fixed hours of instruction and a broad curriculum. Vernacular education was promoted by producing books in Indian languages. English education was also introduced at this time. William Carey, a Baptist missionary from England continued the work of the early Danish missionaries and is credited with promoting English education further in India. Carey was also based in Serampore near Calcutta.

Education in the 19th Century

Several significant and consequential changes were implemented during the
19th century. An influential survey during the British rule in India that was
conducted by William Adam and entitled the "Survey of indigenous education
in Bengal" (1835–1838), argued for greater investment in education. Adam's
report indicated that there were 100,000 schools (practically one in every village)
in the Indian states of Bengal and Bihar even prior to the advent of the British.

Raja Rammohon Roy, a very influential reformer in Calcutta, argued for the
promotion of the spread of Western knowledge through English education.
The use of Persian as the official language was replaced with English and Indian
languages and this strengthened the demand for English education. A resolution
passed in 1844 declared that preference would be given to those with knowledge
of English for all government appointments which increased the demand for
English education even further. This policy had a particularly profound impact
on the Muslims population in the state of Bengal since few of them had been
educated in English and had the necessary prerequisites to enter the civil service.
As late as the 1901 census, there was no English literacy among Muslim men in
Bengal, and the overall English literacy was only 0.9 percent and concentrated
among affluent Hindus.

British administrator Charles Wood presented the education dispatch of 1854
which summarized the recommendations of a Select Committee of the House of
Commons in England.[2] The mandate of the committee was to conduct a thor-
ough enquiry into educational development in Colonial India. The Wood's
dispatch resulted in the establishment of the three Indian universities in Calcutta
(now known as Kolkata), Madras (now known as Chennai), and Bombay (now
called Mumbai). It asserted that "conferring upon the natives of India those vast
moral and material blessings which flow from the general diffusion of useful
knowledge" was a moral responsibility of colonial rulers. Education was promoted "not only to produce a higher degree of intellectual fitness, but to raise
the moral character of those who partake of its advantages, and so to supply you
with servants to whose probity you may with increased confidence commit offices
to trust" (Woods dispatch as cited in Jalaluddin and Chowdhury, 1996). It
further recommended that while English language should be taught where
there was demand, there should also be careful attention to vernacular education
particular for the masses who may be not be equipped to learn in English. To this
end it recommended the translation of English books into local languages.
Another strategy to promote local acceptability was to promote secular education
recognizing there was considerable misapprehension among the populace with
regard to religion. The dispatch emphasized the importance of female education
and cited the importance of benevolent contributions by native gentlemen in
setting up girls' schools. Finally the committee noted that any expense toward
the promotion of education would be amply rewarded because "the general
diffusion of knowledge is inseparably followed by more orderly habits, by

increasing industry, by a taste for the comforts of life, by exertion to acquire them, and by the growing prosperity of the people" (cited in Jalaluddin and Chowdhury, 1996).

By the end of the 19th century, rising nationalism reinforced the demand for vernacular education, particularly from Muslim Associations. A survey commissioned by one of the Viceroys in India, Lord Curzon, around the end of the century found that only one in every four boys had an education and four out of five villages in Bengal did not have schools. To remedy this situation he recommended the promotion of state-supported schools. A Resolution on Muslim Education was passed in 1871 in recognition of the poor state of education among Muslims of Bengal, and is thought to have been influenced by Hunter's description of radicalization of Muslims through the Faraizi Movement,[3] thought in part to be due to lack of educational opportunities. This involved a system of quotas being put into place to encourage Muslim participation in education and employment. This system of giving preference to Muslims continued into the early 20th century.

Education in the 20th Century

Despite the above affirmative action policies, Muslim representation continued to be low in government services and educational institutions. Nationalist demands for vernacular education increased in strength and favored the introduction of compulsory elementary education. In 1901, the Director of Public Instruction reported that only 26 out of a total of 382 teachers in government employment were Muslim. A report written by Earle, an officer on special duty in charge of Muslim education in Bengal, attributed the under representation to the indifference of Education Inspectors toward the issue of Muslim education. In 1907, in a letter of demands to the Lieutenant-General of Bengal, a civil group of Muslims in Calcutta called for the designation of a Muslim to the post of Deputy Director of Public Education. The recommendation was not accepted but a special Muslim inspecting staff was appointed in each Division.

A more intractable problem faced by Muslims was access to education. The majority of Muslims who lacked education lived in rural areas, far away from urban centers where education was available. It was suggested that special boarding houses or hostels should be set up for those Muslim students who were from the eastern districts of Bengal. Despite a growing appreciation for English education, supported by resources from wealthier Muslims, the sentiment that they needed a separate system of education persisted among Muslims. Despite several pointed efforts to improve education among Muslims, they continued to be under represented at all levels of education as compared with the Hindus and Christians. It is generally held that the ambiguity of parents towards purely secular education, and the value placed on Persian and Urdu as the languages for Muslim gentlemen, prevented the successful implementation of a fully satisfactory solution to the problem of poor educational achievement.

After the partition of India in 1947 into India and Pakistan, the provincial government of East Pakistan (present day Bangladesh) appointed an education commission that recommended some important changes to the curriculum. It proposed that all primary education should be offered in Bangla. Overall levels of schooling continued to be low during the time that Bangladesh was part of Pakistan. In 1971, overall proportions of men and women who had had schooling remained as low with less than one in five children completing primary school. After Bangladesh emerged as an independent country, the number of schools expanded and primary education was nationalized by its government. During the last twenty-five years of the 20th century the total number of schools doubled with a considerable expansion of the role of the private sector in offering education.

EDUCATION DURING THE PRESENT TIMES

Educational systems and policy in present-day Bangladesh are strongly influenced by the recommendations of the education commissions of 1974. The state subsidizes education but to different degrees. Education is most subsidized at the primary school level and the degree of subsidy diminishes at the secondary and higher secondary levels. The medium of education is in the vernacular. Most of the curriculum is secular but religious education is offered from the third grade and up even in mainstream schools. The Ministry of Education is responsible for administering policy at all levels and all public school employees report to the Ministry through a series of intermediaries. The Ministry operates through separate directorates for primary, secondary, tertiary, and vocational education. It also supervises the roles of the regional education Boards responsible for administering examinations. These are merit scholarship examinations in the fifth and eighth grades, the secondary school certificate examinations at the end of the tenth grade, and the higher secondary examinations at the end of the twelfth grade. Two separate curriculum Boards are responsible for setting curricula for mainstream schools and religious schools, or *madrashas*.

The Education Ministry retains strict control over school policies for public schools and enlisted private schools. While the majority of primary schools are fully state run, the majority of secondary schools are private schools that receive government subventions, often up to 90 percent of their operating budgets. All such schools that are enlisted have to follow a uniform official policy and curricula. However, the majority of schools dependent on non-governmental organizations (NGOs) and private individuals for financial accounting and taxes are not supervised by the Ministry. They are free to set their own policies including determining tuition fees and employment policies, and designing curricula. There is great variation in the quality of education provided by these institutions. While all of the Bengali medium schools follow the government curriculum and their students take the regional Board examinations, the English medium schools typically follow their own curricula following guidelines for the

O' Levels set in the United Kingdom and administered through the British Council. They are free to charge market rates for tuition and often charge substantial additional entrance fees.

Primary Education

In present-day Bangladesh nearly all children above the age of 5 years attend school for some time in their lives. School enrollment levels reached 95 percent in 1995 with boys and girls equally likely to attend school. There are nearly 80,000 primary schools in the country or roughly one school in every village. Schools vary in terms of their sources of funding and approaches to teaching curriculum. Nearly 50 percent of all primary schools are completely run or managed by the government. The remaining 50 percent are funded and operated by NGOs, religious institutions, or private individuals. One in every four schools is privately run; another 6 percent are religious schools (*maktabs* and *madrashas*) that teach Islam and Arabic in addition to other subjects; and the remainder are schools operated by the myriad development organizations that operate in the country. The NGO affiliated schools typically cater to older children from poor families who have either never attended schools or have dropped out at an early age. All primary schools are mixed gender schools with the exception of *madrashas* that are usually single-sex institutions. Some NGO schools give preference to girls.

Children attending school at the primary level attend school six days a week with Fridays being observed as school closing. Daily school hours are extremely short compared to international standards with school hours at the primary level ranging from two to four hours. Students in Grades 1 and 2 attend for two hours while students in Grades 3 and 4 attend for four hours. Most students attending NGO schools attend school for about three hours on days that school is in session. The actual contact hours between teachers and students is even shorter, rarely exceeding 40 minutes each day, because teachers often have other duties that compete with classroom responsibilities. There are few sanctions against teacher absenteeism, and low contact hours with teachers may be an important reason for the poor performance of children in schools.

Schooling is also hampered by early dropout rates. Approximately ten percent of students drop out at every grade level through primary school. Dropout rates are highest among the poorest students and low schooling is an important correlate of persistent poverty. The need to work for basic subsistence is a common reason for dropping out of school. Children who work in agriculture earn a wage and one or two meals a day when they work. These meals are an important part of household subsistence for poor families. In 1994, the government of Bangladesh started a new program to provide financial incentives to poor families to motivate them to send children to school. This program was initiated in 25 percent of the rural areas of the country initially and later extended to the entire country. During the first ten years of the program the financial incentive was in the form of 15 kilograms of wheat to each eligible student every month. Primary school teachers bore the responsibility of implementing a significant portion of the program. The teachers were required to identify eligible children and track attendance to ensure that children's attendance met the eligibility criteria. Children are required to maintain 85 percent attendance. In 2004 this program was changed to substitute the wheat with cash handouts as incentives. As a result of the Food for Education Program and other efforts to boost enrollment, current demand for schooling has led to considerable overcrowding in schools. Most rural schools run on double shifts with younger students attending earlier in the day and older students attending the later shifts. Urban private schools have longer school hours and the students attend school for at least four hours per day.

The basic requirement for primary school teachers is that they should have passed the tenth grade qualifying Secondary School Certificate (SSC) examinations. According to a UNICEF report almost half of all teachers have a SSC level education, and only 13 percent hold a college degree. However, 9 out of 10 teachers have received some form of training in education through the government's training institutions. Approximately one in three primary school teachers is a woman, but women overwhelmingly out-number men in the non-governmental schools. There is no formal teacher's training for *madrasha* teachers and all these teachers are themselves graduates of the *madrasha* system.

Government primary schools follow curricula set by the National Curriculum Board. Books are supplied to students free of cost according to the curriculum along with teaching guides for teachers. The medium of instruction is Bangla in all government schools and most NGO schools. English is the medium of education in a small number of private schools mostly in urban areas though the number of English medium schools is increasing steadily. While English medium schools are primarily an urban phenomenon, they are also being established increasingly in urbanized rural areas and small towns. The number of private schools has increased from less than 4000 to over 17,000 while the number of government primary schools remained at 40,000 in the country. English is taught as a second language in secondary schools. Subjects taught in first and second grade are Bangla, arithmetic and social studies.

The school day is divided up into 45-minute segments. A different teacher is responsible for each of the segments although teachers of a school do not necessarily specialize in subjects that they teach. Classroom interaction is influenced by teaching guides provided to teachers along with text-books. These teaching guides also emphasize learning and retention of facts. Classroom activities consist of collective review rather than individual work. Students are assigned homework regularly but written homework assignments are less common than assignments to require students to read and memorize. Although there are strict rules against physical punishment, reports of such disciplinary action in schools are still common. Examinations are administered twice a year. Methods of evaluation rely on testing how much information a student is able to retain from the texts taught. Relatively little attention is paid to problem solving or analytical abilities. The following section provides a glimpse into a typical school day of a primary school child.

Everyday Life in a Primary School

Rubina Akhtar was born on February 13, 1995. Her father died when she began school at the age of five years. Along with her mother and two siblings she lives with her maternal grandfather in Uttar para of Gokarna village. She describes how she spent the previous day:

"I woke up at 6 A.M. After brushing my teeth and doing *oju* (ritual ablutions before prayer) I went to study Arabic with the local religious teacher at the neighborhood mosque. I studied for an hour. Then I came home, took a bath in the pond and ate breakfast. After breakfast I took my schoolbag and walked to my coaching class at the school from 10 A.M. to 12 noon.[4] My shift for school began at 12 P.M. The first two periods of study were Bangla and mathematics. I went home for tiffin break. Then I came back to school for lunch. I had only one class after lunch because we only have half a day of school on Thursdays. We had English language lessons during the period after lunch. School was over at 2 P.M. I came home, washed up, and studied for two hours. Then I played *kutkut* (a game like hopscotch) with my younger sister and other kids who live near my house. After that I washed my hands and feet and sat down to study. I studied from 7 P.M. to 10 P.M. I studied English. The assignment from school was to memorize a paragraph with the title 'At the Zoo'. I memorized another paragraph called 'Sports Day'. At 10 P.M. I ate dinner with my sister and my mother and then went to bed."

Secondary Schools

In the 1990s, the government of Bangladesh put in place two programs that had important implications for raising attendance in schools. These programs provide incentives for poor children to attend classes and have resulted in dramatic improvements in school attendance at the secondary level. However, despite this effort the number of students who do not complete primary school still remains high. Secondary schools are considerably fewer in number as compared to primary schools. In 2002 there were a total of 16,562 secondary schools of which approximately 1 out of every 7 is located in an urban area. The ratio of secondary schools to primary schools is a little less than one to four.

While most primary schools are mixed gender, secondary schools are equally likely to be either single-sex or mixed gender institutions. A secondary school scholarship program for female students in rural areas was introduced to provide families the incentive to send their daughters to schools. There is no poverty related inclusion criteria but students have to attend regularly, pass the annual examinations, and parents have to sign a bond that their daughters will not be married before the age of 18 years. This program has been credited with improving girls' education significantly in the ten years it has been in operation. Improved attendance has now resulted in gender parity in schools at all levels but Grade 10. In fact, from Grades 6 to 9 more girls than boys attend school, and an overall 53 percent of all secondary school students are girls. Students attending secondary school spend over four hours in school when it is in session. They also spend more time commuting to school since secondary schools are typically located further away than neighborhood primary schools.

Secondary school teachers are required to have passed at least a two-year bachelors degree. Secondary school teachers appointed to government-operated schools are recruited through special service examinations administered by the government at the national level. Mass recruitment efforts took place in the mid-1990s, but since then recruitment is more limited and on an as needed basis. After they become official, new recruits teach in schools fully operated by the government as well as in schools that are privately run with support from the government. Teachers recruited for private schools are trained in a variety of ways and demonstrate a range of quality in their teaching and are usually local from the immediate area.

All secondary schools are required to follow a standard curriculum. The only exceptions are private English medium schools where students sit for the O' Level examinations administered by the British Council. The Bangladesh school textbook Board sets the school curriculum. The Ministry is responsible for making books available at the school level at the beginning of each school year. Between Grade 5 and Grade 8, in addition to Bangla and English language and literature, students are also required to take English as a second language, history, geography, social studies (or civics), and religious studies, with physical education being mandatory. Beginning in Grade 9, students are tracked into science, humanities or commerce according to the type of national examination they will appear for at the end of Grade 10. Students have to pass in all except the optional subject in order to successfully complete and get a school-leaving certificate. If they fail in one subject all subjects have to be retaken the following year. A plan, yet to be implemented, has been developed to reform the tracking system so that all students follow a uniform curriculum. There is a striking gender distinction in the track of studies chosen at the secondary level. The country is divided into Regional Education Boards and students take the Board Examination for their own region. According to published statistics on examination success rates, the six Boards of the country have variable success rates. However there are certain common gender patterns. Girls are considerably more likely than boys to be in the humanities track that has shown consistently lower passing rates in every Board. For every Board, a student is half as likely to pass the examination if she is in the humanities track than if she is in the science track. Girls are considerably more likely to be in the humanities track, for example in the Dhaka Board, 70 percent of girls study in the humanities track where the overall pass rate in the SSC examination is 30 percent. By comparison 60 percent of boys take examinations in the science track where the successful completion rate is 60 percent. This choice in track of studies is consequential in terms of the quality of education received and it is also consequential in terms of educational and career options available to the students later in life. It is difficult, if not impossible, to later switch into the science track if a student has already chosen one of the other tracks at this stage. Given the importance of national examinations and the overall low success rates particularly in rural areas, teaching methods are strongly oriented towards success in the examinations. At the secondary stage most students have to attend extra classes in order to pass examinations. Teachers rely on class lectures and bi-annual examinations. Each class begins with a lecture, a demonstration, and a question and answer session, and teachers often call on students to test them during lectures and to demonstrate their work on the board. The following excerpt provides an enlightening glimpse into a typical day experienced by a secondary school student:

Everyday Life in a Secondary School

Syeda Shamim Akhtar, 13, studies in Grade 9 in Gokarna High School. She is one of five children. Her father is a high school teacher. All students in Grade 9 have to take English, Bangla, mathematics and religious studies and then choose from among three tracks of studies. Shamim has chosen the humanities track in which the students study history, geography, and civics. She has also taken home economics as an extra optional subject. Following is a description of how Shamim spent a typical day.

"I woke up at 6:15 A.M. brushed my teeth, prayed and sat down to study. I studied English till 7:30 A.M., then Bangla from 7:30 to 8:00 A.M., and math from 8:00 to 9:00 A.M. I solved eight to ten problems during this time. At 9:00 A.M. I went for my private tutoring lessons in English grammar. My father pays 200 takas (about U.S. $3.30) per month for these lessons. At 10:30 A.M. I went to school. Yesterday was half day so I had school from 10:00 A.M. to 2:30 P.M. with no lunch break. Normally we have school from 10:00 A.M. to 4:00 P.M. Each of our study periods is 45 minutes long. We began the day with English period where the lesson was a chapter on computers. We learnt the names of different parts of the computer from a book. From 10:45 to 11:30 A.M. we had mathematics. Yesterday's topic was inequalities. The teacher reviewed five homework problems that were assigned and worked out two problems on the board. Next we had civics lessons and learnt about the relationship between state and government. Between 12:45 and 1:30 P.M. we had history and we discussed the social history of rivers in Bangladesh. The day ended with a lesson in Bangla comprehension. The teacher assigned a piece that the class had to analyze.

I came home from school and took a bath. I said my *Zohr* (noon prayers) and then ate rice and fish for lunch. After lunch I went for a short walk and then

I took a nap from 4:00 to 5:30 P.M. I woke up, did ablutions for prayer and said my *Asr* (early afternoon prayers). After the prayers at about 6:00 P.M., I studied for objective examinations. This is a new examination that is being introduced and we have to learn how to answer short multiple-choice questions. At 6:30 P.M. I went to the roof of our house for a short walk and then I prayed *Maghreb* (prayers at sunset). After prayers I had some tea and biscuits at around 7:00 P.M. and sat down to study till 9:30 P.M. At 9:30 I said my *Esha* (evening prayers), ate dinner and studied again from 10:30 P.M. to 12:30 A.M. This is how I usually spend my day. Sometimes I watch TV instead of napping during the day."

Post-secondary Schools

Post-secondary education is similar to secondary education in many ways. Since passing rates at the Grade 10 level is relatively low with only about 50 percent of all students who appear in the examination qualifying to get to the next level, post-secondary education is much more selective. Passing rates are similar within each track of studies for boys and girls but the gender composition of each track varies. Girls favor humanities while boys favor the science and commerce tracks. There were 2634 post-secondary institutions in the country in 2002 out of which 151 were completely run by the government through the Ministry of Education. All the remaining institutions are privately run but receive support from the government for teacher salaries.

At the highest level of education there are a total of 54 universities of which 17 are state supported. The remaining are private universities that operate without any public funding. There are four engineering universities in the country. The total enrollment at public universities was 92,152, out of which 26 percent reflect female students. However, enrollment in the national university and the open university, both of which allow part-time enrollment, is not included in this statistic. In addition to these academically oriented institutions there is a burgeoning number of technical institutes and training centers providing specialized education at the post-secondary level. In 2002 there were 1562 such institutes of which 1405 are private with a total enrollment of 134,016. The percent of students who are female in these institutions is 26 percent. During the first two years of post-secondary level schooling, students are oriented towards taking a Board examination at the end of 12 years of schooling. This examination tests at a higher skills level but is administered through the same mechanism as described earlier for the SSC examination. 19.5 percent of the teachers at the post-secondary level are female, and all teachers at this level typically qualified with a Masters degree or the equivalent from a recognized university in the country. All college teachers, as they are called, have to appear for national qualifying examinations if they are to teach in government colleges. Government college positions are transferable and a teacher is typically posted for about five years in each college.

CONCLUSION

Despite the considerable achievements in providing universal education, schools in Bangladesh face important challenges in the years ahead. The expansion of the education system may have been achieved at the cost of some decline in the quality of schooling as greater numbers of students compete for the scarce resources in the field of education. Although the state plays a substantial role in the provision of schools at the lowest levels and for the poorest segments of children, access to quality education remains a function of private investments. Some of this takes the form of private tutoring in addition to the formal education received in school. It can also take the form of considerable parental investment. At the highest levels, public education is limited to a small segment of students who are able to compete successfully. For the majority, education remains a privilege of only those who can afford the increasing costs of a private education in the fast expanding private sector. For students from poor families who cannot afford these increased costs, another option is to turn to *madrasha* or NGO schools. A recent national survey conducted among adolescents by the author suggests that in some rural areas boys and girls are switching to from mainstream to *madrasha* schools. The growth of religious education is not well understood but deserves attention as an emerging alternative to mainstream schools.

MAJOR EDUCATION REFORMS OVER THE PAST 80 YEARS

1930   The Bengal Rural Primary Education Act
1973   Nationalization of all primary schools
1974   *Qudrat-e-Khuda* education Commission
1981   School Management Committee Act
1990   Compulsory Primary Education Act
        Tuition-free primary education for girls
1994   Food for Education Program
1994   Female Secondary School Scholarship Scheme
1995   *Madrasha* education brought under general school system

APPENDIX CASE STUDY: GOKARNA SYED WALIULLAH HIGH SCHOOL (ESTABLISHED IN 1915 BY NAWAB SYED SHAMSUL HUDA CHOWDHURY)

Gokarna is located in a remote area of eastern Bangladesh. Its topographical characteristics make it relatively inaccessible by modern standards whereas most of the rest of Bangladesh is accessible by road transport from the capital city of Dhaka. In the past when river ways were the main system of transport, Gokarna was not a remote village. It was easily accessible by river and train from Calcutta and Dhaka. As a result there were several well-to-do families who sent young men to study in Calcutta. Among them was Syed Shamsul Huda Chowdhury (?–1922), an advocate who practiced in the Calcutta courts and eventually joined politics to become a member of the Indian Legislative Council. Among his many other official activities, Nawab Chowdhury was also a member of an education commission. Nawab established a high school in the name of his uncle, Syed Waliulla, on their ancestral land adjacent to the Nawab's palatial home in the village. The school now enrolls 1200 students and offers residential facilities to students who travel long distances. In the past residential students were more common than now when there are more schooling options available.

The school traditionally catered to boys. Teachers were usually residents of the village and a disproportionate number of them came from the large Hindu enclave of the village. In the early years schooling rates were higher among Hindus than among Muslims. While a few of the more religiously oriented Muslim families from the village preferred to send their children to *madrashas*, most residents of Gokarna attended the local school. Currently the school's gender composition has changed substantially, and according to an estimate made by a teacher the ratio of girls to boys is 60:40.

The school has 20 members on the teaching staff who receive their salaries from the Ministry of Education. It is common for private schools such as the Gokarna High School to receive subsidies from the government in the form of teacher salaries, books, scholarships, and other resources. The teacher-student ratio at Gokarna is higher than that of the average private school in rural Bangladesh, possibly because it is a long-established school with a good reputation. All the teachers reside in the village and have permanent non-transferable positions. The salary levels for teachers and the number of teaching positions are determined according to sanctions from the government that are dependent on enrollment levels. The basic budget is about 800,000–900,000 takas[5] per year and that is inclusive of teacher salaries. Head teachers get 9100 takas senior teachers are paid 6800 takas, junior teachers 5100 takas, and the clerical staff 3100 takas.

The school offers education in the science, humanities, and commerce tracks. There is a laboratory for chemistry, physics, and biology. There are separate toilet facilities for boys and girls, and all the classrooms have electricity. There is a school Management Committee. The school has recently received three computers through a government grant.

The general opinion in the village is that the quality of education imparted in the school has declined over the years as enrollment has increased and large numbers of students compete for scarce resources. At the same time rules have become lax and 80 to 90 percent of students are promoted every year, regardless of whether they have mastered the basic competencies. Not all children in the village attend school. Students attending the high school come from Gokarna and the surrounding villages. The village is most easily accessed by boat during the monsoon.

A primary school is located on the same premises as the high school. There are residential facilities in the school. Most students who continue schooling after the high school level go to Nasirnagar degree college, located approximately 10 kilometers away in the Thana headquarters. Enrollment, total budget, and courses taught at the college are similar to the high school. The college receives generous support from a local benevolent Trust set up by a wealthy family in the area. Funds from this trust are used to meet a regular shortfall in the college budget of some 150,000–200,000 takas.

NOTES

The author gratefully acknowledges support from the U.K. Department of International Development and the Hewlett Foundation, and thanks the people of Gokarna village, Nasirnagar Thana in Brahmanbaria district. In particular she is grateful to her father-in-law, Syed Abdul Wahed (1925–2005) for providing much of the oral history on Gokarna High School based on his own experience as a student in that school.

1. http://www.cia.gov/cia/publications/factbook/rankorder/2119rank.html.

2. Charles Wood was then the President of the Board of Control of the English East India Company.

3. The *Faraizi* Movement (1830–1857) was led by a Bengali Muslim leader from East Bengal, Haji Shariatullah, upon his return from *Hajj*. The name is derived from the Arabic word *Faraiz* meaning duty. The movement encouraged reform in religious practices to conform to the leaders own preferences as well as to protest against specific issues of social justice with regard to British colonial rule.

4. Upon probing she explained that these are classes that are held only for students who have been selected for the Class Five scholarship examination. A neighbor who was watching explained that about 15 students from a total of 65 enrolled in Class Five are selected to sit for a national merit scholarship examination each year. Rubina ranked sixth in her class by order of merit in the past year's final exam so she qualified by dint of merit.

5. Taka: Bangladesh currency with approximately 71 takas equivalent to U.S. $1.

BIBLIOGRAPHY

Ahmed, Sufia (1996) *Muslim Community in Bengal 1884–1912*. Dhaka: University Press Limited.

Amin, Sajeda and Gilda Sedgh (1998) "Incentive Schemes for School Attendance in Rural Bangladesh." Population Council Research Division Working Paper No. 106. http://www.popcouncil.org/pdfs/wp/106.pdf, last accessed August 11, 2005.

Amin, Sajeda and Mary Arends-Kuenning (2000) "The Effects of Schooling Incentive Programs on Household Resource Allocation in Bangladesh." Population Council Research Division Working Paper No. 133. http://www.popcouncil.org/pdfs/wp/106.pdf, last accessed August 11, 2005.

Arends-Kuenning, Mary and Sajeda Amin (2004) "School Incentive Programs and Children's Activities: The Case of Bangladesh." *Comparative Education Review* 48(3): 295–317.

BANBEIS (2003) Bangladesh Education Statistics, 2003. BANBEIS Publication No. 362. Dhaka: Bangladesh Bureau of Educational Information and Statistics, Ministry of Education.

Banglapedia at http://www.banglapedia.org

Cleland, John C., James F. Phillips, Sajeda Amin, and Gholam M. Kamal (1994) *The Determinants of Reproductive Change in Bangladesh: Success in a Challenging*

Environment. World Bank Regional and Sector Studies. Washington D.C., The World Bank.

Hunter, W. W. (2002). *The Indian Musalmans.* Reprint. New Delhi: Rupa & Co.

Islam, Sirajul (Edited) (2004) "Education (Zillur Rahman Siddiqui). Society of Bangladesh." In *Banglapedia: National Encyclopedia of Bangladesh, Volume 4.* Dhaka: Asiatic.

Jalaluddin, A. K. and A. Mushtaque R. Chowdhury (1996) *Getting Started: Universalizing Quality Primary Education in Bangladesh.* Dhaka: University Press Limited.

Murshid, Tazeen M. (1996) *The Sacred and the Secular: Bengal Muslim Discourses 1871–1977.* Dhaka: University Press Limited.

National Institute of Population Research and Training (NIPORT), Mitra and Associates, and ORC Macro, 2005. *Bangladesh: Demographic and Health Survey 2004.* Dhaka, Bangladesh and Calverton, Maryland (USA): National Institute of Population Research and Training (NIPORT), Mitra and Associates, and ORC Macro.

National Research Council (1981) *Estimates of Recent Trends in Fertility and Mortality in Bangladesh.* National Academy Press: Washington D.C.

UNICEF (1992) *Assessment of Basic Competencies in Children in Bangladesh: A Status Paper.* Dhaka: UNICEF.

World Bank (2000) *Bangladesh Education Sector Review: Volumes 1–3.* Dhaka: University Press Limited.

Chapter 4

SCHOOLING IN BHUTAN

Tenzin Chhoeda

OVERVIEW OF THE COUNTRY

Bhutan is a Himalayan kingdom located between India and China. This kingdom of 38,394 square kilometers is completely landlocked, with rugged mountainous terrain rising steeply from 100 meters at the southern borders to over 7000 meters in the north. The country can be broadly divided into three geographical divisions corresponding to three distinct climatic zones. These are the sub-tropical southern belt, the central inner Himalayan temperate zone, and the higher Himalayan region. The population of Bhutan is widely scattered across the steep mountain slopes and narrow valleys, which makes the provision of social services such as education and training, extremely difficult. The total population of Bhutan is about 635,000 and over 69 percent of this population is engaged in subsistence farming (2005 census). The country has never been colonized and has a unique and rich culture. Thimphu is the capital and largest city.

Most Bhutanese follow the school of Tibetan Buddhism. The national language is Dzonkha, and there are 15 other languages and dialects spoken in different parts of the country. The most dominant is Tshangla, spoken in the east. Mangdipkha and Khengkha are spoken in the central parts. Nepali is spoken by the late settlers in the southern part of the kingdom. In the schools, English is the medium of instruction and Dzongkha is taught as the national language although English now has official status as well.

Stone tools, weapons, and archaeological evidence suggest that Bhutan was inhabited as early as 2000 B.C. The earliest transcribed event in Bhutan mentions the passage of the saint Padmasambhava in the 8th century. Bhutan's early history is unclear because most of the records were lost after a fire destroyed Punakha Dzong, the ancient capital in 1827. By the 10th century, Bhutan's political development was heavily influenced by its religious history. Various sub-sects of

Buddhism emerged and were patronized by various Mongol and Tibetan over-lords. The decline of the Mongols in the 14th century eventually led to the ascendancy of the Drukpa sub-sect by the 16th century. Until the early 17th century, Bhutan consisted of minor warring fiefdoms until it was unified by Shabdrung Ngawang Namgyal, a Tibetan lama. Both during and immediately after Shabdrung's rule the country came under constant attacks by the Tibetans and their Mongol allies. All these attacks were unsuccessful and gave the Bhutanese a new confidence in their new nation. During the 1870s, power struggles between the rival valleys of Paro and Trongsa led to Civil war in Bhutan, and eventually to the ascendancy of Ugyen Wangchuk, the *ponlop* (governor) of Tongsa. From his power base in central Bhutan, Ugyen Wangchuck defeated his political enemies and united the country following several civil wars and rebellions in the period 1882–1885. In 1907, Ugyen Wangchuk was unani-mously chosen as the hereditary king of the country by an assembly of leading Buddhist monks, government officials, and heads of important families. The current king is Jigme Singye Wangchuk and he has initiated a move toward constitutional government.

Because of its geophysical and political situation, Bhutan remained isolated from the larger world until the middle of the 20th century. It was only in the early 1960s that Bhutan chose to break its isolation and make contact with the outside world. It embarked on the path of modernization with the launch of its First Five-Year Development Plan in 1960. The overarching priority for development has been the establishment of a basic infrastructure including roadways, telecom-munications, health and education services, and modernization of the agricultural sector. Strengthening its national identity, enhancing the quality of life for the Bhutanese people, ensuring the sustainability of services, conserving its rich biodiversity and natural resources, and achieving self-sufficiency in basic food items have been the key themes underpinning Bhutan's development policies in the subsequent Five-Year Plans. This has been balanced by investments in key economic sectors such as hydropower, mining, forestry, and limited tourism. Bhutan's development strategy has been cautious to ensure that the pace of change does not destroy its unique natural and cultural heritage. The govern-ment's strict environmental policies have been reinforced by a strong conserva-tion ethic amongst the people, and this has ensured that 70 percent of the country has been kept under forest cover. Considered as one of the most important locations for biodiversity, Bhutan aims to maintain a minimum of 60 percent of its land under forest cover. A basic road network and telecommunication system now links major population centers of the country and this has served to bring a large proportion of the population out of isolation. This infrastructure also facilitates the marketing of agricultural products and easier access to goods and services. However, still over half the population remains more than a half-day's walk from the nearest road, and completely dependent on rough trails and mule tracks for getting from one village to another. A comprehensive primary health care system and investment in secondary education are some of the current priorities of the government. The economy is being progressively trans-formed from one based on subsistence farming to one that is broader and cash-based. Bhutan has abundant water resources and immense hydropower potential. The tourism industry, while contributing less than 3 percent of the GDP, is important in terms of its capacity to generate convertible currency earnings. However, in keeping with the country's overall objective of preserving its cultural heritage, tourism is kept to a manageable number of about 5000 visitors per year.

BHUTANESE EDUCATION SYSTEM

The educational system in Bhutan will be discussed under three main time periods, the ancient times, the 20th century, and the present times.

Ancient and Medieval: Up until the Advent of Western Education

From as early as the 8th century, there seems to have been an organized system of institutional learning to promote and propagate Buddhism in Bhutan. Over the course of centuries, various religious leaders set up their own establishments to promote individual Buddhist sects they were affiliated with. There is very little research undertaken on the content and extent of such an education system in ancient times. However, an evolved form of this indigenous system of education has survived the test of times and continues to flourish even in this time. Although at a very small scale compared to the system of modern education (enrollment in indigenous educational systems estimated at 10,000 as compared to the 150,000 in the system of Western education), the monastic education system still plays a critical role in the promotion of the Buddhist religion and culture in Bhutan. These schools cater exclusively to the novices and monks, and lessons are imparted in Buddhist philosophy, logic, astrology, traditional medicine, and literature by way of traditional teaching methodologies characterized by a strict regime of rote learning, recitation, and repetitive practice. The schools follow the strict code of a monastic order commonly associated with a Spartan lifestyle and harsh treatment of the errant student not excluding corporal punishment. The schools are all residential schools and the students live on the school premises.

Since religion has always provided a central force in the lives of the Bhutanese people, these institutions and their students have helped define and promote the various facets of Bhutanese culture as manifested exogenously in the imposing and beautiful architecture of wood and masonry. The best examples are those which are manifested in its *Dzongs* (fortresses) and monasteries, the rich colors and intricacies of its murals and paintings depicting the lives and practices of Buddhist saints, the treatises on Buddhist texts and the flourishing traditional medicine. Religion has also contributed to the deeply ingrained cultural traits of the Bhutanese such as their deep respect for life in any form; non-violence and tolerance; and the high value and respect given to parents, elders, and teachers in Bhutanese society.

Enrollment in the monastic education system was open to all, and not exclusive to any cast or creed. In fact, Bhutan is one of the few countries in South Asia that has historically always been largely egalitarian and not divided by a system of castes or classes. Nevertheless, enrollment in these educational institutions was often defined by the abilities of families to afford it. While the students did not have to pay any monetary fees, in an agrarian society a high premium was placed on the support that children provided in the farm by contributing toward domestic chores, sibling care, or tending to domestic animals. Therefore only those families who were relatively well off or had multiple sons were able to send some of their children to schools. Although a child could be admitted in the institution at as young an age as six years, enrollment in such a system theoretically implied the commitment of a lifetime to serve in the monastic order. Just as there were monasteries for the boys, so also there were nunneries for the girls. But the latter have always been fewer in number and have generally offered a curriculum that was less rigorous and less wide-ranging. There were no formal degrees conferred to the graduates by the institutions. However the monks assumed roles and titles in the monasteries commensurate with their competencies and knowledge. Many of the students themselves became teachers to take new students and continued the process of disseminating age-old knowledge and practices.

In the 1980s, the Central Monastic Body of the Royal Government of Bhutan standardized the curriculum in the schools and institutes that fell within its jurisdiction. It also appointed a board of examiners.

Education in the 20th Century

It is popularly believed that the first modern school was set up in the court of Bhutan's first hereditary ruler Gongsa Ugyen Wangchuck (1907–1926) some time in the early 1920s. During the reign of the second king Jigme Wangchuck, a number of such schools were set up in different parts of the country and staffed with teachers who were graduates from the court school. These schools did not attract many students, which subsequently forced the authorities to coerce and conscript the students from different parts of the country. On completion of a basic literacy program these students, who were exclusively boys, were sent for further studies to neighboring India. Upon their return some of these graduates helped in further establishing new schools. Meanwhile, immigrants from Nepal in Bhutan's southern region had also set up a number of private schools modeled after the schools in India. According to official records, by 1960 there were a total of only 11 schools with an enrollment of 400 students. In 1961 the third king, Jigme Dorji Wangchuck, abandoned the age-old policy of self-imposed isolation and embarked on the path to socio-economic development. The setting up of a modern system of education was one of the priorities accorded in the plan. This was seen as a critical step for carrying out activities for future socio-economic development of the country. The government established a number of schools in different parts of the country and recruited teachers from India. The schools also adopted a curriculum from neighboring Indian states.

Until the late 1970s, parents still had to be persuaded and coerced into sending their children to schools. There are many Bhutanese elders today who still recount how their parents had to resort to hiding their children in the forests or attics of their houses to prevent them from being conscripted into these schools. Still other families tried to offer farm produce as persuasive offers to appease the school officials and strike off their children's name from the school register. Gradually, as those who graduated secondary or even primary schools began to assume new responsibilities in a society that was slowly modernizing, the perception and the value of education changed. By the 1980s, several communities were even offering to set up their own local schools.

In the early 1980s, a curriculum of national relevance assumed a central theme amongst the policy makers and administrators of the Bhutanese educational system. The government initiated a number of activities to localize the curriculum and move it away from the Indian system. It also embarked on an ambitious plan of localizing the teaching force which, until then, had been dominated by expatriates from India. The government invested in new curricular materials with Bhutanese content. Initially, the Indian history and geography books were replaced with new Bhutanese texts. This was accompanied by infusing Bhutanese context in the learning of languages, mathematics, and arts. It also tried to move away from the traditional teacher-chalk-board method to what was seen as more progressive activity-based and inquiry-based learning. The changes were targeted at the primary education level, and the whole effort was titled New Approach to Primary Education (NAPE).

This effort was followed by attempts at providing more Bhutanese related content at the secondary education level also, and this inadvertently became linked to the secondary school leaving certificate examinations. Since 1974, Bhutanese students had appeared for the Grade 10 examinations of the Council of Indian School Certificate Examinations in New Delhi, India. The same board also examined and certified its students at the Grade 12 level since 1978. At that time this seemed a pragmatic approach considering the small number of school graduates as well as the nature of the curriculum that the children had to cover. The certificate enabled these students to be accepted in the colleges and institutes in India where most Bhutanese students sought admission for higher education and training. During the latter part of the 1990s, the Bhutanese Ministry of Education gradually built up the capacity to examine and certify its own students for these two examinations. The Grade 10 examinations were localized in 2001, and the Grade 12 examinations were localized in 2003. Both the examinations are now conducted by the Bhutan Board of Examinations of Bhutan's Ministry of Education. Along with the localization of the examination came the freedom for curriculum innovation and provided flexibility for Bhutanese educators to introduce new Bhutanese content and value systems in the education program.

At the same time education was further diversified to include a school of vocational training and a polytechnic institution. The graduates of these programs were employed to carry out infrastructure development in the country such as roads, communication, and buildings for the social infrastructure. Two teacher training colleges, a school for health science, an institute for forestry, and an institute for natural resources training were also established to help train human resources to staff the other development programs. One of the most significant developments has been the establishment of the Royal University of Bhutan in July 2004. This consolidated the seven institutes of higher education in different parts of the country and put them together within the framework of a federated university. A non-formal education program also provides literacy training to people who have missed out on formal schooling. The enrollment in the education system in Bhutan has increased from about 400 students in the early 1960s to 160,000 in 2005. Currently, the government spends over 15 percent of its budget on supporting education, making this sector one of the largest consumers of government resources.

Education System in Present-day Bhutan

The structure of formal education in Bhutan consists of seven years of primary education, followed by six years of secondary education including of two years each of lower, middle, and Higher Secondary. This is followed by degree programs of three to four years duration offered by the Royal University of Bhutan. The official minimum entry age into the formal education system is six years. The Royal Government provides free education until Middle Secondary level (or Grade 10). This level of education is termed the basic education level, and the government aims to provide this to every child in the kingdom. Post basic education level is highly competitive but is free for those who pass the selection scheme that is based on the Grade 10 examination results. These students are admitted to Grade 11 and Grade 12, and those who do well in the Grade 12 national examinations continue to the higher education program under government scholarship. Those who do not qualify to continue into the academic program have the option of choosing one of the vocational training programs provided both by the government as well as by private institutions.

SOCIAL CLASS AND EDUCATION

Bhutan has maintained an egalitarian society over the course of its history. The majority of the population lives in the rural areas subsisting on their small farms. With modern development, there is a growing urban population that is thriving on trade and services. This is estimated at less than 20 percent of the population. Many of these people however still maintain their rural links through an extended family system. The per capita income of the Bhutanese in 2003 was estimated at U.S. $834. Likewise, its education caters to all sections of the population. In the early history of modern education it was often the children of those parents who did not have the clout and the resources to have their children's name removed from the school roster who, in fact, benefited from education. Later, the government's own policy has been to ensure equitable distribution of schools and educational opportunities throughout the kingdom.

RACE, ETHNICITY, AND EDUCATION

There are two major ethnic and racial groups in Bhutan. These include the Drukpas who are the original inhabitants of Bhutan, and the immigrants who came into the country as laborers from Nepal in the latter half of the 20th century. The Drukpas and the original inhabitants of Bhutan are Buddhists, while the immigrants are mostly Hindus. But because of the concerted efforts of the Royal Government to integrate the people into mainstream Bhutanese cultural and socio-economic life, schools throughout the kingdom offer a single uniform curriculum and schooling system.

GENDER AND EDUCATION

In general, more boys are enrolled in the educational system because of the physical hardships associated with traveling over long distances to reach the schools, and the rudimentary boarding facilities discourage parents from enrolling girls. However, with the large number of schools being established closer to populated areas, there is now almost the same number of girls entering primary schools as there are boys. The percentage of girls enrolled in the primary grades from Pre-primary to Grade 6 was 49 percent in the year 2005. This percentage is almost the same as the proportion of girls in the total population of Bhutan.

LEVELS OF EDUCATION

Primary Education

All children who have attained the age of 6 years are eligible for admissions into the primary schools. The children are admitted into the Pre-primary grade which is a one-year program. After the successful completion of the one-year program the children are promoted to Grade 1. By the end of their seventh year in school most children are expected to complete Grade 6 which signifies the completion of the primary education stage. Primary school teachers these days are recruited after students have completed Grade 12. Thereafter, they undertake a three year-long teacher training program in one of the two National Institutes of Education in Bhutan. After the successful completion of the courses they are awarded a Bachelor of Education (B.Ed) degree and are assigned by the Ministry of

Education to any of the primary schools in the kingdom. The Ministry also has on its pay roll a large number of older teachers who were recruited earlier with a lower level of academic qualifications and training. The Ministry is undertaking an extensive program for upgrading these teachers.

In terms of the curriculum studied in primary schools, by the end of the primary cycle each child is expected to have learned or mastered: (1) basic skills in reading and understanding both in English and Dzongkha. Students passing out from the primary schooling system should be in a position to read and understand the national paper, *Kuensel*, in both English and Dzongkha; (2) writing simple letters, applications and reports in both languages; (3) speaking and understanding Dzongkha and English fluently; (4) the functions of addition, subtraction, multiplication, division, and be able to maintain everyday accounts; (5) basic knowledge of health, hygiene, and social studies, and in particular, the geography and history of Bhutan; (6) a deep sense of respect and pride in being Bhutanese, and in being citizens who are loyal, dedicated, productive, contented, and happy with a high standard of moral ethics and discipline; (7) a greater understanding of and appreciation for the predominantly agriculture based rural lifestyle, and develop a sense of resourcefulness and dignity of labor. The national education curriculum is devised to fulfill these objectives. Right from the very first day of school students are taught two languages, Dzongkha (the national language) and English. They also study mathematics, environmental studies, social studies, and moral and value education. Children are taught through activity-based methods, and recitation, art and craft, and sports are also encouraged.

A Typical Day in Primary School

Although the school experience of an urban student is very different from that of a village student, and between students at day schools or boarding schools, a typical day for a student in primary school may look somewhat similar. Generally all across the kingdom, a school day starts with the morning assembly bell at 8:30 A.M. All the students line up in classes in front of the school building and offer their morning prayers. This is followed with the head teacher addressing the students on selected topics, followed next with announcements for the day. In some schools, students are required to deliver a short speech on a topic of their choice, and this is followed by the singing of the national anthem. Each study period is of 35 minutes duration. The lower grades, Pre-primary to Grade 3, are organized as a class-teacher system whereby the class teacher of each class teaches all the subjects to the students in that class. In the higher primary classes, the subject teachers teach a particular subject across grade levels and thus move around to the different classrooms. A morning recess of 15 minutes is provided for students to go to the washroom. This is usually a busy time and the students mill about, playing games and generally releasing their energy in different ways. Lunch break is from 12:30 P.M. to 1:30 P.M. and most students in the urban areas bring their own lunch from home. In the rural areas, some children are provided lunch by the school through the World Food Program. The afternoon classes usually conclude by 3:30 P.M. for the higher grades and a little earlier for the lower primary grades. In the urban schools most students go home with their parents in cars. Others walk to and from school. In the rural areas, children may walk as long as two hours each way to get to and from the schools depending on the distance between their homes and the schools. Some village primary schools provide boarding facilities for children whose houses are too far from their school. The big events in the school calendar are the sports day and the school concert. Every child is encouraged to participate in some games with the most popular game being soccer. Every primary school has a playing field of sorts cut from the steep mountainside. In their spare time during the lunch recess and after school, both boys and girls organize playful matches amongst themselves. Inter-house and inter-school competitions are also regular features of the school activities. Other games include volleyball and basketball. The schools in Bhutan open in the third week of February. There is a mid-term break for three weeks during the month of July. The academic year formally ends on December 18, although regular classes end by late November. The rest of the time is spent in preparation for the annual examinations, organization of the end-of-the-year events such as the school concert, and other co-curricular activities.

Secondary Education

Secondary education in Bhutan comprises of a two-year Junior Secondary, a two-year Middle Secondary, and a two-year Higher Secondary system. In order to be admitted into Junior Secondary (Grades 7–8) all children are required to have passed the All Bhutan Grade 6 examinations set by the Bhutan Board of Examinations, but administered and evaluated by the teachers of the respective schools. Many of the students move from their primary schools to the nearest Junior Secondary school. For students who cannot be enrolled as day scholars because of the long distances to the school, the school provides boarding facilities which includes a dormitory for sleeping as well as three meals a day. The parents have to also contribute in cash or kind for one of the meals.

For children to be admitted into the Middle Secondary, they are required to have passed the All Bhutan Grade 8 examination which is designed, administered, and evaluated by the Bhutan Board of Examinations. As in the Junior Secondary, many students have to move to new schools and often study as boarders. Similarly for students to progress to the Higher Secondary educational stage, they are required to score high grades in the Grade 10 examination which is administered externally by the Bhutan Board of Examinations. Only about 50 percent of the students qualify to continue on government scholarships in the Higher Secondary Schools. The remaining students either leave to undertake vocational training or help their parents with their farms or businesses. Increasingly, however, a large number of Bhutanese are opting to enroll their children in the numerous private Higher Secondary schools both in Bhutan and in neighboring India.

There is no separate teacher training program for Secondary Education. The two National Institutes of Education (NIEs) mentioned earlier offer teacher training program for both primary and secondary teachers. Some of the recruits from Grade 12 inducted into the B.Ed program enter primary level teaching, while others enter secondary level teaching. In addition, the NIEs also offer a Post Graduate degree in Education to those who already hold a Bachelor's degree in arts, sciences, or commerce. This is a one-year course, and after its successful completion the teachers are usually assigned to teach the Higher Secondary grades.

Curriculum in the Junior Secondary is an extension of the foundation built at the primary level. Languages and mathematics continue to be the core area of development at this stage while value education is also emphasized as a subject. In addition, Bhutanese History and Bhutanese Geography are added to the curriculum. Basic vocational skills are also introduced as co-curricular activities along with sports, agriculture, art and craft, and performing arts. At the secondary education level, more science subjects are introduced including, physics, chemistry, and biology. Students are also offered a choice of computer applications and economics at this level. At the Higher Secondary level, students can choose between three streams of studies: general science, commerce, and arts. General science students can either take up physical science which includes mathematics, physics, and chemistry. Commerce students take up commercial accounting. Arts students have a choice of taking economics, geography, history, or literature in Dzongkha or in English. All the students however have to take up Dzongkha and English as additional subjects. Students are also provided basic orientations to the world of work and can participate in a limited number of basic vocational training programs as part of co-curricular learning such as carpentry, hairdressing, shoe repairs, and so forth. Lectures, project work, and drills dominate the teaching methods at the secondary level. Homework is an important teaching-learning component to continue the learning process beyond the school hours.

A Typical Day in Secondary School

A typical school day in secondary schools might be described in a very general way. Most of the day students walk to school each morning. Depending on the distance of their homes, some may need to start walking as early as 6:00 A.M. to get to school in time for the morning assembly which starts at 8:15 A.M. The morning assembly begins with prayers, followed by lectures and announcements by the principal. The assembly ends with the singing of the national anthem. Classes are normally 35–40 minutes long. Except for lab work and practicals, subject teachers move from class to class. As in the primary grades, the students get a morning recess of 15 minutes followed by an hour of lunch break. Formal classes end by 3:30 P.M. after which the students may organize games and various co-curricular activities. Most students walk back to their homes late in the evenings when they are expected to do their homework and also help with the chores at home.

Boarding students have to get up at 5:00 A.M., attend to physical exercise at 5:30 A.M. followed by the morning study at 6:30 A.M. The students are required to clean the school premises before breakfast, normally served around 7:30 A.M. Lunch is at 12:30 noon, followed by tea at 3:30 P.M. This is followed by games and other organized co-curricular activities. Evening study is at 6:00–7:00 P.M., followed by evening prayers. Evening supper is served at 7:30 P.M. after which there is a night study, normally for an hour starting at 8:00 P.M. Bed time for boarders is observed at 9:30 P.M. The warden puts the lights out at 10 P.M. Boarding students get more time for studies and organized games, whereas day students get more time to help with chores at home. Some boarding schools require students to collect firewood for the school kitchen on Saturday afternoons. Sunday is usually the day off and the time is usually utilized for clean up and laundry.

Post-secondary Education

There are seven post-secondary institutes in the country, all under the umbrella of the Royal University of Bhutan. Admissions to post-secondary institutes are highly competitive and students are selected based primarily on their performance in the Grade 12 examinations. Students who have scored highest in the sciences are selected for fellowships to undertake the five-year medicine program in medical schools and colleges in India and other countries. These fellowships are funded by bilateral official development assistance or by multilateral donors. Before the establishment of the Bhutan Institute of Technology (BIT) in 2002, Bhutanese students were sent out of the country to study engineering also. But with the establishment of BIT, students can now complete a three-year degree program in mechanical, civil, or electrical engineering in Bhutan. *Sherubtse*, one of the premier institutes of post-secondary learning in Bhutan, offers a three-year Bachelors degree in science, arts, and commerce, and a four-year Bachelors degree in computer science. A three-year Bachelors in education is available in the two NIEs. The other educational opportunities in the country are a five-year degree course in traditional medicine offered by the National Institute of Traditional Medicine, and a three-year Bachelors degree program for nursing in the Royal Institute of Health Sciences. There is also a plan to introduce a three-year Bachelors degree program in Agriculture and Natural Resources in the National Resource Training Institute which currently offers diploma-level programs. The admissions to the programs are open to all the students irrespective of age or gender. The selection is based on the academic performance of the students, as well as on their aptitude and interest. However, because of the earlier history where relatively fewer girls were enrolled in the primary schools due to long distances and other hardships, fewer girls have been able to make it to this level. This is gradually improving every year as a result of an increasing number of girls now being enrolled in the primary school system.

Unlike in the primary and secondary schools, a high proportion of the teachers in the post-secondary or higher education are expatriates, mostly recruited from India. This is because of the general shortage of teachers with the requisite qualifications to teach this level. The Royal Government is currently in the process of reversing this through an aggressive policy of recruitment, improving salaries and benefits, and providing scholarships to attract qualified and competent Bhutanese individuals to take up teaching at this level. Unlike the general education program, post-secondary institutes are usually one of a kind and their curriculum is designed to meet specific education and training needs of a particular clientele. For example the curriculums in the two NIEs have been designed with the help of the Ministry of Education in order to prepare teachers for teaching in the Bhutanese schools. The curriculum is a mix of upgrading the subject knowledge of the students as well as good pedagogical practices including child psychology, curriculum theory, and classroom management and organization. The courses in the National Institute of Traditional Medicine has been designed internally to meet the training and educational needs of the traditional medical practitioners. The engineering courses offered by the RBIT (Royal Bhutan Institute of Technology) have been designed by the Institute and offers a mixed program of theory and practical work. The courses in *Sherubtse* continue to be affiliated to the Delhi University in India, and apart from Dzongkha and computer studies and specific modules drawn up by the college faculty, the larger part of the course content continues to be dictated by the requirements of Delhi University. Similarly the Bachelor of science nursing course offered by the National Institute of Health Science is an extension of a program offered by LaTrobe University in Australia. At this post-secondary level, the course work is offered as a series of lectures, practical demonstrations, project works and research assignments. A typical day in post-secondary education is generally less organized and closely associated with learning at the post-secondary level. However students are encouraged to attend the classes on a regular basis, and many courses require a minimum attendance to qualify the students for examinations. There is greater freedom for the students to organize co-curricular activities of their choices. Besides, many campuses provide diverse opportunities for social activities such as dances, clubs, sports, and other recreation activities. Many of the campuses started as boarding facilities, but recently these are opening up for day students too. These students usually rent private houses and rooms and cook their own meals. A significant number of Bhutanese students continue to be sent to Universities in the region and abroad for specialized training and education especially in medicine, engineering, agriculture sciences, education, and management.

CONCLUSION

Bhutan is a country which has recently opened up to the world outside its borders. Its public education system began only in the 1960s, and it introduced the television and internet to its society only in 1999. Bhutan now has schools at all levels across most of the country and rotates the teachers between urban and rural areas to ensure equal access to good teachers. Hospitals offer both Western and traditional medicine as options for patients. What is most striking about this country is its commitment to balance the preservation of its cultural traditions, the protection of its environment, and maintain a responsive government in its mission to ensure that prosperity and advancement is shared across the nation. This mission is supported by the overall spiritual philosophy of this Buddhist kingdom: that happiness, contentment, and wellbeing are defined not by material wealth but by a sense of harmony between the individual and the environment.

BIBLIOGRAPHY

Jagar Dorji (2005) *Quality of Education in Bhutan. The Story of Growth and Change in the Bhutanese Education System*. Thimphu, Bhutan: KMT Publisher.

Ministry of Education, Royal Government of Bhutan (1988–1995) Quarterly Policy Guidelines.

Ministry of Education, Royal Government of Bhutan (1996–2004) Education Policy Guidelines.

Ministry of Education, Royal Government of Bhutan (2001) "Education Sector Strategy, Realizing the Vision 2020, Policy and Strategy."

Ministry of Education, Royal Government of Bhutan (2005) "General Education Statistics."

Planning Commission (1999) Royal Government "Bhutan 2020: A Vision for Peace, Prosperity and Happiness."

Royal Government of Bhutan (2005) "Bhutan National Human Development Report."

Chapter 5

SCHOOLING IN INDIA

Amita Gupta

OVERVIEW OF COUNTRY

Geographical and Historical Overview

The Republic of India is the seventh largest country in the world, with the second largest population consisting of about 1.1 billion people. This vast country lies bounded by Pakistan and Afghanistan in the west and northwest; by China, Nepal, and Bhutan in the north and northeast; and by Bangladesh and Myanmar in the east. The southern half of India is a peninsular coastline surrounded by three large bodies of water namely the Arabian Sea on the southwest, the Indian Ocean in the south and the Bay of Bengal on the southeast. The island nation of Sri Lanka lies just south of India's southern tip. In addition to the main land mass there are groups of islands that also belong to India. These are the Andaman & Nicobar Islands that lie to the southeast in the Bay of Bengal and the Indian Ocean, and the Lakshadweep Islands to the west that are located in the Arabian Sea. The mainland of India has roughly three well-defined geographical regions: the mountainous zone formed by the lofty Himalayan mountains which include some of the tallest peaks in the world; the vast Gangetic plain formed by the basins of the mighty rivers Ganga (or Ganges), Brahmaputra, and their tributaries; and the central and southern peninsula comprising of the Deccan Plateau. The distance between India's northern apex in the Himalayan Mountains down to its southernmost tip at Kanyakumari is approximately 2000 miles, and the total area of the country is roughly equivalent to that of all of Europe.

Historically, the inhabitants of the Indian-subcontinent are considered as constituting one of the oldest living and continuing civilizations in history.

The earliest human activity in the Indian subcontinent can be traced back to the Stone Age (400,000–200,000 B.C.). Implements from the early, middle, and late stone-age periods have been found in the Indian states of Rajasthan, Gujarat, Bihar, and parts of what is now Pakistan. These Paleolithic people were semi-nomadic hunters and gatherers for many millennia. Historical and archaeological records indicate that people who lived in India around the middle of the 9th century B.C. represented five main racial categories namely the Negrito, the Proto-Australoid, the Mediterranean, the Mongoloid, and the Alpine races. The first evidences of agricultural settlements on the western plains of India are roughly contemporaneous with similar developments in Egypt, Mesopotamia, and Persia. These settlements grew quickly and records suggest that inhabitants in ancient India made extensive use of copper and bronze. They also domesticated animals, made pottery, and engaged in some of the earliest trade activities known.

The ancient Indian civilization flourished as a sophisticated and advanced society about 5000 years ago. The ruins of the Indus valley civilizations found at Mohenjo Daro and Harappa are said to date back to about 3300 B.C. according to recent excavations and are evidence of a highly organized and developed community. There are archaeological evidences of a distinct pottery style that point to people living in India in 3000 B.C. who had already progressed to building houses and tilling the land. But Harappa and Mohenjo Daro, separated by a distance of 600 kilometers, form only the core sites of a civilization that was much more extensive than Egypt's ancient civilization or Mesopotamia's Sumeria. Excavations have revealed other cities that were part of the Indus Valley Civilization in the Sindh and Punjab regions of modern-day Pakistan;[1] as far away as the Iranian frontier of Baluchistan; in the North-West Frontier Province; and clusters of sites in the Indian states of Gujarat, Rajasthan, Punjab, Haryana, Uttar Pradesh; and Jammu & Kashmir. A full inventory of Harappan artifacts include standardized bricks, pots, terracotta items, decorative items made from beads and shell work, copper and bronze hardware, and several seals and tablets engraved with an archaic script. There is also evidence of regular streets constructed above a network of well-built sewage system of ducts. It is thought that Mohenjo Daro might have had a population of about 30,000–50,000 inhabitants which implies that there must have been the need for effective transportation by river and road, a large labor force, and a crop storage system. It is not clear what led to the disintegration of this highly developed civilization in the Indus valley, but floods and migrations are some of the suggested factors.

In the ensuing centuries of recorded Indian history a number of major monarchies and dynasties ruled a substantial part of the country's total land mass. Some of the more prominent events and periods in Indian history are highlighted below.[2]

2500–1550 B.C.	Harrapan civilization
1500–500 B.C.	Peak Vedic Period
563–334 B.C.	Peak Buddhist Period (Kingdom of Magadha was ruled by kings such as Bimbisara, Ajatshatru, Mahapadma Nanda)
327–325 B.C.	Invasion by Alexander of Macedonia
322–183 B.C.	Mauryan Period (important kings included Chandragupta Maurya, Bindusara, and Ashoka)
A.D. 300–888	Pallava kings of Kanchi (Madras State)
A.D. 320–647	Gupta Period (important kings included Chandra Gupta I, Samudra Gupta, Chandra Gupta II, Kumara Gupta I, Skanda Gupta, Harsha)
A.D. 550–757	Chalukya kings of western and central Deccan
A.D. 630–970	Chalukyas of eastern Deccan
A.D. 760–1142	Pala kings of Bengal and Bihar
A.D. 850–1267	Chola kings of Tanjore (Madras State)
A.D. 916–1203	Chandela kings of Bundelkhand
A.D. 974–1238	Chalukya kings of Gujarat
A.D. 1100–1400	Delhi Sultanate
A.D. 1190–1294	Yadav dynasty of Devgiri (northern Deccan)
A.D. 1216–1327	Pandya kings of Madurai (Madras State)
A.D. 1336–1565	Vijayanagar Empire
A.D. 1500–late 1800s	Mughal Empire
A.D. 1650–1900s	Maratha kings
A.D. 1700–1947	British colonial rule
A.D. 1947	India gains independence from British colonial rule

Ancient texts such as the *Veda*[3] were written in India using the Vedic language, an archaic form of Sanskrit, sometime between 1500 and 2000 B.C. These texts have been considered by scholars from all over the world as being rich sources of philosophy, spiritual insights, and treatises on subjects such as medicine, science, math, astronomy, and so forth. The material richness and spiritual wealth of this land have consistently attracted foreign kings and scholars respectively since the very beginning, and historical records abound with stories about conquering armies and learned travelers who came to India. From the ancient through the modern period, India had been ruled by numerous kings and emperors, and the reign of each ruler left a significant impact on the country's culture, social customs, and educational systems. In medieval and modern history two significant and long-lasting foreign influences were established in India. The first was that of Muslim rulers beginning in about A.D. 1000, and culminating with the establishment of the Mughal dynasty in 1526 that lingered on till approximately A.D. 1857. The Mughal Empire covered approximately one million square miles in India. The second influence was that of the British who began to establish their colonizing presence in India from about the mid-1600s A.D. and continued to rule the country until 1947 when India attained independence from their rule. At the very prime of their rule, the British Empire had complete control of about 1.5 million square miles in India.

Today, almost 70 percent of India's total population lives in rural areas, and India has a strong agricultural industry producing a wide variety of crops and vegetables, as well as well-developed animal husbandry, dairy, poultry, and fishing industries. But with growing industrialization and urbanization, modern India has emerged as one of the world's five top industrialized nations producing every conceivable item in industrial and consumer goods, and has achieved significant success in cutting edge research in science and technology. Currently, with a massive middle class population of nearly 350 million, India not only has one of the largest pools of scientifically and technologically skilled person-power, but with the increasingly large consumer market the country is predicted to soon becoming the third largest economy in the world.

Government and Constitution of India

At the time of her independence from the colonial rule of the British Empire in 1947, India adopted a parliamentary system of government with a union of states and declared the nation to be a democratic republic. Today India is the world's largest democracy with more than a billion people residing in 28 states and 7 union territories. The democratic government exists in the form of the Central government as well as the State governments, and at the village level one also finds an extensive and highly organized system of local governance known as the *Panchayati Raj*. The chief of state in India is the President and the head of government is the Prime Minister who is usually the leader of the ruling political party.

There are more than 1600 dialects spoken in India, and the Indian Constitution recognizes 22 official languages. Of these, Hindi is considered to be the national language, and post-colonization English continues to be the official working language. Most of the educated population in India may be said to be at least bilingual if not trilingual. Apart from being multilingual, India as a nation is also multiethnic with multiple religions as well. Hindus form the largest community comprising of more than 80 percent of the total population, which accounts for more than 800 million Hindus living in India alone. Other main religious groups include Muslims (12 percent), Roman Catholics and Protestant Christians (2.6 percent), Sikhs (2 percent), Buddhists (0.7 percent), Jains (0.4 percent), Parsis (0.3 percent) and Jews (0.1 percent). Although the Indian Jewish population constitutes only a small fraction of India's total population, it still works out to be a community of 1 million Jewish people who currently live in India. It is interesting to note that the Jewish community in India does not comprise of recent immigrants but was established centuries ago. India's legal system recognizes separate personal law codes for Hindus, Muslims, and Christians. A structure is thus built into Indian society that strives to ensure and protect the rights of minority groups. Another feature is the national educational policy of the three-language formula whereby all school-going children learn three languages. This attempts to ensure that no one language is recognized as the only correct language. India's Constitution also supports a secular approach to education. However, in India the word "secular" is commonly understood by the public to mean an equal recognition for all religions, and does not imply the rigid separation of church and state as it does in the United States. Thus many religious days in India are written into annual calendars as national holidays in several educational and non-educational institutions, and observed as school closings. For example, in addition to all the Hindu holidays, other holidays recognized on the calendars include *Id-ul-Fikr, Id-ul-Zuha, Moharram*, and other Muslim holidays; *Buddh Purnima* which is the birth date of Lord Buddha; *Mahavira Jayanti* which recognizes the Jain religion; *Guru Nanak's* Birthday which is an important Sikh holiday; Christmas and Easter as the Christian holidays; and so forth.

HISTORICAL DEVELOPMENT OF EDUCATION

The current systems of education in India reflect the diverse cultural, political, social, and spiritual influences that the country has experienced over the course of her history. Few countries have systems of education that have had such a long, continuous and relatively stable history as is the case in India. Educational records in India date back a few millennia and there is ample evidence to suggest that schools, or *ashrams*, as formal institutions of education commonly existed as early as 3500 years ago. More recently, a British survey conducted by William Adam in 1835 reported on an already existing extensive system of popular indigenous education throughout India. According to this report, even during the early part of the 19th century there were about 100,000 schools in the Indian states of Bengal and Bihar alone. This implied that there was a school in almost every village in India much before British colonial initiatives in education were implemented. Going back further in time, written records indicate that even from 250 B.C. to A.D. 250 free education for all except for unskilled workers was spread throughout India and was easily available.

Hindu Spiritual Ideas

The primary reason for a well-developed system of education in India from the earliest of times is the high value placed on teaching and learning in Indian philosophy. Indian philosophy itself represents an ancient tradition that goes back thousands of years and is based directly on the teachings of texts such as the *Veda*. The *Veda* are the ancient Hindu scriptures and form the foundations for numerous other texts such as the *Upanishad, Purana, Brahmana, Bhgavad Gita*, and so forth. Contrary to common belief, the *Veda* are not merely religious texts. The very word *Veda* comes from the root "vid" which means "to know." They consist of four books and together they are six times as long as the Bible.

The philosophical speculations from the *Veda* were compiled in another text, the *Upanishad,* which were written in about 800 B.C. Together the two texts offer extensive discourses on various subjects including religion, rituals and ceremonies, philosophy, literature, science, medicine, ethics, social conduct, morality, politics, civics, weaponry, arts, music, and dance. The emphasis in the *Upanishad* is on the search for truth, and on knowledge of the self. One finds comprehensive recommendations for leading a good and worthwhile life based primarily on the Hindu concepts of *dharma* and *karma.* Although India reflects a very multicultural history and her culture has incorporated elements from various other traditions in terms of language, art, music, education, worship, and litera-ture, its philosophy is largely a Hindu philosophy based on the core concepts that are taught in the Vedic scriptures and that continue to be enacted by Indians in their daily lives. Some of these core concepts are the following: recognizing the self in relation to others; a high degree of respect accorded to one's elders, teachers, and guests; a high value placed on the pursuit of knowledge and intellectual growth; and striving to live within one's *dharma* while being mindful of one's *karma.*

The concepts of *dharma* and *karma* are two examples of the underlying premises of Hindu philosophy. *Dharma* is a hard-to-define concept but can be generally understood as that which maintains the order of the universe; a social cement that holds a society together. *Dharma* is explained as being the principle and the vision of an organic society, with all the members who participate in this organic society being interdependent and their roles being complimentary. To *dharma* are ascribed such social concepts as duty, responsibility, and morality. In other words, each individual is positioned in multiple roles and must carry out the responsibilities of those roles. That would be the individual's *dharma.* *Karma* refers to the actions of the individual human being, and the consequences of those actions. This views human actions within a cause-effect paradigm, emphasizing the careful selection of words and deeds by an individual. Although the *dharma* we are born into is not our choice, it is our *karma,* the decisions and actions that we consciously choose to act upon that determines the quality of our lives. Thus *karma* is not a doctrine of reincarnation, nor does it imply fatalism or pre-destination, but rather is a promise of hope and responsi-bility for one's own actions. A third concept is that of *moksha,* the final liberation from human suffering. It is the purpose that human life works toward, and it is understood by Hindus that the attainment of *moksha* is not dependent on a third entity but is determined by the actions of one's own self. Liberation from human suffering cannot be attained if we do not live by our *dharma* while being mindful of our *karma.*

Thus the conscious recognition of one's *dharma* and *karma* has been supremely important for living the good life. Subsequently, cognitive develop-ment and the skills related to cognition were important in the making of the right decisions in life. These skills included intellectual clarity; comprehension and understanding; the pursuit of knowledge; different ways of knowing and learning; developing memory as an important step in the learning process; and academic proficiency. The ideal conditions for learning were stated to be, first and foremost, the desire to learn and a love for truth. The sequence of stages in the learning process were: receiving lessons daily; understanding them; retaining them in memory; reflecting upon them; and exercising judgment or discrimination between right and wrong. Memory was considered to be an innate attribute of the human mind. The concept of memory has also been specifically discussed and defined in various ancient Indian texts and it has been traditionally viewed within the context of four distinct cognitive processes: *avagraha*, when a general knowledge of an external object is obtained through contact with sensory organs; *iha*, when we desire to have detailed knowledge of the object by comparing its similarities and differences with other known objects; *avaya*, when we desire to get the knowledge corroborated; and *dharana*, when the permanent impression of an object assists our knowledge. These educational values and skills came to be accorded high value in the process of education in ancient India, and have been historically prioritized in Indian education.

Although this Vedic philosophy has directly informed education in India from ancient times to the present day, other educational objectives and strategies came into play under various religious and cultural influences in India. Most prominent of such influences were those from Buddhism, after the Buddhist religion was established as an offshoot of Hinduism in 600 B.C.; from Islam, after Muslim rulers from Arabia, Persia and Asia Minor began to make forays into India around A.D. 1000; and from Christianity, which entered the life of Indian culture and society through the colonizing work of European missionaries and traders ultimately resulting in India being established as a prominent British colony until her independence in 1947. Under the Islamic rulers and monarchs, a stronger focus on the three R's appeared, and under the British colonial administration the educational system in India was transformed into a textbook-driven, examination-oriented bureaucratic system. However, manifestations of many of the ancient Vedic values in school curricula, philosophy, and teaching strategies are still evident in many schools in India even today. A detailed and comprehensive discussion on the same can be found in the author's earlier book which is based on a study conducted in schools in India.[4]

The historical periods in the examination of the educational systems in India may be divided into time periods according to the various religious and cultural influences as different spiritual traditions entered into the life of Indian society. Primarily, four periods may be specified here for discussion with regard to education under the Vedic, Buddhist, Islamic, and European Christian influences. Vedic and Buddhist influences dominated education and schooling in the ancient period, Islamic influences predominated during the medieval period, and European influences predominated during the modern period, although lasting influences of each earlier period linger on and are often juxtaposed with later influences at any given stage.

ANCIENT INDIA: APPROXIMATE TIME PERIOD
FROM 2000 B.C. TO A.D. 700

Education When Vedic/Hindu Influences Were Predominant (2000–600 B.C.)

From time immemorial, India has been a center for learning. Hindu texts and scriptures of ancient India formed the basis of the very first recorded educational systems in India that dominated from approximately 2000 B.C. to 600 B.C. During that time education was based primarily on the teachings of the *Veda* and *Upanishad*, and encouraged philosophical reflections, spiritual and secular learning, and intellectual development. Although education was available freely during the early Vedic stage, over time it became more discriminatory as the caste system evolved and began to crystallize. The castes were initially based on occupational groups and were divided into four categories: *brahman* (priests), *kshatriya* (noblemen and warriors), *vaishya* (traders and agriculturists), and *shudra* (artisans and sanitation workers). The study of the *Veda* was common to all castes mentioned earlier except *shudra*.

Education was informed by several sources, most notably by the Vedic texts that are believed to have been composed sometime between 2000 and 1500 B.C. and are the earliest known writings on existential philosophy. The *Veda* were written in Vedic, an archaic form of Sanskrit from which most of the Indo-European languages, including Latin, have been derived. The *Veda* consist of four books called *Rig Veda, Sama Veda, Yajur Veda,* and *Atharva Veda,* and together the works are six times as long as the Bible. Other texts included, Kautilya's writings (3rd or 4th centuries B.C.) which provide a detailed study of politics and education; Manu's writings (dating back to the early years of the Christian era) which are considered to be the first law books in India; and the two Indian epics, *Mahabharata* and *Ramayana* (written around 800 B.C.) which include detailed references on social norms, teachings, and education of the times. The famous Indian scholar, Panini, derived and wrote the Sanskrit grammar in the 4th century B.C. and this is considered to be the earliest known form of organized grammar. It was the discovery of Panini's Sanskrit grammar that led to the study of phonetics in the West. The *Rig Veda,* the first book of the *Veda* and earliest known writings, emphasized that knowledge could be gained only after the study of many diverse subjects. Beside the study of the *Veda,* several other subjects were included in a typical curriculum in ancient India. Records indicate that some of the content areas in a typical Vedic curriculum at the secondary or college level in 1500 B.C. included the following:[5]

Shiksha: the teaching of proper pronunciation and recitation of the *Veda*
Kalpa: the rules of sacrifice
Vyakarana: the study of grammar and derivation
Chandas: knowledge of composition, versification and meter
Jyotisha: the understanding of the secrets of nature in a scientific manner,

Reasoning, including logic.
The sciences including medicine, astronomy, physics, chemistry, and metaphysics.

Additionally, Vedic education also taught people the skills to become efficient in their occupations as carpenters, artisans, physicians, farmers, poets, and so forth. There were no class or gender distinctions at that time, and according to the third Vedic book, *Yajur Veda*, Vedic knowledge could be imparted to anyone. There are several instances in Vedic literature that describe the participation of women in higher education, and Apala, Paulomi, Gargi, Urvashi, and Devyani are some among many others named. It is believed that 27 women scholars were responsible for the composition of several mantras (italicize) in Rig Veda. This is not surprising as the Hindu religion recognizes the equal importance of the male and female energies in gods and humans, and the goddess figure has always occupied a powerful position in Hinduism. In ancient India, the progressive nature of Vedic education as education for all disclaimed social and economic barriers and implied some kind of gender equality in society.

Music became an important aspect in Vedic education. Many melodies were discovered and it is said that the seven *svara* or notes on which Indian classical music is based were known in Vedic times. Medical science was developed and systematically taught to students and there is mention in the *Veda* of herbal medicines for conditions or diseases such as fever, leprosy, jaundice, dropsy, cough, baldness, snake bite, and mania, among others. A review of Sanskrit books written as far back as 1500 B.C. reveals extensive discussion and scholarship concerning diseases, speech pathology, and audiology. Details have been provided of the ancient Indian system of disease classification, the classification of speech sounds, causes of speech disorders, and treatment of speech and language disorders. However, over subsequent centuries the business of higher education became more concerned with the requirements of priesthood as the rituals of sacrifice began to gain increasing prominence in Vedic society, thus privileging priests over other groups of people.

Closely linked to the spiritual philosophy of the ancient scriptures was a scientific bent of mind. This allowed the emergence of not only philosophers and spiritual leaders in Ancient India but also scientists, astronomers, engineers, geographers, aeronautical engineers, physicians and surgeons, mathematicians, and so forth. Mention is made of some prominent scholars: Gargya is credited with the enumeration of 27 constellations in the *Veda*; Bharadvaja presided over the first medicinal plant symposium of the world in 700 B.C.; Attreya Punarvasu is mentioned in the *Mahabharata* as having started the Academy of Medicine; Sushruta, known globally as the father of surgery, is said to have invented the technique of rhinoplasty even before the Christian era; Kanada was the first to expound the Law of Causation and the Atomic Theory in his books written in the 6th century B.C.; Medhatithi was the first to extend numerals to billions and has been mentioned several times in the *Rig Veda*; Aryabhata was known to have made great strides in advancing the knowledge of algebra in the 5th century A.D.; and so forth.[6] These are only some of the many more names that appear in India's ancient texts and scriptures.

The *Upanishad* are scriptures that were written after the *Veda* in about 800 B.C. These contain the philosophical conclusions from the *Veda*, and have also strongly influenced Indian education. Steeped with the spirit of inquiry and a passion for finding out the truth about things without tolerance for any dogma standing in the way, the *Upanishad* encouraged the study of the external world as an aspect of the inner reality. Interest in magic and supernatural elements was discouraged and there was a continuous attempt to harmonize social and spiritual activities. The learning process was characterized by a spirit of exploration wherein both teachers and students were perceived as co-travelers on a quest toward truth through discussion, discourse, and reflective dialogue. The emphasis of the curriculum lay on self-realization and knowledge of the individual self and the absolute self. Historians and educators have described at least 24 different subjects the study of which was included in a curriculum within an educational system defined by the *Upanishad*. Some of the content areas in a typical 800 B.C. Upanishadic curriculum for secondary or college level education have been described as including the following:[7]

Anushasan: the study of systems such as phonetics, grammar, metrics, astronomy, and knowledge of rituals.
Vidya: the study of the six schools of Hindu philosophy: *nyaya, yoga, vaisheshika, sankhya, purvamimamsa, uttaramimamsa.*
Vakovakyam: the study of theological discourse, art of argumentation
Itihaas Durana: the study of figures from legends and myths
Akhyana/Anvakhyana: the study of stories and post-narratives
Anuvakhyana: the study of the explanations of various *mantras*
Brahamana: the study of books on religious explanations
Kshatyavidya: the study of the science of wielding weaponry
Rashi: the study of numbers and arithmetic
Nakshatra vidya: the study of the science of astronomy
Bhuta vidya: the study of the science of life forms
Upanishad: the study of knowledge about the supreme reality
Ved Veda: the study of the grammar of the ancient *Vedic* texts
Dev vidya: the study of the science of the worship of gods
Brahma vidya: the study of the different branches of the *Veda*
Deya jana vidya: the study of arts such as the making of perfume, dyeing, dancing, singing, or playing a musical instrument.

Thus, education based on Vedic and Upanishadic texts was not necessarily restricted to only religious study but in fact included a curriculum that supported the study of many different content areas and ideas. It was believed at that time that a study of a combination of subjects on practical utility as well as spiritual upliftment would lead to the development of a balanced personality. The Upanishadic passion for finding out the truth about things holds a scientific method in its approach. The teaching methodology strongly utilized the science of reasoning and questioning, as can be inferred from the frequent use of terms like *prasnin* (questioner), *abhi-prasnin* (cross-questioner), *prasna-vivaka* (answerer). The curricular content was differentiated into two categories—*preyas* (leading to worldly pleasure and utility), and *sreyas* (leading to salvation from worldly suffering). The concept of humility was so entrenched in the ancient Indian educator's mind that nothing was labeled as the final or ultimate answer or truth. Written works in ancient Indian education and philosophy usually ended with the word "*nethi*" (this is not the last word), implying the on-going and continuing nature of inquiry.

It was about this time in India's history that the concept of social classes and castes began to emerge and became crystallized under the then existing social influences, and education started to gradually become more discriminating and selective. Education was largely open to students from the *brahman* caste (the priests), the *kshatriya* caste (the kings and warriors) and the *vaishya* caste (the merchants and traders). The study of the *Veda* was common to all of the above, and thereafter students could be trained in occupation-related areas of study. Thus there was both spiritual and secular education available to most except for members of the *shudra* caste (the artisans and sanitation workers), who although they could train in menial jobs, were denied religious and spiritual learning. Based on ancient scriptures and texts, the general aims of education in ancient India might be summarized as being an infusion of a spirit of piety; character formation; personality development; inculcation of civic and social duties; promotion of social efficiency; and preservation of the national culture.

During the Upanishadic period, Benares or modern-day Varanasi, became a major center of learning, and the *Upanishad* refer to a philosopher named Ajatshatru who was also one of the kings of Benares. In the 7th century B.C. Benares was one of the most famous centers of education in eastern India, and continued to be so through the rise of Buddhism and Islam in India. Even today, the Benares Hindu University is very well known and is one of the more prominent universities in India. Schools that impart traditional Vedic education today in Indian society can be found in places that are usually associated with temples and are attended by students training to become Hindu priests, in centers for Hindu studies, and in many major universities that offer courses in Vedic education and the study of Sanskrit texts. Recent interest in Vedic education has also led to government and non-government sponsored initiatives for starting schools based on the concept of the ancient *gurukuls* and other Vedic schools.

Education When Buddhist Influences Were Predominant (600 B.C.–A.D. 700)

Buddhist influence on the educational system in India occurred approximately between 600 B.C. and A.D. 700 when Buddhism developed as a religious offshoot of Hinduism and began to spread not only within India but also to the countries east of India. Although Buddhist philosophy is embedded in the ancient Hindu concepts of *dharma* and *karma*, it rejected the rigidity and dogma that had begun to dominate Hinduism by that time in history. Thus Buddhism rejected rituals, ceremonies, and caste discrimination, and ensured that education was made freely available to any person who desired to learn including women. Students were entrusted to the care of *bhikkus* (Buddhist monks) in the monasteries to be instructed by them in spiritual and secular subjects. Written records by Chinese scholars such as I-Tsing and Fa-Hien make mention of the fact that the student population at the monasteries included not only the professed monks and novices, but also those who were learning the Buddhist scriptures with the intention of joining the order, as well as those who were residing at the monastery only for the sake of receiving an education. Learning continued to be based on Vedic texts as well as Buddhist scriptures such as *Dhammapada*. There are written records of scholars from around the world including China and Greece, who came to study at universities such as Nalanda and Vikramashila that flourished in India around that time. Such was the reputation of these powerful centers of higher learning that there was a long waiting list of scholars from all around the world with the admission rate being only 20 percent. Descriptions of the curriculum of studies at Nalanda have been found in the journals of the Chinese scholar, I-Tsing. They indicate that the study of grammar received great attention and grammar was the foundation of all other studies. There were five bodies of knowledge or *vidya*: *sabdavidya* (grammar and lexicography), *silpasthanavidya* (arts), *chikitsavidya* (medicine), *hetuvidya* (logic), and *adhyatmavidya* (science of the universal soul, or philosophy). The main course was founded on an elaborate study of Sanskrit grammar which led onto the study of logic, and finally to metaphysics and philosophy. Written records provide detailed descriptions of these world-famous universities. The ruins of Nalanda University can still be seen today in the modern-day Indian state of Bihar, close to Bodh Gaya where the Buddha is said to have attained enlightenment under a tree known as the Bodhi Tree. Records suggest that there existed a grand library at Nalanda University which comprised of three separate buildings. One of the library buildings was named Ratnodadhi, and has been described as being nine-stories tall and as housing several sacred scriptures. Another university, Vikramashila, was also located in Bihar on the banks of the river Ganga, and comprised 107 temples and 6 colleges. Educational opportunities at Buddhist monasteries were available to all, and this subsequently led to the establishment of a widespread system of popular education in India.

Buddhism was founded by a Hindu prince, Siddhartha who later came to be known as Gautam Buddha. The word *buddh* in Sanskrit refers to wisdom and *buddha* is one who has attained a supreme level of enlightenment or wisdom. As a religion, it flourished for a while in most of India, especially under the reign of Emperor Ashoka and the Mauryan dynasty. Ashoka is credited with the spread of Buddhism beyond India, into other parts of Asia and as far east as Japan. Although Buddhism continued as a religion in India for 1500 years, it did not find strong or lasting success within India itself where Hinduism was, and has been, the dominant force. Consequently, Buddhist schools too gradually diminished in number. Chinese scholar Huan Tsang, who studied at some of the Buddhist universities named above, mentions in his work *Life and Travels*, that even though Buddhism was on the decline in India by the 7th century A.D., many monasteries continued to flourish as centers of Buddhist learning. Today, Buddhist education is imparted in monasteries in the northeastern regions of India which are closest to predominantly Buddhist countries such as Tibet, Bhutan, and Myanmar, as well as in Dharamsala in northern India which is the home of the Dalai Lama who is in exile from Tibet. Buddhism is still practiced extensively in many other Asian countries such as Sri Lanka, Thailand, Vietnam, Cambodia, and Japan, among others.

Primary Education in Ancient and Medieval India[8]

In Ancient India, formal schooling for children was said to have begun only at the age of seven or eight years. Up until about 1000 B.C., writing was used only for the preservation of sacred literature, and secular literature had not yet been created. Thus knowledge of the 3 R's was not yet a part of the primary curriculum. Records indicate that in the early school years both girls and boys were taught not how to read and write the Vedic *mantras* or chants, but how to pronounce them properly, and to precisely differentiate between long and short vowel sounds, accents, and the rules of conjunction and coalescence of vowels and consonants. Thus primary education equipped young students to later successfully pursue higher education which, in turn, was essentially comprised of Vedic studies.

1000–200 B.C.

There is evidence to show that around 1000 B.C. the art of writing started to become freely available, and reading and writing would have gradually become an integral part of primary education. New sciences such as grammar, etymology, and metrics were developed at this time, and reading and writing would have been pre-requisites for the study of these subjects. Another social ritual that became widely integrated into people's ways of life during this period was the ritual of initiation or *upanayana,* which can be roughly translated as signifying the social birth of a child into the larger community outside the home, and being handed over to a teacher for the latter to initiate the student's formal education. The ritual was performed when the student was ready to commence his/her Vedic education under the supervision of the teacher with whom he/she would live. Over time this ritual became mandatory and it was held that without formal education a person would be unfit for marriage and society. Thus *upanayana* and Vedic studies were mandated for all in the community, both boys and girls. Doubtless, this helped in the spread of Vedic learning and also promoted primary education whereby students would be prepared for the higher education curriculum that now included grammar, arithmetic, astronomy, metrics, and philology. Ancient texts suggest that the percentage of literacy at this time was very high, reaching almost 80 percent. Sanskrit was the spoken language, and reading and writing in Sanskrit, with elementary arithmetic, grammar, phonology, and metrics formed the primary curriculum. Public institutions had not yet evolved at this time, and so schools must have been private enterprises with the family priest being the main educator and teacher.

200 B.C.–A.D. 800

During this period, primary education was recognized as a fully developed and essential part of education. Another ceremony observed by families was called *aksharavikarana* and this was performed for children at the age of five or six years which marked the beginning of a child's primary education. About six months were spent by the students in mastering the letters of the alphabet, after which a year was spent in mastering elementary arithmetic. During the later stages of primary education (8–11 years), students would also study grammatical works including Panini's *sutras* (Sanskrit grammar). Those students who could afford it were able to practice writing on wooden boards using some kind of color or dye. Poorer children would practice writing on the sand or dust on the ground, using pointed sticks or even their fingers. Using their fingers also worked to develop and strengthen the children's fine motor muscles. This method is described in great detail in many written records and continued to prevail until very recent times, and can still be seen practiced in remoter rural areas in India. Once the students had mastered the writing of the alphabet on the sand or board, they would graduate to writing on palm leaves and plantain leaves using charcoal ink. There was a strong emphasis on math, and tables of multiplication were recited by all the students in a class led by a teacher or a class monitor. By about A.D. 500 a number of public secondary schools and colleges were developed, and this also gave the impetus for public primary schools to be started. There are indications of such primary schools existing in the states of Kashmir, Bengal, and Madras (now called Tamil Nadu). Primary teachers belonged to not only the priestly or *brahman* class, but also came from families who were accountants, writers, and traders. Around A.D. 800 as the class system became increasingly rigid, the ritual of *upanayana*, which automatically initiated a child into the learning of the 3 R's, gradually became restricted to only *brahman* families and ceased to be performed in the families belonging to the *kshatriya*, *vaishya*, and *sudra* castes. This proved to be an immense setback in the spread of literacy in Indian society, and the percentage of the population who were literate fell dramatically. There was also a marked decrease in literacy levels among women at this time.

A.D. 800–1200

During this period there was a gradual increase in the development and spread of vernaculars and the common person ceased to understand Sanskrit. Primary education thus became increasingly preoccupied with the study of vernaculars. As long as Sanskrit had been the commonly spoken language, primary education had been viewed as a pre-requisite to, and an integral part of, higher education which was imparted entirely in Sanskrit. But when vernaculars began to be spoken commonly and primary education came to be dominated by vernaculars, the purpose of primary education as being a pre-requisite to higher education was lost. Vernacular education was no longer viewed with the objective of developing good Sanskrit scholars, but rather for the purpose of helping people succeed in ordinary walks of life. The curriculum during this period included reading, writing, commercial arithmetic, accountancy, and a good knowledge of vernaculars with perhaps a little bit of Sanskrit. Sanskrit dominated in the education of *brahman* boys who came from priestly families and would go on to becoming priests themselves, whereas agriculture and commercial arithmetic dominated the syllabus for students belonging to other castes who were taught such problems as how to measure the area of fields, how to deduce monthly wages, how to find the price of corn per unit of weight, and so forth. The extent of literacy in India went down even further during this period, even though the spread of public education was quite extensive. Several written records make reference to the fact that although most villages possessed schools for primary education, the percentage of boys attending them varied tremendously. This period also coincided with the time when the Muslim presence in India became stronger and more controlling, and under that influence literacy levels plummeted even further, especially for women.

The Historical Image of the Teacher: Role and Responsibilities

Traditionally, the teacher in India has been highly respected and revered. It was the teacher's responsibility to facilitate the individual's intellectual development and to lead the student away from the darkness of ignorance and toward the light of knowledge. Therefore the teacher was known as *guru*, or one who removes darkness. The word is derived from two roots, "gu" meaning darkness and "ru" meaning its removal. It was believed that parents were responsible for one's physical birth but the *guru* was responsible for one's intellectual or spiritual regeneration. The role that a teacher plays in an individual's education is far more important and influential than any building, equipment, classroom materials, or other resources. This belief that was established in Ancient India is still very much recognized, and teachers in India even today are accorded a high degree of respect as compared to many other nations around the world. Teachers in India were not prepared in teacher education institutions until the 18th century when Dutch missionaries established the first teacher education college in India. In order to become a teacher, students were called upon to pass an ordeal of debates in learning how to defend their own positions and attack that of their opponents. Thus the skill and power of debate and discussion, questioning and cross-questioning, were remarkably developed by the end of an individual's education.

However, with respect and veneration given to a teacher came a great deal of responsibility attached to the role of teaching. The *guru* had to be one of very high character in being patient and just, well grounded in his area of expertise, and demonstrating a commitment to lifelong reading and learning. In addition to profound scholarship, the *guru* was also required to have fluent delivery of instruction, readiness of wit, presence of mind, and a stock of interesting anec- dotal examples to share with his students. The *guru* was to be pious and a source of inspiration, and was morally obliged never to withhold knowledge in the apprehension that his students might one day surpass him. Teachers were not expected to charge a regular fee, and their duty was to teach all their students regardless of how poor the latter might be. There is little doubt that in ancient India teaching was considered to be a profession nobler than any other profession. Although today the teaching profession has become commercialized in many ways, and teaching continues to remain a low paying job, teachers and professors continue to be held in high regard and are greatly respected professionals in Indian society in general.

The Daily Life of a Student in Ancient India

Most formal schools in Ancient India were like boarding schools in the resi- dence of the *guru*, and such schools were called *gurukul*. The term literally means the household and family of the *guru* and it included his own family as well his students. Up until the age of about 8 years, children had a life free of restrictions after which they would start the educational stage of their lives, usually in a *gurukul* which was often situated in environments that were calm and serene such as within the grounds of a temple, or in a forest, or in a quiet area within a city. Of course, the daily life of a student in ancient India would have varied according to many factors such as type of education, location, regional cultures, age of students, and so forth. But for students whose education focused on religious and literary studies, it can be safely assumed that their daily schedule was characterized by the following routines. Students would be required to awake at about 4:30 A.M., have their baths and say their prayers. Vedic students would spend additional time in the early morning performing various morning rituals in order to learn how they were conducted. Other students would, after their prayers, learn new lessons and revise old ones. The morning's work would cease at 11:00 A.M. and the students would break off for meals. A period of rest followed and then teaching would begin at 2:00 P.M. and continue for the rest of the afternoon. In the evenings students might engage in physical exercises, and at sunset the students would pray, offer fire sacrifices and then eat dinner. Students of sculpture, architecture, painting, and carpentry would spend a considerable part of the day in the teachers' workshops. The poorer students would help out with household chores and other work as payment toward their education. Students were expected to develop and demonstrate dignity, decorum, and self- discipline. They were to be respectful and courteous to their teachers and elders, never indulge in lying and slander, and always demonstrate plain living and high thinking. Even royal students living in a *gurukul* were not allowed to have access to their personal money. All students were required to attend their classes regularly and be attentive to their lessons. The relationship between an ideal *guru* and an equally ideal student built on a process of teaching and learning that was defined by mutual respect and trust; and a high code of conduct lay the foundation for the well-known *guru-shishya parampara* in India, or the traditional teacher-student relationship.

MEDIEVAL AND EARLY MODERN INDIA: APPROXIMATE TIME PERIOD A.D. 700—1700

Education When Islamic Influences Were Predominant

Islamic influences on the educational system in India began gradually around A.D. 1000 and predominated after that until the 1700s. The 11th century marked the start of several frequent and regular Islamic invasions into India from Persia and Asia Minor, and resulted in the establishment of monarchies such as those of Mahmud of Ghazni in A.D. 1001, Muhammad Ghauri in A.D. 1175, Qutab-ud-din Aibak who made Delhi the seat of Islamic power in India in A.D. 1193, Bhaktiya Khilji who destroyed the famed Nalanda University in A.D. 1200, Raziya Sultana who became the first woman ruler of Delhi in A.D. 1236, and Mohammad bin Tughlaq who came to power in A.D. 1323. This period also included the rise of the Mughal Empire which was founded by Babar in A.D. 1526 and which remained in place for almost three hundred years, until its demise under the British colonial rule. During this period, the system of education in India was marked by the rapid development of Islamic schools that were closely associated with mosques. The languages of instruction became primarily Arabic and Farsi (Persian), and the curriculum in these schools became intimately informed by the Islamic religion. Gender segregation became prominent in Indian society and education under the influence of Islam. Women could not be seen or heard in public, and with the implementation of the *purdah* system, women's lives in Muslim dominated regions of India became even more sheltered and homebound with decreasing rights to education in general, as was the case with members of certain social castes. Educational philosophy in general advocated conformity and discouraged the critical thinking or speculation that had been valued in the earlier educational philosophies as discussed.

However, the development of a healthy encounter between Hindu and Muslim cultures was also possible in the reigns of those kings and emperors who were keen to promote the meeting of these cultures. Some prominent names in the spread of education are the early Muslim monarchs of the Khalji and Tughlak dynasties in the 12th and 14th centuries; Raziya Sultana in the early 13th century; and emperors of the Mughal dynasty between the 16th and 18th centuries namely Humayun, Akbar, and Jehangir. In fact, education under these emperors was considered to be the birthright of every citizen and indigenous education was greatly promoted. A college was in existence in Delhi when Raziya Sultana came to power in early 13th century. Raziya herself was a patron of learning and an educated woman and under her patronage, as well as that of Nasir-ud-din (1246–1256) and Balban (1266–1287), literary societies flourished in Delhi and by the end of the 13th century Delhi had become a great center of learning and continued to be so. High standards of education under the administrations of other Muslim rulers also led to the establishment of many village schools and colleges. Mention can be made of some prominent centers of learning such as those at Firuzabad, Badaun, Agra, Jaunpur, Bijapur, Golkonda, Malwa, and Bengal, among others.

The second Mughal emperor Humayun, ruled from 1530 to 1556 and was an accomplished scholar who built a college and library in Delhi. He met his death by falling off the balcony of his own library. Humanyun's son, Akbar (1556–1605) was instrumental in the spread of education and learning of not only Islamic literature and arts but also of Hindu texts, arts, and music. Under Akbar's reign, Hindu literature such as *Ramayana, Mahabharata*, and the *Atharva Veda* were translated into Farsi. He even tried to initiate a new but short-lived religion called *Din-e-Ilahi* which eclectically blended the spiritual aspects of Hinduism and Islam. Akbar's son and successor, Jehangir, was a lover of books and paintings. He ordered the repair and building of dozens of libraries, schools, and colleges during his reign. Jehangir's grandson, Dara Shikoh, was a great scholar with a strong leaning toward Hindu philosophy and translated many Sanskrit works such as the *Upanishad* into Farsi. In south/central India, several colleges and schools were founded under the rule of Muhammad Shah (1463–1482). The library at Bidar is said to have possessed over 3000 volumes, provisions were made for the education of orphans, and hundreds of village schools were started. There were several other Muslim kings throughout the country under whose leadership education was greatly promoted. During their reigns there was a predominance of Muslim influences including the great importance given to Persian poetry, music, dance, and the arts; Farsi being made the language of the court in India; and a rise in the teaching of Arabic and Farsi languages. Although Arabic was the sacred language of Islam, Farsi was the court language of the Mughal rulers and thus extensively used in India. Knowledge of either Arabic or Farsi was necessary for Hindus to hold important offices in the government. In the military camps of the Mughal kings which included both Persian and Indian soldiers, a new language called Urdu emerged from the intermingling of Hindi and Farsi. Urdu quickly became the language used for general instruction in many schools that encouraged both Hindu and Muslim students. The study of the *Koran*, the sacred book of the Muslims, entered the life and culture of the country. At this time in Indian history, education became largely defined by the learning of the three R's, religious instruction, and other subjects such as literature, languages, grammar, logic, metaphysics, science, and politics.

In the *Ain-e-Akbari*, which constitutes an account of Akbar's administration written by Abul Fazl, an interesting description is found that highlights the standards of learning expected from a student. Schoolboys were to first learn how to write the letters of the alphabet by tracing their shapes and learning their names. Then the schoolboy was to learn how to join the letters in cursive writing. After this the student had to learn some poetry and prose by heart, as well as some verses in praise of God. He was to practice writing daily in order to improve his penmanship. All students were to read books on morals, arithmetic, geometry, astronomy, physiognomy, household matters, agriculture, the rules of the government, medicine, logic, sciences and history, as well as Sanskrit. Unlike the usual Islamic education, Akbar's vision served to broaden the notion of education provided in the *madrasahs* under the Islamic influence, at least during his reign.

Today, Islamic education in India is imparted in *maktabs* and *madrasahs*, which are religious schools and colleges run by mosques, as well as in specific centers of Islamic studies. After Hinduism, Islam is the second largest religious group in India with about 12 percent of the Indian population being Muslim.

MODERN TO MID-20TH CENTURY INDIA: APPROXIMATE TIME PERIOD A.D. 1700–1947

Education When British Colonial Influences Were Predominant

From about A.D. 1600 onwards the presence of French, Portuguese, Dutch, and British missionaries, traders, and subsequent trading companies in India led to the start of European and Christian influences on the educational system. This stage saw the emergence of missionary schools in India with their predominantly Roman Catholic beliefs and Christianity's focus on individual salvation. By the time the British had established their control in India in the late 18th century, the educational system in many parts of India had already begun to suffer under poor management, and under the influence of various dynasties education had become a privilege that was primarily available only to the rich excluding the poor and women. According to evaluations by the British rulers in India the standard of education was low, the course of studies was limited, literature and science were in a state of decay, and there was a clear absence of a spirit of inquiry and the full development of an individual's character and personality. It is clear that this state of education was vastly different from the robust system of education that prevailed in some of the earlier periods in India's history. Later, as the British gained supremacy and control over all of India, Protestant forms of Christianity as well as education in the scientific methods of modern Europe were implemented. A mammoth task of converting the national system of education in India from a traditional one to a modern Western one was thus begun at the primary, secondary, technical, and university levels. The parties who took charge of this massive reorganization included the British government, foreign Christian missions, and

Indian nationals who were pre-disposed toward Western education. Under the influence of Britain's imperial rule, Western values permeated the intelligentsia and literati of India.

The turning point of the British influence on education in colonial India was the adoption of English as the language of instruction in all the schools supported by the British administration. Lord Minto, Lord Dalhousie, Sir Warren Hastings, Lord Macaulay, and most other Viceroys of India were instrumental in shaping the country's educational system during their individual administrations. It was Lord Macaulay who dismissed all the collective Indian literary works over the centuries proclaiming them to be inferior to English literature. In the early part of the 19th century colleges were founded in India modeled after the prominent universities in England: in 1817 Hindu College (now known as Presidency College) was established in Calcutta, and in 1834 Elphinstone College was set up in Bombay. A detailed and comprehensive account of the history of English education in India from 1781–1893 appears in a historical document which includes a rare chronological account of the extracts from Parliamentary papers, official reports, dispatches, minutes, and resolutions of the government.[9] Highlighted below are some of the more important educational initiatives in 19th century British India:

1813: Sanskrit learning was to be encouraged for its excellent systems of ethics and codes of law.

1815: Missionary movements in starting colleges of education were begun.

1829: English was adopted as the language of official business in colonial India.

1835: The debate between comparative benefits of English and Oriental learning resulted in Lord Macaulay's Minute which proclaimed English to be the language of instruction in schools in India.

1844: Lord Hardinge supported the employment of those native Indians who were successful in the system of education administered by the British.

1854: Governor-General Lord William Bentinck declared religious neutrality in education in schools. This was received with much disapproval by the Missionaries and was followed by the gradual conversion of Hindu students in Missionary schools.

1857: By this time, the Universities of Calcutta, Madras, and Bombay had all been founded, modeled after the University of London. Sanskrit, Arabic, and Persian languages were included among the subjects offered but only when consistent with religious neutrality.

1882: The Indian Education Commission was established to report on the subject of education. Members included both European and native Indian representatives.

1889: The Indian Education Commission proposed that schools include textbooks for moral education, and yet stay secular in terms of religious neutrality.

1892: By this time a total of 144 colleges had been established by the British administration in India. Of them there were 108 liberal arts colleges, 28 law colleges, 4 medical colleges, and 4 engineering colleges.

The process of colonization in India began with a physical conquest of territories followed by the conquest of minds, selves, and cultures. In order for

Europe to be established as the site of civilization, the colonized world had to be emptied of its own knowledge and value. The West, thus, had to be established not only in physical structures but also in people's minds. To establish and maintain control, the colonizer had to essentially become the educator and proclaim that the only way colonized Indians could be properly educated was through the language and canon of the educator. In British India, this required the implementation of a system of education that would bureaucratically control the way natives would be educated. The assumption that proper education must be defined by the language and canon of the colonizer became the underlying basis for the famous Macaulay's Minute of 1835 in which the then Viceroy of India, Lord Macaulay, proclaimed that the English language would become the medium of instruction in schools in India. The declaration of Macaulay's Minute was the beginning of a system of education in India that would tend to forsake its own history and philosophy and become more Western. Two very significant moments in the relationship between Indian and European philosophy were first, the separation of Indian thought into Philosophy and Religion, and second, the process of erasure of Indian philosophy under the conditions of colonization and the hegemonies of Western society. One of the more significant of the lasting legacies of the British colonial era is the textbook-centered pedagogy that began to, and continues to, dominate education in India. In the mid-19th century, the colonial administrators implemented a new bureaucratic format for the educational system in India. The new system would be governed by a bureaucracy tightly controlling all aspects of schooling the purposes of which were: (1) to acculturate Indian children and youth in European attitudes and prepare them to work at the lower and middle levels of colonial administrative services; (2) to insist on English as the medium of instruction; (3) to have indigenous schools conform to the syllabus and textbooks prescribed by the colonial government if they wanted to qualify for government aid; and (4) to use centralized examinations as assessment tools to determine eligibility of students for promotions. The examinations were designed by the British administrators and were based on the content of textbooks that had also been designed by the British. Subsequently, employment in the public services and private firms became conditional on passing these examinations, and demonstrating a command and mastery of the English language and literature, as well as British culture and etiquette. Thus, the rote memorization and examination-based system of education became largely a means whereby a class of Indian clerks and low-level bureaucrats were produced to fill key administrative positions for British officers. Almost 60 years after her independence in 1947, much of this examination-based and textbook-driven educational approach is still in practice and shapes the overall system of schooling in India even today.

One of the results of this colonizing presence of Western powers was a post-colonial hybridization of culture and language. The British influence on Indian culture and language was also accompanied by an export of Indian language and culture into the English world of the West. Scores of words that are now a part of

English vocabulary have come from Indian languages. It is said that by the middle of the 19th century, 26,000 words had made their way from India to England.[10] Some examples of Indian words that were absorbed into the English language are verandah, pajamas, cashmere, loot, tycoon, pundit, thug, guru, mantra, bungalow, juggernaut, avatar, karma, jodhpur, and so forth.

EDUCATIONAL TRENDS FOR POST-1947 INDEPENDENT INDIA

In the early and mid-20th century, with the prospect of political freedom looming ahead, appraisals conducted by Indian leaders and educators of the existing educational system led to the conclusions that in the interest of the country changes were required to bring back the historical prestige of Indian studies as well as to promote economic development of India by encouraging industrialization and technical education. Further, education was to be made available to all. The majority of the educators and philosophers recognized the fact that independent India could not discard many of the elements of Western culture that had permeated Indian society and the Indian mind over the course of the last several hundred years. Thus new ventures in education sought to combine and synthesize Indian and Western cultures. Leaders like Lala Lajpat Rai, J. Ghoshal, Atulananda Chakrabarti, and Rabindranath Tagore specifically sought to combine in education the elements that were best in the Indian and Western traditions. They recommended that although the essence of the relationship between the ancient Indian *guru* and his student was based on mutual respect and commitment, the authoritarian nature of the all-knowing *guru* should not be encouraged. And although India should cherish all her best traditions, Indians should also be able to develop themselves as competent players on the international field. Several of the above mentioned and other leaders in India at that time held that the brilliancy of the ideal of humankind was constituted by the converging forces that came from various different directions of the world, an idea that is rooted in ancient Indian texts and scriptures. In line with this thinking was the implementation of several educational initiatives. In the eastern state of Bengal, Tagore founded a school at Shanti Niketan, and later a university known as Vishwabharati (World University) where education would be open to all, and its principles would be based on the best values underlying Indian and Western cultures.

Even before India's independence, Swami Dayanand Saraswati founded the Arya Samaj movement in the 19th century, and established a large system of numerous Anglo-Vedic schools and colleges that were based on both Western and Indian Vedic studies. These schools are known as the D.A.V. or Dayanand Anglo-Vedic schools and are actively operating even today. Provisions were made in many of these institutions to educate girls and individuals from the under-privileged classes. Swami Dayanand Saraswati made it a point to note that nowhere in the *Veda* was it written that girls should be excluded from education. The Swami also set up several traditional *gurukuls* in the tradition of the ancient

Indian schools where students would live in residence with their teacher. The better known modern *gurukuls* were those that had been established at Kangri near Hardwar, and at Vrindavan near Mathura.

Another educational system set up in the late 19th century to specifically serve the needs of women is the S.N.D.T. Women's University in Mumbai where it has a distinguished teacher education program, and a special emphasis on Indian languages. The initials S-N-D-T stand for Shrimati Nathibai Damodar Thakersey, the mother of the founder of the college. The S.N.D.T. Womens' institution was officially recognized as a university by the state government in 1916.

Under the British administration there was no provision for the intensive study of Indian culture and Indian languages in schools and colleges. A system of institutions established in the early 20th century to meet this need were the *Vidyapiths* or Centers of Learning such as those in Pune and Ahmedabad offering courses of study in Sanskrit and the Hindu tradition. In a similar manner, the Jamia Milia Islamia, or the Muslim National University, was founded in Aligarh at the same time for Muslims to have opportunities to study their culture and languages more extensively. There are many more examples of schools, colleges, and universities that were established all over India.

India's foremost freedom fighter and spiritual leader of modern times, Mahatma Gandhi, promoted a system of education called Basic Education. His educational beliefs focused strongly on vocational education and the use of vernaculars as the medium of instruction. He desired to adopt a new method of education that would be more closely related to the conditions of life as experienced in India, and this implied the removal of English as an alien or foreign language of instruction in schools. Education in the new method must be imparted through the mother tongue, and this would strive to close the gap between the education that a child receives at school and the environment of his home. Not only should vernaculars be encouraged, but education should also work for the spread of Hindi, the national language. Gandhi's conceptualization of Basic Education was centered around some form of manual and productive work because he believed that manual work in addition to intellectual work was necessary for the holistic and spiritual development of a person. In addition, all education was recommended to be free, and special attention was to be paid to character development that required the teachers in primary classrooms themselves to be competent and of good character. To Gandhi, character building was the essence of education and purity of life was the one indispensable condition for it. He laid great emphasis on religious education, where religion for him meant Truth and *Ahimsa* (non-violence). The objective of education is not only to turn out good individuals but also those who are socially useful. Thus the national system of education, according to Gandhi's vision, should aim to train 10 percent of the students for national service.

Several other scholars, philosophers, and educators contributed extensively toward the development of education in independent India. Some of the more prominent names are Dr. Radhakrishnan, Dr. Zakir Husain, Prof. Humayun

Kabir, Dr. Shankar Dayal Sharma, among many others. Dr. Zakir Husain was the Vice-Chancellor of the Jamia Milia Islamia University from 1920–1946, and later became appointed as the third President of India. He was a close associate of Gandhi and became one of the chief exponents of Basic Education. He viewed true education to include self-realization and the growth of an individual's latent and obvious aptitudes, and made a clear distinction between indoctrination and education, the latter resulting in the acquisition of a set of values, good character, and a perpetuation of objective culture. Dr. Radhakrishnan, a professor of Eastern Religions and Ethics at Oxford University, was independent India's second President. He was a great philosopher and proponent of higher education and emphasized that the value of university training included not only the information acquired, but also the development of scientific habits, free inquiry and rational reflection, and learning to distinguish between knowledge, opinion, fact, and theory. He was of the belief that wisdom comes through austere meditation and the inward journey of the spirit. These sentiments were echoed by Krishnamurti, the 20th century educator and philosopher, who believed that a really good educator should be concerned not only with the immediate but be prepared for the future—the future not in terms of the next day or the next thousand days, but the future as in the potential of the extraordinary development of the human mind. Thus children needed to be educated in totality: to be good on the outside and on the inside, with the most important goal of education being the knowledge of oneself. Despite these various ideas on education the larger system of education in India continued to be predominantly an examination-driven one as had been put into place by the British administrators.

At the time of her independence in 1947, the Indian population reflected a wide spectrum of diversity. However, despite the diversity India was still a predominantly Hindu land and all other religious groups were certainly in the minority. Recognizing this, the framers of the Indian Constitution were aware that in this newly created and hugely diverse democracy the complexity and rights of minority groups would definitely become an issue that could lead to deep divisiveness of Indian society if safeguards for the minority groups were not clearly articulated in the Indian Constitution. Thus they made every effort so that fundamental political and social rights were guaranteed to all Indian citizens regardless of their caste, creed, sex, language, race, or culture. The Constitution articulated the provision of not only basic rights to minority groups but also rights that would allow them to conserve their religion, culture, and language. More importantly, according to Articles 29 and 30 of the Indian Constitution, all minority religious or linguistic groups have the right to establish and administer educational institutions of their choice. Further, in granting aid to educational institutions, the state cannot discriminate against any institution that is under the management of any minority group; and it would be expected that the state and every local authority within the state would provide adequate facilities for instruction in the mother tongue at the primary grade levels to children belonging to minority groups. In 1964, the Education Commission proposed a Three

Language Formula which became generally accepted, and whereby a school-going child would study (1) the mother tongue or the regional language of the state; (2) the official language of the Union (Hindi) or the associate official language of the Union (English); and (3) a modern Indian or foreign language not covered under (1) or (2), and other than that used as the medium of instruction. Despite such efforts, however, the complexities of power relationships between the different languages does come into play and there is a definite marginalization of people who speak languages other than those recognized as the official national languages, especially those who belong to the tribal or indigenous populations.

Also in 1964, the Central government appointed a committee to frame a national policy that would give definition to a school education system in a nation that had recently become independent. The committee, headed by Dr. D. S. Kothari, issued a report titled the Kothari Commission Report on Education (1964–1966), which is even today considered to be the most in-depth and comprehensive study of primary and secondary education in India. The report recommended a common school system that would include:

- Publicly funded schools open to all children irrespective of caste, creed, community, religion, and socio-economic status;
- Adequate standards maintained in all schools;
- Schools free of any tuition fee;
- Schools that would meet the expectations of average parents so they would not feel the need to send their children to fee-charging private schools;
- Significant increase in funding to enable elementary schools to develop a level of infrastructure that would transform government schools into good neighborhood schools;
- Free education to be provided for all in their mother tongue at the primary level, especially for minorities;
- Ways of creating partnerships between expensive private schools and the common school system to be explored with regard to incentives and legislation.

The National Policy on Education, formulated in 1986 and further updated in 1992, endorsed the Kothari Commission but these recommendations have not been implemented. The Central Advisory Board of Education (CABE) issued the Acharya Ramamurthi Report in 1990 which outlined the following impediments to the common school system:

- Socio-economic disparities resulted in richer families sending their children to private schools with better infrastructure, higher teaching standards, and teachers who were better qualified. Government schools were less sought after and consequently less invested in;
- The constitutional protection that was granted to minorities to establish and administer their own schools was conflicted with the notion of the common school system;
- The quality of education offered in government schools has thus far remained inferior to the curricular standards of private schools;

- Politics has interfered with the implementation of a common school system due to lack of interest on the part of politicians;
- There was rapid and prolific emergence of private, English-medium, fee-charging schools as well as a proliferation of exclusive government schools such as Sainik and Kendriya Vidyalayas catering to government employees only.

Today, India continues to negotiate a balance between low literacy rates on one hand, and becoming a technological superpower on the other hand; between the importance of promoting national and indigenous languages and the more practical need to continue to promote English, the language of the colonizers, as the country inches closer to becoming the third largest economy in the 21st century world.

CURRENT EDUCATIONAL SYSTEMS IN INDIA

India is home to more than 17 percent of the world's total population and to 325 languages of the total of 2820 languages in the whole world. Since her independence in 1947, India has seen tremendous growth in the educational arena. Currently, India has the world's second largest educational system after China, according to a World Bank report. Independent India's commitment to the spread of knowledge and freedom of thought is reflected in her Constitution: "The State shall endeavour to provide within a period of ten years from the commencement of this Constitution, for free and compulsory education for all children until they complete the age of fourteen years" (Article 45). But given the sheer magnitude of her population and the vastness of her cultural and linguistic diversity, the national goals of universal elementary education and complete eradication of illiteracy have yet to be realized. With 272 universities and thousands of colleges affiliated with them, 428 engineering colleges and technological institutes, more than 1200 medical colleges, scores of agricultural institutes and many other specialized centers of learning and research, India can be considered to be one of the leading countries in providing quality education from the primary through the secondary and post-secondary levels. Since education is such a priority in Indian society a large percentage of high school graduates do go onto college. At the same time, because of the overwhelmingly large population and a subsequent acute job shortage, there have been millions of college graduates who do not have jobs. However, with the recent trends in the globalization of commerce and economy, that is changing rapidly and jobs are becoming more easily available to the college-educated skilled workforce. So although India has the largest number of out-of-school children in the world who come mostly from poorer and rural households, the nation at the same time also has the largest pool of trained and skilled person power in the world that reflects a largely middle class and urban background.

There is a large system of government schools throughout the country, and also an extensive system of private schools, especially in urbanized areas, catering to India's massive middle class population of 350 million. Traditionally, children of poorer families from low socio-economic classes and rural areas have usually attended government schools as these are affordable in being free or subsidized, whereas private urban schools with higher tuitions are more accessible to the middle class population. The Ministry of Education in India provides the following statistics on the numbers of government and other recognized institutions at the various levels of education as of 2002:[11]

Primary schools (Grades 1–5)	664,041
Upper Primary schools (Grades 6–8)	219,626
Secondary schools (Grades 9–12)	133,492
Colleges for general education	8737
Colleges for professional education	2609 (medicine, law, engineering, etc.)
Universities	272

According to reports by the Ministry of Education, about 90 percent of the schools at the primary level are under government and local body management, and only about 10 percent are privately managed. At the secondary school level, only 42 percent of schools are under government and local body management whereas about 58 percent of schools are privately managed. But these figures take into account only government institutions and private institutions that are recognized. There is a huge number of private unrecognized schools that are not a part of these statistics but which might be offering a reasonable quality of education. The government statistics on enrolment at the primary level (Grades 1–5) is said to be about 63.6 million boys and 50.3 million girls. At the secondary level (Grades 9–12), the enrolment for boys is 18.4 million and for girls it is 12.1 million. The total enrolment at the elementary level for children between the ages of 6–14 years is about 150 million, making it the second largest elementary education system in the world. This number constitutes about 82 percent of the total number of children in India within that age group.

India's educational system continues to be driven by a strong focus on the assessment of students through a rigid examination system. Government organizations such as the National Council for Educational Research and Training (NCERT) promote a national curriculum that becomes translated into a prescribed syllabus and a set of corresponding textbooks for each grade level. These are then subsequently recommended to all 42 examination boards in the country. In addition to the Central Board of Secondary Education (CBSE) which is the world's largest educational board at the operational level, some of the other examination boards in India include the Indian Certified School Examination (ICSE), State Board of Examinations (SBE), and the Matriculation Board of Examination (MBE). Of these, the most widely used by urban schools are CBSE or the ICSE. Students are individually assessed at the end of each academic year for the content of the textbooks they have studied. The policy on language instruction in all schools generally follows the Three-Language Formula as proposed by the National Policy Resolution of 1968, and reiterated in the 1986 National Policy on Education, the three languages being the regional language; Hindi or English, and a modern Indian language. In most cases, Hindi is taught by virtue of being the national language of

India; English is taught for being the official and business language; and the third language taught is the native or regional language of the state, one of the eighteen dominant regional languages recognized as official from the 845 spoken in India. In support of this multi-language system, the Constitution requires all states to publish books in up to a dozen or more languages. Given the extent of diversity in India the system of education is a complex multi-tiered system that encompasses an infinite variety of schools. Apart from the CBSE, each state has an independent role in defining the details of education offered in its schools. So although education is primarily in the jurisdiction of the central government, the state governments play a major role in educational development. The National Policy on Education has provided a comprehensive policy framework for the development of education and a Plan of Action that assigns specific responsibilities for organizing, implementing, and financing its proposals. All the States and Union Territories in India have adopted a uniform structure of school education that consists of the 10+2 system. But there is variation between states and union territories regarding the following:

- Age for admission to Grade 1: this is generally between five and six years of age;
- The language of instruction: usually the regional language is the medium of instruction at the primary level in government schools in most of the states and union territories, whereas most private schools utilize English as the language of instruction;
- Public examinations: In all government and private schools throughout the nation, public examinations are held at the end of Grades 10 and 12 by the respective State Boards of Secondary and Higher Secondary Education. Promotion after Grade 10 and high school graduation after Grade 12 are based largely on these examinations.
- The teaching of Hindi and English languages: Hindi is the national language and in addition to the regional language that school children learn, the teaching of Hindi is compulsory in all but two of the States. The teaching of English is also compulsory in all States but is usually taught in Grades 6–10.
- The number of working days in a year: The number of school days in a year is 200 in all States nationwide.
- The academic session: The academic session begins and ends variously and is quite different in all the States.
- Vacation time and holidays: Usually the long vacation period coincides with the long hot summer months, but in the hilly and mountainous states the longer vacation could be availed of in the winter months.
- Compulsory education and free education: Compulsory education (mandating school attendance) covering the entire elementary stage of education has been implemented only in 8 States and Union Territories as of 1998. However, free education for Grades 1–12 has been introduced in all government schools in the majority of the States and Union Territories of India.

Pre-primary Education

The establishment of the National Policy on Education (NPE) in 1986 and its subsequent modification in 1992 accorded a great deal of importance to Early Childhood Care and Education (ECCE) and recognized it as playing a critical part in the development of human resources. Development of ECCE programs was seen as not only providing the individual child with early care and education, but also releasing women for other activities besides child rearing, and facilitating the access to schools by older girls who would have been otherwise providing sibling care. The predominant system of education in most government and many private schools has followed, until recently, the pre-independence traditional colonial model characterized by a structured approach with a tightly prescribed content-based curriculum; a strong focus on reading, writing, and arithmetic dominated by rote learning; children seated most of the time at individual desks placed in rows; and a large amount of homework assignments required to be completed by the children everyday. At the early childhood level there is seen a wide range of schools, and differences may be attributed to whether the school administration is government controlled or privately controlled; whether schools exist in rural areas, small towns, or in large urban centers; whether they provide services as day care centers or nursery schools; whether they are religious or secular in nature; and so forth. However, according to the Sixth All India Educational Survey in 1996, the total coverage of young children in all kinds of pre-primary schools was only 25 percent of the total number of children. Primarily, the following kinds of pre-primary or early childhood settings may be seen:[12]

- the *Anganwadis* are run by the centrally sponsored Integrated Child Development Services (ICDS), and the *Balwadis* run by State Government or local bodies. The goal of ICDS is to empower underprivileged children younger than the age of six years, and ensure that they are physically healthy, mentally alert, emotionally secure, socially competent, and intellectually ready to learn when they reach primary school age.
- the non-governmental organization (NGO)-sponsored early childhood centers also exist in large numbers. NGO's have played a critical role in advancing childcare services in India, with their unique capacity in mobilizing local communities to bridge the gap between the government and the people. NGO-sponsored education centers may be found primarily in low socio-economic urban settlements and in rural districts.
- the independent private nursery school is commonly seen in urban residential centers. Usually this school is started as a business by stay at home middle class wives and mothers, either in a portion of their own homes or in a separate residential building. Such schools are small and most often offer a curriculum to prepare children to be admitted to larger on-going private schools.
- the nursery or kindergarten grades housed within larger, on-going private schools in large urban centers and metropolitan cities comprise yet another type of early education program. Usually, the coveted private schools hold parent interviews and admissions tests for the children, and getting admission into some of the more elite schools is very difficult. As of 2006, a court ruling has eliminated such admission tests in private schools.
- the mobile crèche is usually a temporary structure set up at a construction site to care for the children of women workers and is run by the Central Social Welfare Board. The children cared for are usually zero to three years of age, with the primary objectives of the crèche determined by the child's biological rhythm, alternating sleep, feeding, play, and rest.
- the urban day care center is usually run by voluntary and governmental organizations such as the Central Welfare Social Board for disadvantaged families.

- in villages one can even see a school under the trees with an adult member of the village taking on the teacher's role, and instructing a group of children in the outdoors, equipped with only a portable chalkboard and chalk, while the children use slates and chalk to substitute for notebooks and pencils.

Among these diverse early childhood settings listed, those run by the ICDS (including the *Anganwadis* and *Balwadis*) form the largest group for children in the age range zero to six years. ICDS is considered to be one of the world's largest integrated early childhood education and care program which serves more than 12 million children between 3 and 6 years of age along with about 3 million pregnant and lactating mothers. But even this number is grossly inadequate when the total number of children between 0 and 6 years is 157 million. The goal of ICDS is to not only empower young children, but also empower women ages 15 to 45 years, thus promoting school readiness in children and basic education skills in mothers.

The 2002 National Conference on Early Childhood Care and Education organized by the Department of Elementary Education at NCERT reports that although in 1999 there were 22.9 million children in the zero to six years age group receiving Supplemental Nutrition Program services, the main area of concern of pre-school education offered by *Anganwadis* and *Balwadis* has been quality, specifically with regard to a lack of resources, lack of awareness, lack of indicators, distortions in curriculum, poor training, lack of institutional capacity, and inadequate advocacy about the need and significance of early care and education programs. Although the purpose and philosophy of these educational initiatives is good, the resources are scarce and the training of staff is inadequate. The private nursery schools and kindergartens, on the other hand, may be financially supported by high tuitions and/or other private funds, and definitely have the resources to offer better facilities and services, as well as hire teachers who are better qualified and experienced. This can have negative and positive consequences. The competition and reliance on private tuitions may lead to higher academic standards but also to overcrowding of classrooms and social inequity.

Primary Education

The primary grades include Grades 1–8, and are divided into Lower Primary and Upper Primary. The curriculum basically becomes more academic and is essentially a preparation for the board exams that the students will be taking in the secondary grades. All students generally have to study all subject areas at all grade levels. In the Lower Primary grades the subject areas will include English, Hindi, math, science, and environmental studies. But in the upper primary grades (usually by fifth grade) the subject areas will be more specific such as English language, English literature, Hindi language, Hindi literature, third language, physics, chemistry, biology, geometry, algebra, and so forth. In addition to academic content areas, schools also offer extra-curricular activities such as sports, art, music, dance, and so forth. The choices and time allotted for these non-academic subjects will depend on individual schools and resources.

Secondary Education

The school curriculum determined by the NCERT and implemented by the CBSE is the most widely adopted by schools across the country, and this also determines both the primary and secondary school curriculum. The CBSE Scheme of Studies for secondary high schools includes a basic scheme that must be followed by all private or government schools:

The *Academic Stream* which offers the following learning areas:

Learning areas 1 and 2: Two Languages (in addition to the language of instruction): Out of the two, one shall be Hindi or English (or both), and the second language may be chosen from: Assamese, Bengali, Gujarati, Kashmiri, Kannada, Marathi, Malayalam, Manipuri, Oriya, Punjabi, Sindhi, Tamil, Telugu, Urdu, Sanskrit, Arabic, Persian, Limboo, Lepcha, Bhutia, Nepali, Tibetan, French, German, Portuguese, Russian, and Spanish.

Learning areas 3, 4, and 5: Three electives out of the following subjects: mathematics, physics, chemistry, biology, engineering drawing, economics, political science, history, business studies, accountancy, home science, fine arts, agriculture, computer science, sociology, psychology, philosophy, physical education, music, and dance.

Learning area 6: General studies

Learning area 7: Work experience

Learning area 8: Physical and health education

The NCERT and CBSE require that while translating the curriculum due emphasis should be laid on national identity and values education.

There is also the *Vocational Stream* of studies that offers students electives such as: typewriting in English, stenography in English, typewriting in Hindi, stenography in Hindi, marketing, consumer behavior and protection, storekeeping, and store accounting.

As an example of how the CBSE basic requirements are adapted by a private school in New Delhi, the following curriculum for Grades 11 and 12 is presented. The second and third languages are required only till Grade 10 and may be dropped after that. There are three Courses offered which include science, commerce, and humanities, and students can choose to take one.

The science course includes the required or mandatory subjects English, physics, and chemistry. Students can then further opt for the:

a. Medical stream within which the fourth subject required is biology, and the fifth can be either math or psychology;

b. Non-medical stream within which the fourth subject required is math, and the fifth can be either computer science or economics.

The commerce course includes the required or mandatory subjects English, accountancy, business studies and economics; the fifth subject is an option between math and computer applications.

The humanities course includes the required or mandatory subjects English, psychology, and economics; the fourth subject is an option between history and political science; and the fifth subject is an option between math, computer application, fine arts (graphics or painting), and geography.

In addition to the above, physical education can be opted for as a sixth subject in all streams.

Some Examples of Recent Government Educational Initiatives and Schemes

Several proposals or Centrally Sponsored Schemes are financed by the Education Department including Mid-Day Meal Scheme, Operation Blackboard, Non-formal Education, Teacher education, Post-literacy and Continuing education, and Vocational Education. Many of these initiatives have been implemented by state and central governments to expand the provision of primary formal and non-formal education in the goal toward Universalization of Elementary Education (UEE). Some examples are as follows:

The Total Literacy Campaign includes effective and sustained advocacy, massive community mobilization, and consciousness building that aims to target teachers, students and parents, and community opinion leaders.

The Kasturba Gandhi Shiksha Yojana is a program that will aim to establish residential schools for girls in all districts that have a low female literacy rate. The central government will grant financial incentives and scholarships to the girl child born in families living below the poverty level.

Operation Blackboard was launched in 1987 with the goal of improving school environments, increasing retention of students in schools, and enhancing learning achievement of children by providing the minimum essential facilities in schools. As of the year 2000, a total of 523,000 primary schools had thus far been improved under this scheme.

Decentralization was a goal set by the NPE in 1986 whereby there would be a decentralization of power, with the facilitation of the transfer of power and participation to the local self-governing institutions or the *Panchayati Raj* Institutions. This has enhanced the voices of women and minorities especially from the marginalized castes and tribes.

The School Meal Program was launched in 1995 and its aim has been to provide a nutritious and wholesome cooked meal of 100 grams of food grains per school day, free of cost to all children in Grades 1–5.

The District Primary Education Program was launched in 1994 with the objectives of providing all children with access to primary education through formal or non-formal programs; to minimize differences in enrollment, drop out rates, and learning achievement based on gender and social classes; to ensure basic competencies in literacy and numeracy and raise the average achievement levels by at least 25 percent; and to move toward a holistic view of primary education with an emphasis on decentralized, community-based management.

The Bihar Education Project was launched in 1991 with the specific purpose of improving elementary education in Bihar, one of India's poorest states.

The Andhra Pradesh Primary Education Project was implemented in the southern Indian state of Andhra Pradesh which houses Hyderabad, one of the cities that contribute to the region that has come to be known as the Silicon Valley of the East, but which also has one of the lowest female literacy rates of 34 percent. The project aims toward classroom improvements through two methods: training teachers and emphasizing school construction activities. This project has trained more than 80,000 teachers in 23 districts and more than 3000 teaching centers have been activated.

The Lok Jumbish Project has made a significant contribution to the primary educational system in the state of Rajasthan reaching a population of more than 12 million. It has found a high degree of success in bringing together government agencies, teachers, NGO's, elected officials, and the community into a unified group working toward the universalization of primary education.

The Alternative Schools initiative operates under the District Primary Education Program and consists of schools following several different models: (1) In the Employment Guarantee Scheme of the state of Madhya Pradesh the government starts a school within 90 days if an area without a school within a 1.5 kilometer radius is identified and if there are at least 40 out-of-school children. These schools are managed by the village *Panchayat*; (2) The Multi-grade Schools in the state of Kerala have been opened in collaboration with the privately run Rishi Valley School Group in those villages that do not qualify for new schools. The project emphasizes group learning and the use of self-learning materials; (3) The Alternative Schools in the state of Tamil Nadu have been started to bring back out-of-school children to mainstream schools after one year of preparation; (4) The Sugar Schools in the state of Maharashtra are schools that are close to sugar fields and factories and are meant for children of those families who migrate to the areas of sugar factories during the season.

More recently as of 2006, the Department of School Education and the Ministry of Human Resource Development have listed several other developments. Under the Kasturba Gandhi Balika Vidyalaya scheme, 1000 new schools will be added to the 1180 already approved schools for girls belonging predominantly to the Scheduled Caste, tribal and minority communities. The Jawahar Navodaya Vidyalaya scheme offers rural children access to high quality school education with the approval and opening of more than 530 schools. The National Institute of Open Schooling, which is the largest open schooling system in the world, now has an enrolment of about 1.4 million students from the primary (elementary) to the pre-college level. At the higher education level, the University Grants Commission has substantially increased its financial assistance to Central and State universities, and three Indian Institute of Science Education and Research facilities have been set up in Kolkata, Pune and Chandigarh.

Higher Education

Historically, India has had a highly developed system at the university level starting with some of the earliest recorded university systems at Vikramashila, Nalanda, and Takshashila (the last of which is in what is now Pakistan) which were established between 600 B.C. and A.D. 700. Colleges and universities have existed in India ever since then and grown exponentially in number. There were 4 medical colleges in all of India until the 1950s, and today there are more than 1200 medical colleges. According to a University Grants Report of 2002–2003, there are more than 15,000 colleges in India today. Of these are 11,128 arts, science, and commerce colleges; 784 teacher training colleges; 368 law colleges; 1077 engineering, technology, and architectural colleges; and 1253 medical colleges. The best known colleges in India are the world-renowned Indian Institutes of Technology (IIT) that offer degrees in the engineering and technical fields. The idea of the IITs was originally conceived at the time of India's independence when the leaders of this newly liberated country understood the vitality of educating a pool of a skilled workforce in science and technology. The first five IITs were established soon after independence in the 1950s and 1960s and ever since then its graduates have made a profound mark on global economy. Postgraduate and doctoral degrees are awarded in almost any discipline in India, and more recently, several Indian universities have established partnerships with colleges and universities in the United States, United Kingdom, and Australia whereby students are able to transfer between the two institutions. Until about 20 years ago, higher education in India was mostly a government establishment and some of the best college education was available at a very nominal cost. However, an interesting dynamic emerged as a result of low college tuition (as compared to college costs in countries such as the United States); India's large number of high school graduates; and the high value attached by Indian society in general to education and learning. The result was always stiff competition and gaining admission into a good college has always been solely dependant on the applicant's academic merit. It is only within the last couple of decades that private colleges have mushroomed everywhere in India, bringing with them additional possibilities but also astronomical college costs.

The Private School Phenomenon in India

It might be fairly accurate to conclude that currently in India there seems to exist a system of schools that can be grouped into four different categories: government schools; government-aided schools; private schools in slums and low poverty areas; and private schools that are affordable to the middle class and the rich. In spite of massive governmental efforts toward improving state-run schools, there are still inadequacies and inequities in the education that students receive in many of the government schools. Recently, a substantial rise in the number of small, English-medium private schools in rural and densely populated, poor urban neighborhoods has been reported. It is important to observe that private schools in India today are not merely for the privileged any more. With a growing educational shift over the past several years, the current growth of private schools even in the poorest villages has become an unstoppable force. The primary reasons are dissatisfaction over the inadequacies and inequities of government schools, and the growing awareness of the need to learn the English language. With global capitalist values increasingly permeating the fabric of Indian society, and the resulting growth in economics amongst middle class families, the poorer families are increasingly realizing the need for their children to know fluent English in order to get a piece of the pie, and are seeking out schools which will offer that and more. This has led people such as former teachers, landowners, and entrepreneurs to establish private schools which are less bureaucratic, have better facilities, and which offer an English-medium curriculum. Consequently, poor parents in slums and villages across India are pulling their children out of government schools if not satisfied and are enrolling them in smaller private schools which may not necessarily have exorbitant tuitions. In the state of Bihar, one small town of 300,000 people now has 100 private schools. In the state capital of Patna, hundreds more of private schools are to be found. In a recent study conducted in the state of Andhra Pradesh, 1000 schools were identified in the slums of its cyber-city Hyderabad, out of which two-thirds were private schools. In one slum locality of Shahadra, one of the poorest and most densely populated sections of Delhi, the capital of India, researchers have recently surveyed schools that included 71 government schools, 121 private schools, and 72 private unrecognized schools. According to official data from three other states in India, two-thirds of the children in urban Maharashtra, Uttar Pradesh, and Tamil Nadu are now in private schools. According to one report, 36 percent of school children in Uttar Pradesh, India's largest state and one of her poorest, attend private schools. The number of parents willing to pay tuition fees only goes to indicate how much a good education is valued by them. Their dissatisfaction with state schools is not unfounded. According to the 1999 Public Report on Basic Education, 20 percent of government schools in the country are single teacher institutions without proper buildings, 58 percent lack drinking water for students and more than 70 percent lack toilet facilities. Additional data indicate that although government school teachers earn a third more than private school teachers, one out of four teachers in government primary schools is absent, and one out of two teachers who are present is not teaching. The purpose for government schools seems to be mainly to make people literate at a basic level, and prepare them for such jobs as low-level government clerks.

In the face of mushrooming private schools, current educational debates in India are centered on a growing awareness and need to universalize education and offer public access to quality schools, and identifying the best possible directions in which to proceed so as to achieve this goal. Suggestions from economic and educational advisors point toward ideas such as voucher systems, and a simplification of the current four-tiered school system in India. However, parents will increasingly opt for English-medium private schools unless the standards of teaching; qualification and experience of teachers; academic performance of students; availability of basic resources such as water, electricity, toilets, desks, chairs, and blackboards show marked and consistent improvement in government schools at all levels.

Moving toward abolishing private schools without a comparable alternative is certainly not an answer as an education that equips a massive group of people with high-quality technical and research skills and a high level of English fluency is immensely valuable for India's economy. But it can be reiterated that one certainly does not find in India the instance where private schools are only for the rich and privileged. The poor are making the distinction between adequate and inadequate levels of education, and are finding remarkable ways of helping their children into private schools even in the poorest sections of urban and rural India in an attempt to break the cycle of poverty and socio-economic oppression.

New Trends in the National Curriculum Framework

Post-globalization changes in Indian society have led to a stronger focus on issues in global and comparative education. In very recent attempts to move away from the centuries-old rigid academic approach, the National Curriculum Framework committee has proposed significant pedagogical changes that have gone into effect just this year in 2006. These changes include making the process of learning more "fun and child-friendly." Several things are being done to achieve this end such as re-designing text books with more illustrations and cartoons to make them more appealing and interesting to students; simplifying subjects such as math; eliminating the study of grammar as a separate segment; moving away from the basic premises of phonics and more toward the ideas of whole language; nation-wide teacher training workshops to re-train teachers in the new pedagogy; and implementation of social promotion in elementary schools. It is interesting to note that these changes are occurring in India just at the time when the opposite seems to be taking place in the U.S. where a concern over the low academic scores by U.S. primary and high school students has led to a more rigorous approach in the teaching of academics and the elimination of social promotion in many states. The extent to which this fundamental change toward "child-friendly" pedagogy will be successful in the Indian context with its overcrowded classrooms, examination boards and tough college admission requirements can only be determined after the next few years.

21ST CENTURY INDIA: CONTINUING CHALLENGES

As the world's largest democracy today, India has the largest pool of skilled person-power and is rapidly emerging as the world's third largest economy in the 21st century. Her massive educated and skilled middle class of nearly 350 million people (which is estimated to grow to 550 million by the year 2025) is contributing to the workforce of multinational companies across the world. One significant reason for this economic growth and expansion is that the Indian middle class has proven to be skilled, successful, and competent on the global playing field. This in turn has been the result of a society that has valued learning and promoted education for thousands of years, held students up to high academic and moral standards, and has equipped them with the necessary skills to compete with the rest of a now "flat" world.

However, the picture is not entirely a rosy one. Over the course of several centuries the emergence and continuation of certain social practices and attitudes have created obstacles in the spread and availability of education to all in Indian society. In many parts of India those practices continue to exist in conscious or unconscious forms and include exclusions and oppression of groups of individuals within various sections of Indian society. Even though the government has deemed many of these practices illegal and works toward abolishing them, many practices and customs still persist to greater or lesser extents in parts of India, but they certainly do not characterize all of India. Some of these social evils include (1) the infamous caste system, which much like racism in the United States has prevented members of the "lower" castes to have equal access to education and jobs; (2) the attitude of male privileging which has given preference and more importance to boys and men through various social structures such as exaggerated joy on the birth and marriage of sons as compared to daughters, more inheritance rights to sons, and more access to education and jobs for men; (3) the dowry system, whereby the worth of a daughter-in-law has been measured solely by the wealth she brings into her husband's family, and which has led to numerous instances of a daughter-in-law being mentally and physically abused or even being killed by her husband's family; (4) the old practice of *sati* which required a new widow to consume herself on the funeral pyre of her dead husband; (5) the plight of widows themselves amongst certain regional and ethnic groups where they are relegated to the margins and lose the right of being cared for by their husband's family. Such practices over the last several hundred years have stymied the educational opportunities for girls and women.

But India, the world's largest democracy, is a nation of contradictions and a land of opposites. Where there are inhuman and immoral social practices, there is also an acute consciousness of care, duty, and family responsibility; where there are low literacy rates, there is also Kerala, a state with 100 percent literacy; where there are schools which do not have even the basic resources and facilities, there are also high educational standards leading to cutting edge research and development in schools and universities which are among some of the best in the world; where there is suppression of girls there is also an enormous degree of active participation by women in the fields of science, medicine, engineering, politics, and education, and several political leaders in India are women; where there is abject poverty there is also enormous wealth; where there is widespread disease there is also access to health and medical care, and some of the largest pharmaceutical companies in the world; where there is malnutrition there is also an India which leads in agricultural production; where there is crude vulgarity and modernism there is also a society deeply rooted in moral and spiritual values, and tradition. The biggest challenge that faces India today with regard to education is how to provide free, accessible, and quality education to all her children, and also maintain a skilled, English-speaking workforce that will continue to compete successfully with the rest of the world.

VOICES, VIGNETTES, AND STORIES OF STUDENTS FROM DIFFERENT TIME PERIODS

1915: Schooling in a Small Town Government School

It was the year 1915. Manmohan was a seven year old boy who lived with his family in a small town in Northern India called Ambala. His father was a bank manager, and his mother a homemaker. Along with Manmohan were also his younger brother and older sister and they all attended the local school. Ambala was situated in the foothills of the Simla mountains. The total population of Ambala was then about 10,000–15,000 people. India was then ruled by the British and the seat of the British government was in New Delhi, but moved to the cool hills of Simla during the searing heat of summers. Manmohan started school at the age of six years and attended the local government primary school in Ambala. The school hours were 10 A.M.–3 P.M. Each morning upon arrival, all the students had to line up under the supervision of the monitors. A prayer meeting followed and the students usually sang the patriotic song "*sare jahan se achha hindustan hamara*" (our India is better than all the world). Manmohan's class had about 25 other students and they studied all subjects in primary school including English, science, and arithmetic, with each class being 45 minutes long. Manmohan usually ate a morning meal before leaving for school and then ate lunch at home after school. He did not carry any water or food with him to school. After primary school, his family moved to Saharanpur, a small town in the state of Uttar Pradesh. He attended the local government school and here there was a strong emphasis on English. His geometry books were a popular series of math books by Hall and Stevens that had been published in England. This school did not offer Science and Manmohan, much to his regret had to drop that subject. He then attended the Kashi Ram High School where there was a strong emphasis on translating phrases from English into Urdu and vice versa. No Hindi was taught but Urdu and Farsi were. Manmohan recalls one of his favorite books being the then popular "Maneaters of Tsavo."[13] There were 22 students for matriculating from tenth grade with the School Leaving Certificate. Only two students passed that year, and Manmohan was not one of them. Consequently he had to go to another school to complete high school. The students did not wear school uniforms, and the school did not offer any sports as there was no space for play. One year the high school acquired some neighboring land which was developed into a playing field. This was where the boys would play hockey after school hours. Girls' education was not encouraged in government schools, and most girls who went to school attended private or missionary schools, and usually only up to primary or middle grades. After graduating from high school, Manmohan attended Hindu College which was one of the two colleges in Delhi at that time in 1915. The other college, St. Stephens, was influenced heavily by Christian ideas, and Hindu College was the cheaper of the two the annual tuition being only Rs. 8. At Hindu College, teachers were referred to as

Shastriji and they taught Sanskrit and Indian culture. Manmohan completed B.A. (Hons), majoring in the arts including philosophy, history, English, and math. Hindu College was co-educational, but there were only about two girls among the 400 boys. Manmohan grew up to find a prominent job in one of the Ministries of the Indian government.

1942: Schooling in a DAV School in Urban Delhi

The year was 1942. India was in political ferment with several freedom fighting movements that were demanding the British government to leave India and go back to England. Leaders of the freedom fighting movements included Mahatma Gandhi, Jawahar Lal Nehru, Sardar Patel, Maulana Azad, Acharya Kripalani, among others. In addition, World War II was at its height. Harimohan and Prem were 12 years old and the best of friends. They came from middle income families and lived on Noorjehan Road in Delhi, the capital of the British government. They both attended Grade 6 at the DAV school in Gole Market in Central Delhi. The DAV schools were part of the Dayanand Anglo-Vedic chain of educational institutions started by Swami Dayanand. The DAV schools were managed by the Arya Samaj Trust, a social organization, and were neither private nor government schools. Most schools at that time were single sex schools. The school hours for Harimohan and Prem were 7 A.M. to 12:30 P.M. during the summers, and 9 A.M. TO 3 P.M. during the winter months. The medium of instruction was Urdu up to Grade 8, and thereafter was English from Grade 9 onward. Classes began at 7 A.M. in the summer. After four periods of instruction would be lunch break, and then classes would resume again for another four periods. The two friends would carry lunch from home some times, and on other days would buy some lunch from the roadside food carts. During school hours, students could play games and sports like hockey and football. After school, Harimohan and Prem walked back home, a distance of about 4–5 kilometers. The school had no bussing. Summer afternoons were hot and after resting a bit and completing their homework, they would then meet other friends in the neighborhood park and play other games such as badminton, cricket, *gulli danda* (a popular local game played with two short sticks), or fly kites. When it got dark, their parents called them home and it was a daily challenge to get the boys to leave their play and go home for dinner.

Some of the subjects Harimohan and Prem had to study included English, Urdu, history, geography, and math. Students could opt for science after Grade 9. One of their subjects was *Dharma* which was based on Vedic philosophy and was taught three days a week. All the teachers in school were Indian, and the Principal and Vice Principal were Arya Samaji, members of that particular social organization. The school text books were all printed in India. Thus the DAV schools had very little British influence. Most boys at that time studied Urdu while the girls studied Hindi. However, in *Kayastha* (particular caste) families such as that of Harimohan's, even the girls studied in Urdu. Even though some Arya Samaji schools were for girls also, Harimohan's three sisters, Sundri, Sabita and Kusum, attended a government all-girls' school. Because of World War II food was rationed and most of it was reserved for the British soldiers. The availability of sugar was limited and eggs were rationed to three eggs per week per family. The mode of transportation during those days was mostly bicycles, and the monthly income of a government employee was Rs. 125–150 including all allowances. In 1942, Mahatma Gandhi initiated the famous Quit India Movement demanding the British to leave and give India her freedom. In Delhi, Harimohan and Prem found themselves right in the midst of the political rioting against the British Government, and they got involved in several freedom revolts as their school took on an active role in the demonstrations and protests. Student leaders from their school organized demonstrations and many students would participate in destroying government property such as electric poles, street lamps, and cinema halls that screened films for the British soldiers. Small as they were, the cumulative effects of these protests soon served to finally free India in 1947. Although later Harimohan went to medical school and became a doctor, and Prem grew up to become the manager of an export company, at the time they were schoolboys they gave no thought to the future and what they would like to become. Life for students like them during the 1940s was all about school, play, and getting swept up in political activism.

1947: Schooling in an All-girls School in a Princely State in Central India

It was 1947 and Usha was going to school for the first time at the age of 12 years in seventh grade. Prior to that, she was home-schooled by her father and a tutor where she learned math, grammar, Marathi (one of the state languages in India), Sanskrit (the classical Indian language) and English, mainly through memorization of math tables and formulae, grammatical rules and verses in all three languages.

Usha belonged to a middle-income *Brahmin* family from central India who greatly valued higher education. Her father was a doctor and her grandfather had been a lawyer. Her mother was a home-maker but had matriculated from a school in Pune. Usha's family comprised of her grandparents, her parents and her two brothers and they all lived in the princely state of Indore which was governed by the royal Holkar family. The Holkars were among several royal families who had been ruling princely kingdoms all over India for several hundred years. Indore itself was a small town at that time, but under the progressive thinking of the Holkar rule education for girls had been greatly promoted and the state of Indore provided free schooling and college education for all girls which was very unusual in India at that time. Private schools, however, were not free and charged their own tuitions. The school Usha attended was the all-girls Ahilya Ashram Chandravati Mahavidyalaya. It was the same school that her grandmother and aunt had also attended.

In the seventh grade, Usha had to study history, geography, math, English, Marathi, and Sanskrit. The school day would begin at 10:30 AM and Usha would leave home after eating an early lunch. The school provided a bus service so every morning Usha would ride to school on the bus. The bus cost Rs. 1.50 per month. Sometimes, she would ride her bike to school. She would carry a snack with her in a tiffin box as the long school day ended only at 4:00 PM. Apart from the academic subjects, the school offered a Sports period 2–3 times a week where the girls got to play dodgeball, basketball, *kho kho* (a common outdoor two-team game played in India), and also physical exercise drills. After she returned home from school, Usha would play with her brothers and their friends since she was the only sister. She learned how to fly kites, play marbles and *pithu* (a game played with seven stones and a ball) which were all considered to be mainly boys' games. After playtime, she would go home and her grandfather would teach Usha and her brothers *bhajans* (devotional songs) and *shlokas* (Sanskrit verses). She would then eat dinner with her family and then go to bed. She did not get any homework.

In the eighth grade she had to choose between studying Sanskrit or science, and between history or geography. Usha's favorite subject was math and she was very good in that subject. She thinks that it was due to an excellent math teacher she had in school. She still carries her passion for math with her. Students were matriculated after tenth grade. The eleventh and twelfth grades were considered to be part of college, where Usha elected to pursue the study of science and biology toward the pre-medical program. She eventually went to medical college and became a pediatrician. Although 1947 was the year India became independent, Usha's school experiences were not greatly influenced by any of the political upheavals and changes that were sweeping India at that time. The education of girls had always been a priority in the Holkar state of Indore where Usha was born and raised.

1999: Schooling in a Government School in a Village in Bihar

It is the year 1999, and 13 year old Kuntalesh Mandal lives in a village called Bhuskaul in Darbhanga District in the eastern state of Bihar. Bhuskaul is a 24 hour train ride from the Indian capital of New Delhi. Bihar is one of the poorest states in India. Kuntalesh, or Kuntu as he is fondly called, belongs to a low-income rural family. He lives with his parents and has four older brothers. The three oldest brothers live in New Delhi and work as domestic help for upper middle class households doing jobs such as cooking and driving. Their wives and children however, live in the village with their husbands' parents. The family survives on the income of the three brothers who work in the city, collect money and send it home regularly. They do not have any other source of income. Kuntu's mother used to, at one time, work in the village in other people's houses. But she is now suffering from terminal cancer and is bedridden. Many families in the village are engaged in farming. The well-to-do ones may own farms and the poorer families work on other people's farms.

Kuntu started going to school at the age of five years. The name of his primary school was Rajkimat Vidyalaya. After Grade 7 he transferred to Janta Unch Vidyalaya at Jeebach Ghat. Both the schools were government schools and the annual examination fee was Rs. 45. School was close to home and he walked to and from school each day. His school had no uniforms, and the school hours were from 10:00 A.M. to 3 P.M. Classes began every morning at 10:30 A.M. and there were one hour periods for the different subjects. His first period was Hindi, followed by English, math (which was taught in Hindi language), science (physics and chemistry), civics, and geography. There was one teacher for each subject, and Kuntu's favorite subject was Hindi. He told me that although his native language is Bihari, Hindi was his favorite subject because it was the national language of his country and he should know it well. Lunchtime was at 1:30 P.M. and he would usually walk home for lunch. Kuntu had 72 students in each of his classes.

Each afternoon, he would come home from school and play with his friends in the large playing field near his house. His favorite games were Bat and Ball (a variation of cricket), football, and kite flying. After one hour of play he would go home, wash up and do his homework for about 30 minutes. Then he would have dinner and go to bed. Kuntu recently dropped out of school because he failed math by five points. His parents urged him to drop out, but given the chance he would like to go back to school. The schools in the village are co-ed. Kuntu told me that the government nowadays is trying to encourage education amongst boys and girls. Government schools are giving Rs. 250 in addition to money for rations and food supplies to families who have children in the schools. All the students are also provided free meals two days a week in the government schools.

Kuntu's older brother shared that over the last 15 years many more students have started attending this school. Even a few years ago, the schools comprised of temporary structures like hutments, and the children used to sit on the floor. But now schools are housed in proper buildings and classrooms are furnished with desks and chairs so that students no longer have to sit on the floor. Electricity is also a recent luxury in the village. The school teachers in the village nowadays are also better educated and come from higher socio-economic backgrounds. School attendance is enforced by the school masters, and moreover, the village families are increasingly desirous of sending their children to school regardless of poverty levels. Kuntu's brother shared that in their state of Bihar and the neighboring state of Bengal rural families living in poor villages are prioritizing education for their children. They sacrifice many necessities in order to collect money to educate their children, and provide them with books, uniforms, and other supplies. Kuntu is proud of his next older brother, Munikant, who attends college in the nearest town to his village called Darbhanga. His college tuition is Rs. 1500 per year and Munikant tutors school children after his classes so that he can collect money to pay for college. He has just successfully completed B.Com (a Bachelor's degree in commerce), ranking first in his class. But Kuntu is most grateful to his three oldest brothers who sacrificed their own education to come to the city and earn enough to support the daily requirements of their family as well as the education of their younger brothers.

2006: Schooling in an Urban Government School

Maya is a bright enthusiastic eight year old girl and lives in a tiny one-room apartment in the bustling city of New Delhi with her parents, her older brother, and her younger sister. The family belongs to a low-income background and is originally from the city of Jhansi in Bihar State. They moved to New Delhi about 10 years ago. Maya's father bores wells for a construction company and her mother cleans houses for a living. Maya attends the neighborhood government primary school called Nagar Nigam Prathmik Vidyalaya. It is a co-educational school and requires her to wear a uniform which consists of a dark purple skirt and a light blue blouse. The school is about a mile away and she walks to and from school every day on a crowded and heavily trafficked road that goes through a busy market. Sometimes she walks alone and sometimes she accompanies her older cousin who attends the same school. Maya studies in Grade 3 and her teacher's name is Aruna Mathur whom she calls Aruna Ma'am. Classes begin each morning at 8:30 A.M. and school gets over at 1:00 P.M. every afternoon. All her schoolwork is done in the Hindi and English languages, although mostly in Hindi. Lunch time is around 10:30 A.M. Sometimes Maya carries her own lunch and at other times it is provided by the school. The school has a large playing field and she plays with her friends every day after eating lunch. After school, Maya walks back home and does her homework. Then at 3:00 P.M. everyday she walks back to school to participate in the free tuition classes that are offered. This includes extra tutoring for children who desire to have it. The tutoring continues until 4:30 P.M. after which Maya spends a little time playing on the school field with her friends. When she returns home around 5:30 P.M. she gets busy trying to complete the tuition homework that the tutors have assigned for that afternoon. By the time that is completed, it is dinner time. Maya eats the meal with her family (her favorite dish being *matar paneer*, which is a curried preparation of green peas and cottage cheese), watches some television, and then goes to bed.

Maya helps her mother with housework sometimes. Once when her younger sister had to be taken to the hospital, her mother was away most of the day. Maya recalls that she and her brother together did a lot of the housework for the day including sweeping and mopping the house, and washing the dishes. Maya told me with a sparkle in her eyes that she wants to be a teacher when she grows up. Her mother, Pushpa's, dream is that Maya be educated and become something more than the poor cleaning lady that she herself is.

2006: Schooling in an Urban Private School

Shivali is a 15 year old girl who lives in the capital city of India, New Delhi. She belongs to a middle class professional family and attends a co-educational private school. Shivali has just completed and passed the annual examination for Grade 9 and will start the academic year in Grade 10 as of the first week of July when the school year begins for most Indian schools. Shivali lives in a joint family with her parents, brother, grandparents, and also her great-grandfather all under one roof. There are thus, four generations of a family living together which is still a common occurrence in India. This is Shivali's description of a typical ninth grade school day:

I wake up 6:30 A.M., take a bath, and get into my school uniform. I usually have a glass of milk and maybe a toast for breakfast. I leave home to catch the school bus at around 7:25 A.M. From 7:30 to 7:45, I'm in the bus and on the way to school. Sometimes I talk to my friends. If there is a test that day, I revise the test material—it helps a lot. Until 8:00, we either talk to friends or again if there is an upcoming test in the day, we all sit and study. The school bell rings at 8:00 A.M. The teacher enters the classroom and we get ready for attendance. Everyday, we have 9 periods—zero period to the 8th period. In the zero period, we either have assembly, or an activity of choice (my activity is the school magazine club where we write articles for the school magazine. Other activities are cricket, basketball, handball, judo, etc.). On each day we have a different schedule for the school day. The subjects that I have are math, English, French, physics, biology, chemistry, history, geography, and economics. School gets over at 2:00 P.M.

From 2:00 to 2:45 P.M. I'm on the bus heading back home. I usually talk to friends. I reach home around 2:50–3:00 P.M. I walk home alone from the bus-stop unless it is too hot. On very hot days my maid meets me at the bus stop and walks me home with a sun umbrella. Sometimes it can be as hot as 115 degrees Fahrenheit. From 3:00 to 3:45 P.M. I eat lunch and change my clothes. Sometimes I take a quick shower. Then on Tuesdays, Thursdays, and Saturdays I go for French tuition from 4:30 to 5:30 P.M. I return home at 6:00 P.M. On other days, I revise what has been done each day in school, and I do my homework. Sometimes if I have time, I play tennis at a local sports club.

I eat dinner between 8:00 and 8:30 P.M. From 8:30 to 10:30 P.M. I do various things, like play on the Xbox, play with my dog Lucky, go on the computer, watch T.V., and finish any other pending work that has to be done. I get ready for bed and sleep around 10:30 P.M.

NOTES

I am deeply grateful to all the participants for sharing their school stories. Their voices and reflections on past or current school experiences help in illustrating the richness and depth of the diversity of schooling in India, and provide the reader with unusual details of how schooling was experienced by the ordinary student in different parts of India during the last 100 years or so.

1. During the partition of India into India and Pakistan in 1947, the region of the subcontinent most directly affected was Punjab. The dividing border cut the region into two, with the western part of Punjab becoming included in Pakistan and the eastern part being left with India. Thus, both India and Pakistan currently have states or regions known as Punjab.

2. Keay, J. (2000) *India: A History.* New York: Grove Press.

3. *Veda*: see Chapter 1.

4. Gupta, A. (2006) *Early Childhood Education, Postcolonial Theory and Teaching Practices in India: Balancing Vygotsky and the Veda.* New York: Palgrave Macmillan.

5. Vyas, R. N. (1981) *Indian and Western Educational Psychologies and their Synthesis.* Ambala Cantt., India: Associated Publishers.

6. Satya Prakash (1965) *Founders of Sciences in Ancient India.* New Delhi, India: The Research Institute of Ancient Scientific Studies.

7. See note 5.

8. Altekar, A. S. (1965) *Education in Ancient India.* Varanasi, India: Nand Kishore & Brothers.

9. Mahmood, S. (1895) *A History of English Education in India: Its Rise, Development, Progress, Present Condition and Prospects being a Narrative of the Various Phases of Educational Policy and Measures Adopted under the British Rule from Its Beginning to the Present Period (1781–1893).* Delhi, India: Idarah-I Adabiyat-I Delli.

10. Iyer, P. (2004) *Sun after Dark: Flights into the Foreign.* New York: Alfred. A. Knopf.

11. National Policy on Education available on Department of Education, Government of India home page at http://www.education.nic.in.

12. Kaul, V. (March 1998) "Minimum standards for quality in early childhood education." Paper presented at a meeting on The National Consultation Meet on Streamlining of Early Childhood Education Services. New Delhi. State Council of Educational Research and Training (September 1994). Early Schooling : Problems and Perspectives. New Delhi.

13. The Man-Eaters of Tsavo by John Henry Patterson (1907) is the story about theTsavo man-eater lions who attacked the builders of the Uganda–Mombasa Railway in 1898. The attacks took place in Kenya and were recorded by Patterson. The book was made into a film in 1996 called "The Ghost and the Darkness."

BIBLIOGRAPHY

Achyuthan, M. (1974) *Educational Practices in Manu, Panini and Kautilya.* Trivandrum, India: College Book House Trivandrum.

Altekar, A. S. (1965) *Education in Ancient India.* Varanasi, India: Nand Kishore & Brothers.

Avinashilingam, T. S. (1960) *Gandhiji's Experiments in Education.* Ministry of Education, Government of India.

Bagulia, A. M. (2004) *Kothari Commission.* New Delhi, India: Anmol Publications.

Basham, A. L.(1998) *The Wonder that was India.* New Delhi, India: Rupa & Co.

Bernard, T. (1995) *Hindu Philosophy.* Bombay, India: Jaico Publishing House.

Chandra, A. N. (1980) *The Rig Vedic Culture and the Indus Civilization.* Calcutta, India: Ratna Prakashan.

Dalrymple, W. (1994) *The City of Djinns.* Great Britain: Flamingo.

Gupta, A. (2006) *Early Childhood Education, Postcolonial Theory and Teaching Practices in India: Balancing Vygotsky and the Veda.* New York: Palgrave Macmillan.

Keay, F. E. (1918/1980) *Ancient Indian Education: An Inquiry into its Origin, Development and Ideals.* New Delhi, India: Cosmo Publications.

Keay, J. (2000) *India: A History.* New York: Grove Press.

Krishnamurti, J. (1974) *Krishnamurti on Education.* London: Krishnamurti Foundation Trust.

Kumar, K. (1992) *What Is Worth Teaching?* New Delhi, India: Orient Longman Publishing.

Kumar, K. (1993) "Literacy and primary education in India." In P. Freebody and A. Welch (Eds) *Knowledge, Culture and Power: International Perspectives on Literacy as Policy and Practice* (pp. 102–113). London: Falmer Press.

Mahmood, S. (1895) *A History of English Education in India. Its Rise, Development, Progress, Present Condition and Prospects Being a Narrative of the Various Phases of Educational Policy and Measures Adopted under the British Rule from its Beginning to the Present Period (1781–1893)*. Delhi, India: Idarah-I Adabiyat-I Delhi.

Miles, M. (1997) "Disabled learners in South Asia: Lessons from the past for educational exporters." *International Journal of Disability, Development and Education*, 44 (2): 97–104.

Nanavaty, J. J. (1973) *Educational Thought. Volume 1*. Poona, India: Joshi and Lokhande Prakashan.

National Council of Educational Research and Training available at www.ncert.nic.in.

Paranjoti, V. (1969) *East and West in Indian Education*. Lucknow, India: Lucknow Publishing House.

Radhakrishnan, S. (1936) *Freedom and Culture*. Madras, India: G.A. Natesan & Company.

Satya Prakash (1965) *Founders of Sciences in Ancient India*. New Delhi, India: The Research Institute of Ancient Scientific Studies.

Sen, A. (2005) *The Argumentative Indian: Writings on Indian History, Culture and Identity*. New York: Farrar, Straus and Giroux.

Sharma, S. D. (1992) *Horizons of Indian Education*. New Delhi, India: Sterling Publishers.

Shridhar, K. K. (1996) "Language in education: Minorities and multilingualism in India." *International Review of Education*, 42: 327–347.

Singh, R. P. (1968) *Zakir Husain: Dynamics of Indigenous Education*. Delhi, India: Sterling Publishers Private Limited.

Tooley, J. and Dixon, P. (2003) "Providing education for the world's poor: A case study of the private sector in India." In B. Davies and J. West-Burnham (Eds) *Handbook of Educational Leadership and Management*. London: Pearson Education.

Tooly, J. (2005) *Private Schools for the Poor*. Published by Hoover Institution and available at www.educationnext.org/20054/22.html.

Varma, M. (1969) *The Philosophy of Indian Education*. Meerut, India: Meenakshi Prakashan.

Varma, P. K. (1999) *The Great Indian Middle Class*. New Delhi, India: Penguin Books.

Vishwanathan, G. (1995) "The beginnings of English literary study in British India." In Bill Ashcroft, Gareth Griffiths, and Helen Tiffin (Eds) *The Post-colonial Studies Reader*. New York: Routledge.

Vyas, R. N. (1981) *Indian & Western Educational Psychologies and their Synthesis*. Ambala Cantt., India: The Associated Publishers.

Chapter 6

SCHOOLING IN MALDIVES

Mohamed Latheef and Amita Gupta

OVERVIEW OF COUNTRY

The Republic of Maldives is situated south west of India and Sri Lanka, and consists of an archipelago made up of 1190 coral islands in the Indian Ocean. The total ocean area covered by the archipelago is about 90,000 square kilometers but the land area is limited to less than 300 square kilometers. The islands are grouped into 24 natural atolls. For administrative purposes these are grouped into 21 units, 20 of which are also called "atolls" and the capital Malè. Only 3 of the islands of Maldives have a land area greater than 3 square kilometers whereas 33 islands have a land area which is more than 1 square kilometer. The islands are all low-lying with the highest elevation less than 3 meters above sea level. The climate in Maldives is tropical and humid with the humidity varying during the monsoon and dry seasons. The coral reefs surround the islands or clusters of islands sometimes allowing for the passage of only small boats wherein it could be the only way to reach the island. Of the 1190 islands, 199 are inhabited of which 74 of the islands have populations less than 500 people and 60 islands have populations of more than 1,000 people (Census 2006).

It is believed that Maldives was inhabited by Aryan immigrants from India and/or Sri Lanka around the 4th or 5th centuries B.C. The state religion in the Maldives has been Islam since the middle of the 12th century and the current population is 100 percent Sunni Muslim. The national language of Maldives is Dhivehi which shares ancestry with several of the languages in India, Sri Lanka, and in countries of south east Asia. The fact that there has been a common language (Dhivehi) and a common religion (Islam) has allowed for a tradition of political stability and cultural homogeneity in the country. The Portuguese ruled the Maldives from Goa in India for 15 years in the 16th century. In 1887 the country became a British protectorate and remained so until it attained independence in 1965. The relative absence of the colonizing rule of foreign powers in the country's history is a key factor in the survival of an education system that is unique to Maldives. The head of the government is the President of the Republic who is elected every five years. *Citizen's Majlis* (the legislative assembly) consists of 50 members of whom 42 represent 21 constituencies and 8 are appointed by the President.

The estimated total population of Maldives is about 300,000 in 2006 and the country is classified as a developing country. The country's population is relatively young due to a rapid growth rate between 1965 with a population of 96,000 and 1995 with the population reaching almost 260,000. The high population growth rate of 2.8 percent reflects both a decrease in the mortality rate and a relatively high fertility rate. Although the rate has declined to 1.96 in 2000, the population spike from 1970s to 1990s has posed several challenges in social and economic development such as the pressure on economic opportunities, widening income disparities, youth unemployment, and increasing social demand for social services. The implications of a rapidly growing population with regard to the education sector can be seen in an increased enrollment and a higher demand for more school buildings, teachers, and educational resources. Since the population in Maldives is very young, almost a third of the population is in schools and the consequent demand for education is very high. Further, the increasing density of the population is a matter of concern, especially in the capital, Malè, where 25.5 percent of the total population resides. According to the 1995 census, 17.3 percent of the population is under 5 years of age and 46.5 percent are under 15 years of age, although in the 2000 census these ratios show a decline, for example, 11.44 percent of the population under 5 years and 40.7 percent under 15 years. However, several implications resulted from the fast rate of growth experienced in earlier years.

Emerging challenges to development efforts include a growing high dependency ratio (the ratio of total population to working age population), which also impacts any attempts to provide education for the young. Although the population to be served is relatively small nevertheless, easy access to people is hampered by the geographical dispersion of the population. Maldivian society also faces emerging social challenges and problems of drug abuse. Maldives used to be a low crime country, but now an upsurge in the crime rate alarms the system. Religious fanaticism and disharmonious alien values, although small in scale at present, remain potential threats to the social fabric of a unified and homogeneous society that has lived together in peace and harmony for thousands of years. While many factors responsible for these problems are beyond its scope, the education system can play a major role especially through various forms of preventive education, values education, and education for tolerance through formal, non-formal and informal education. The new global "information age" particularly highlights the growing role of the media as an agent of socialization. Many students are increasingly learning more of their knowledge, attitudes, and values from new media such as television, internet, and other forms of mass media than from their experiences in schools. It appears that the mass media have already overtaken the school and home as the most influential institutions on the mind and character of the child. The conflict lies in differences of argument on both sides of the objectives of the media: production for entertainment and education.

Maldives is a small very vulnerable economy, easily affected by global developments especially those related to the flow of tourists and the price of tuna. There is an important need for rapid adjustments; to develop new policies to mitigate the consequences of adverse world market development; and to seize new opportunities as they arise. Such adjustments often have educational and training implications. The challenge posed by the changes and potential in fisheries and service industries call for an increased output of persons with higher levels of schooling and training. The growth and maintenance of a society which has so far been supported by the fishing and service industries now demands higher levels of educational qualification.

DEVELOPMENT OF EDUCATION

Traditionally, the school system in Maldives comprised three types of institutions: the *edhuruge* or *kiyavaage* (neighborhood Quranic school), which was a gathering of children in a private home with the objective of making the pupils learn to read the Quran, to read and write *Dhivehi* (the local language), and to provide some rudiments of arithmetic; the *makthab*, which was more formal and offered almost the same curriculum, but was housed in a separate building; and the *madhrasa,* which offered a wider curriculum. These schools, privately-owned or run by the island communities, were self-financing. The overall level of educational attainment in traditional schools was low, but they have contributed toward achieving many educational objectives, including a relatively high rate of literacy and the preservation of national culture and tradition.

In 1927, the first government-provided formal school was established in Malè. This school was initially limited to the education of boys but later, in 1944, a section was opened for girls and young women. General instruction in this school included the teaching of the Dhivehi language, Islam, Arabic, and Arithmetic. The first Constitution of Maldives promulgated in 1932 legislated education as a responsibility of the government for the first time. This resulted in the immediate formation of a special department to oversee the provision of education.

Significant developments in education also took place in the 1940s and 1950s. For the first time in the country's history, education came to be regarded as an agent for national development. It was a period during which the government promoted and encouraged island communities, atoll administrators, and ward committees in Malè to provide educational facilities for their children. Many islands built and administered schools using their own resources. By 1945, a school at least at the level of a *makthab* was in operation on each inhabited island. An atoll *madhrasa* was established in each atoll run by the atoll administration which enrolled outstanding students selected from the entire atoll. Atoll schools provided basic education for successful students to fill administrative and leadership roles on the islands. Some outstanding atoll students were also provided with further education in Malè where two hostels were established to accommodate them as boarders.

The introduction of a modern English-medium education system in Male in 1960 became the land mark turning point in Maldivian educational development. Targeted at the manpower needs for social and economic development, these schools adopted formal organized curricula following syllabuses of international examination systems. With this system also came expatriate teachers and English textbooks. This new system, unlike the traditional schools, sought to enroll students in age-related grade levels. Unfortunately, however, the same period also saw a gradual decline of attention to atolls schools thereby leading to a deterioration of education in the atolls. The introduction of the English-medium schools in Malè resulted in the creation of a dual system of which the traditional schools were relegated to a second-level status.

A revival and growth of educational opportunities in the atolls came about from policy changes that occurred in the late 1970s. Until then, government provided schooling had been concentrated mainly in Malè. The beginning of the departure from this dual system occurred in 1976, with the administrative decision to introduce a national system of education and to expand modern education into the atolls. This program was augmented and reinvigorated by a new government in 1978 promoting a more equitable distribution of facilities and resources. The new policy focused on providing Universal Basic Education for All and thus the strategies highlighted primary schools (Grades 1–5) and middle schools (Grades 6–7); involved the creation of a unified curriculum for Grades 1–7; an improvement in teacher training; and upgrading or establishing new schools in the atolls. Two government schools, the Atoll Education Center (AEC) and the Atoll School (AS), were established in each atoll and today these schools represent the availability of high quality basic education for the children in their localities. Originally the AECs were to serve various roles in administration and dissemination, and as non-formal and model schools but these have been largely unrealized as the AECs have struggled to meet the high social demand for education. Currently, the AECs and APSs (Atoll Primary School) have few real differences in their roles. Other changes have included a move toward the merging of the traditional and the English-medium systems leading to a unified and modern system of education which has aimed to incorporate the positive features of both the traditional and English-medium systems. Educational development of the country has been characterized by a rapid increase in enrollment and number of educational institutions, and the provision of basic education remained the main priority of the sector for a number of years. Thus many of the schools have been newly constructed; a national curriculum has been introduced in 1984; and textbooks and teacher guides have been developed for all the basic education grades (Grades 1–7).

Enrollment in schools has risen sharply (from 15,000 in 1978 to 101,081 in 1999) and access to primary education (Grades 1–5) has been universalized. Current plans for education emphasize the universalization of 7 years of basic education; an expansion of secondary education; the strengthening of educational management information systems; a clearer emphasis on curricular relevance; establishing national capacity for secondary teacher education and post-secondary education; and the strengthening of partnerships with parents and community to support educational expansion and development. Currently, the adult literacy rate is over 98 percent.

CURRENT EDUCATIONAL PRIORITIES AND CONCERNS

Education in modern-day Maldives has been influenced in the past by three main streams: informal training, which children receive from the family and island community; Islamic religious instruction, provided through private tutoring and individualized teaching; and Western-style schooling which emerged in 1960 with the introduction of English-medium schools in Malè as part of a conscious effort to prepare Maldivians to meet the increasing needs for the country's development.

A major challenge has been the large number of widely dispersed small island populations which greatly increases the cost of providing educational services and the necessary infrastructure. A single town or city with a population of 300,000 can be more easily served by one university and a few secondary and primary schools as compared to a population of the same size that is scattered over 199 inhabited islands such as is the case in Maldives. Transport within Maldives is expensive because of several reasons: the distances involved; the small amount of goods entering into trade; the small number of people wishing to travel which makes scheduled transport services uneconomical; and also because coral reefs and the absence and/or lack of harbor facilities often make the loading and unloading of merchandise difficult. Development is seriously constrained by the lack of adequate and qualified person-power. While the country has a high literacy rate and has nearly universalized its primary education, there is an acute shortage of qualified professional technical people commensurate with the rate of social and economic development. This constraint needs to be overcome for Maldives to become independent of the use of expatriate labor especially in higher categories.

Based on the principle of equal educational opportunity for all, the government has worked towards the expansion of educational facilities throughout the country. This has not only served to reduce disparities in access to education for the inhabitants of Malè and those of the atolls, but also to raise public interest and awareness in education. In order to respond to the basic needs and demands of the community, and to help create a vital and self-reliant society prepared for future growth, the government will continue the nationwide program of modernization of the system, which includes upgrading and construction of educational facilities, and upgrading curricula and teaching methods. In addition, non-formal educational programs will be further developed and expanded.

The objectives for educational development of Maldives were aimed at the national development needs together with internationally set targets such as those of the Jomtien Conference of 1990 and later the Millennium Education Conference 2000. The Framework for Action to Meet Basic Learning Needs, prepared for the 1990 Jomtien Conference introduced the shift from universalization of five-year basic education to strategies aimed to enhance universalization of seven-year basic education. The work was followed on by the Education Master Plan (1996–2005) completed with assistance from the Asian Development Bank (ADB). The goal of the Education Master Plan Process (the EMP viewed planning as a process) was that it:

reflects national needs and priorities; is responsive to the existing and projected human resource and financial realities; promotes international understanding and prepares Maldivians for their roles as world citizens; provides the nation with problem solving skills necessary to deal with **major national concerns** including population, environmental, and health concerns; helps assure that Maldivian learners are prepared for both the labour market and for their roles as national citizens and family and community members; and deals with both the complementarities and foregone opportunities inherent in educational decisions about policies and programmes.

The expansion of the secondary education sector is severely impeded due to not only the lack of adequately trained personnel at the basic education level, but also a lack of teachers and the fact that a majority of secondary school teachers are still expatriates. There are two major difficulties in training teachers for secondary schools. The first is the lack of a local training facility which results in having to resort to the high cost of training teachers abroad. The second is the fact that the population pyramid of the country has a wide base, or in other words, the available number of suitable candidates who can be trained in order to address the rapidly increasing population is low and difficult to obtain. The quality of curriculum is also compromised due to an acute shortage of qualified personnel to work in this area.

With regard to higher education, the government has clearly recognized the need to invest in tertiary education opportunities. In 1989, through the use of loan funds from the World Bank's International Development Assistance, the government initiated the Education and Training Project (ETP). This activity provided financial assistance to Maldivians to seek higher education overseas in addition to other components of the project.

STRUCTURE AND ORGANIZATION OF THE EDUCATION SYSTEM

Schooling in Maldives is provided by the government, the community, and the private sectors. In 2004, 36.5 percent of the educational places in the nation were provided by the community while 54.8 percent were provided by the government. As for the geographic distribution, 71.9 percent of the educational places were in the atolls. Most of the atolls schools are able to provide lower levels of education, namely, primary and middle school levels. The proportion of government places increases by level with the government providing most of lower and almost all upper secondary schooling. Lower secondary education, once the monopoly of Malè institutions, has been extended to the atolls through the gradual addition of Grades 8–10 classes in Atoll Education Centers (AECs), Atoll Schools (ASs) and schools with larger school enrollments.

With respect to formal education, Atoll Education Centers (AECs) and Atoll Primary Schools (APSs) were started as model schools to provide a curriculum to the children on the atolls similar to what was offered in Malè schools. This was a specific strategy adopted to cater to the widely dispersed small populations. Apart from being schools the AECs and APCs also carried out other functions such as assisting in the in-service education of teachers and literacy work. There is no inhabited island without a school. Children have access to a school on their own island. Nearly all of them have classes up to Grade 7. The very few schools that do not have classes up to Grade 7 are projected to be upgraded very soon. However there is a very low school enrollment in the majority of schools. There are schools on islands where the school-age population would, under normal circumstances, be considered far too small to sustain even a primary school. Moreover, what started as five-year primary schools had to be extended to the full seven years if access to a basic education of seven years was to be maintained.

The island of Malè is an exception, since it is the capital of the country and sustains 28 percent of the school-going population in the country. Like in other countries, the inevitable development of the capital attracted more and more inhabitants from the peripheral islands. Formal school provision started in Malè and being then the only island on which it was available, children and their families began to migrate to Malè. Policies over the last few decades supporting the development of the atolls, which still continue and are given very high priority, have made significant improvements in the formal educational provision in the atolls. However, the unique physical features impose severe constraints and impediments on the provision of services to the atolls. Transportation of any materials has to be by sea. Any visits by supervisory staff have also to be by sea except for a few islands where travel by air is possible. The weather is such that some islands are not approachable for days. Unlike Ministries of Education elsewhere, the transportation item is a significant component in the education budget of the Maldives government. Even with the financial provision, time is spent mostly on the sea and not on the islands.

Although the physical features impose severe constraints on the provision of basic services, the people of Maldives have a deep and abiding commitment to education. A survey on poverty completed in 1998 has developed a Human Vulnerability Index for Maldives. As a part of the exercise for developing the Index it was necessary to allocate weights to various needs in terms of their priority to the people. Accordingly, the national sample covering all the inhabited islands was asked to rate the selected dimensions. It was seen that even in the most vulnerable islands, education has the highest priority for females. The response of males is also nearly the same. There is no doubt that it is this strong and abiding commitment to education which has enabled Maldives to make very significant progress, during the last decade, to the goals it had set itself despite all the natural difficulties.

Primary Education

The primary education system is a five-year cycle which children in the Maldives are expected to begin at the age of six-years. This is followed by the sixth and seventh years of education which is referred to as the "middle school" or "extended primary" cycle. In Malè, this primary to middle school cycle is preceded by a two-year cycle of pre-primary education (lower kindergarten and upper kindergarten years). In the other atolls this form of pre-primary education is also now becoming common, especially in the highly populated islands. Thus the formal grade cycle of Grades 1–5 (primary level) and Grades 6–7 (middle school level) together make up what the Ministry of Education (MOE) calls the basic education cycle.

Modern pre-schools exist in Malè and informal institutions in the atolls are now being replaced by modern, privately-financed or community-financed facilities on some islands. All pre-schools in Malè are non-government institutions, but unlike in the atolls, in Malè all teachers are supplied by the government and have additional costs for facilities. The result is considerable regional disparity in terms of the quantity and quality provided. Pre-primary curriculum has been effective in increasing children's readiness for primary grades. However, there is concern that an increasing amount of Grade 1 content is being shifted into kindergarten. The policy on the medium of instruction is to use either English or Dhivehi depending upon the availability of resources. There is a steady increase in the number of formal pre-primary schools in Maldives but the vast majority of schools are run by the community or by the private sector. The formal pre-school caters to children aged four–five years and lasts two years. In recent years, pre-schools have expanded into the atolls, as more and more *edhuruge* (gathering of children in a private home to learn to read the Quran) are being transformed into modern pre-schools, with either fully trained or partially trained teachers. Some of these schools are now being converted into Early Childhood Care Development center with assistance from UNICEF.

Secondary Education

Secondary education in the Maldives consists of Grades 8–10 (lower secondary) and Grades 11–12 (upper secondary). Lower secondary education is now being extended to the atolls through the gradual addition of Grades 8–10 in some AECs and ASs, and by the creation of the two regional secondary schools, one in the north and one in the south. The upper secondary education which, until 2000, remained limited to two formal schools, the Center for Higher Secondary Education (CHSE) and the Institute of Islamic Studies, and a few non-formal centers in Malè, has now been extended to the atolls in all regions. Students are prepared to take the University of London General Certificate of Education Ordinary Level (GCE O-Level) and Advanced Level (A-level) examinations after completing the lower and upper secondary levels, respectively. There are two national examinations at secondary levels basically for testing three subjects, namely, Islamic Studies and *Dhivehi*, the national language and Arabic Language. The two examinations are Secondary School Certificate Examination introduced in 1986, and the Higher Secondary School Certificate Examination introduced in 1987.

There is no university in Maldives. However, the Maldives College of Higher Education (MCHE) was established in 1998 with the joining up of five constituent institutions offering post secondary education and training. The institutions signed up as Faculty of Education, Faculty of Management and Computing, Faculty of Engineering Technology, Faculty of Health Sciences, Faculty of Hospitality and Tourism, and Faculty of Sharia and Law, along with a Center for Maritime Studies and Center for Open Learning. MCHE now offers degree programs and will be upgraded to the University of Maldives in 2007. MCHE is able to offer only a very limited number of places and study programs, and is not able to cope with the social demand for tertiary education. Therefore, most of the students completing secondary education and intending to pursue university education have to go abroad, either utilizing various foreign scholarship programs or relying on their own resources.

ADMINISTRATION AND MANAGEMENT OF THE EDUCATION SYSTEM

The principal functions of the Ministry of Education (MOE) until the mid-1970s included the administration of the three government schools in Malè, and testing and certification of candidates entering government jobs and into trades requiring special certification. Schools did exist outside Malè, but they were private and community undertakings and were largely left to operate by themselves. The recent development and expansion of education has required many new responsibilities. These include state-financed programs for school construction, curriculum development, textbook production, teacher training, non-formal education, and distance education.

The MOE is divided into seven sections and four specialized agencies. The heads of the sections and specialized agencies report directly to the Minister of Education, who is not only the political head of the Ministry but is often perceived as the professional and intellectual leader. This is made possible by an absence of marked distinctions between political, civil service, and professional functions.

The MOE works directly under the President of the Republic. The Minister of Education is assisted by Deputy Ministers, and receives policy advice from the National Education Council and the Advisory Committee on Basic Education.

The Educational Development Center (EDC) was evolved in 1979 out of the Educational Projects Office of the Ministry of Education, established in 1976 with responsibilities for expansion of primary education, teacher education, curriculum and textbook development, schools construction, science education, non-formal and community education, and educational radio programs. The EDC is now responsible for developing the national curriculum for Grades 1–12; identifying and producing textbooks and teaching aids; identifying and developing appropriate educational technologies for schools; designing and testing special educational projects; and conducting support and training activities.

All the island schools managed and administered by the local island communities with the island chief serving as the head are now administered with full responsibility by the Ministry of Education. Owing to duties and responsibilities other than those of education, the island chief was able to devote little time to the affairs of the school which are generally entrusted to the senior teacher in the school. Moreover, due to a lack of formal education and training, the island chief is often unable to provide professional and administrative support to the school. This used to be one of the weaknesses of the education system. The Ministry of Education is taking steps to meet the new challenge by training supervisors and head teachers for all schools.

CURRENT CHALLENGES AND FUTURE DIRECTIONS

Several directions have been identified by the MOE and experts that the government needs to take in order to meet the challenges facing education in the Maldives. These include, among others, improving educational efficiency through quality enhancement; improving early childhood care and development; improving the quality of basic education and teaching; enhancing the provision of basic education for youth and adults; and creating an informational management system.

Improving Educational Quality and Efficiency

There need to be increased efforts in Maldives to reduce the number of dropouts, failures, and repetitions in order to maximize the current funds available for education. To maintain quality only at current levels or to allow quality to decline would have neither a favorable human resource development nor a healthy political outcome. Properly trained and motivated teachers, effective management and supervision, appropriate facilities and learning materials and a curriculum with increased relevance to the individual and national development needs, suitable subject distribution and content are basic requirements for acceptable educational quality.

Improving Early Care and Education

The challenge in improving early education is the imbalance between the services and facilities offered in Malè and on the atolls. Nurseries and pre-schools have been established on the atolls but the support for them from the government is for training the teachers and for obtaining educational materials whereas in Malè the salaries of the teachers are paid by the government in addition to providing other supports. Another issue is the role of the traditional *Edhuruge* and *Kiviyaage* in the face of emerging and more modern educational institutions. The concept of education at this level basically comprises care and development constituting a wide range of concerns such as health and nutrition of mothers and children, and development of children from birth to age of entry into nursery. To address these concerns and challenges, a new program for Early Childhood Care and Development has been tried out in Maldives with assistance from UNICEF and is now being expanded into the atolls for ages from birth to school.

Improving the Quality of Basic Education and Teaching

This is a major issue that is being addressed in the country and a large part of the required physical infrastructure has been put into place. The provision of facilities, instructional materials, and other learning resources to schools are considered a priority. However, an emphasis on the quality and appropriateness of facilities, furnishings and equipment and the adequacy of provision with respect to the curricular requirements will constitute a baseline in terms of quality assurance. At this level, all the teachers are expected to be nationals rather than expatriates. But this remains far from being achieved. To improve the professional competencies of the current cadre of teachers, rigorous in-service training, stringent recruitment procedures and standardization of the entry levels of teacher training at this level are required. The latter is only a long-term possibility that is also dependent on increasing the capacity of the teacher education system. The short-term measure is to improve the competencies of the current cadre for which also the teacher education system has to contribute.

Additionally, a systematic mechanism for monitoring student learning is essential for the improvement of basic education. Regular, periodic assessment of the education system on the basis of previously established standards of achievement for children at the end of Grade 3, Grade 5, and Grade 7 are necessary. Current practice does not allow for comparison of the performance of students. Hence it is necessary to establish and sustain a monitoring culture through capacity building to improve the performance of the education system. Further, there are several groups of children needing special attention for a variety of reasons, such as those children on the outer and more remote islands, and children with disabilities and special issues.

A target set for the millennium was that all students who complete Grade 10 after the year 2000 would be computer literate and that target was achieved.

Other major efforts are being made to improve performance quality of school staff, particularly on the islands, through the training of the heads of schools; regular and closer supervision of schools by trained supervisors; stronger emphasis on continuing in-service education of teachers; provision of incentives to teachers such as bonuses and housing to work in remote schools; recognition and rewarding of good teachers; and motivating teachers for self-learning through incentives and salary adjustments.

Provision of Basic Education for Youth and Adults

While various ministries and agencies have made provisions and worked hard toward meeting goals in this category, there has been very little coordinated and sustained effort. Although there are increasing services to the atoll populations on the atolls themselves, the adequacy levels of these services need to be examined and assessed. In order to serve small and widely dispersed island populations new strategies using modern technologies need to be explored. It is also necessary to co-ordinate the basic education provision for youth and adults to ensure that no areas are neglected, that minimum standards are met in conducting systematic courses, and that there is no duplication of efforts.

Creating an Education Management Information System

Efforts need to be made to initiate a broad-based Educational Management Information System (EMIS) to facilitate all decision-making at the policy and administrative levels. Such an EMIS will need to address at least five major areas: labor market information; details on content and activities of educational programs; cost and expenditure data; student flow and student performance measures; and the preparation and support of teachers.

CONCLUSION

With swift open economic development there is the tendency for developing countries to emulate what may not be a sustainable life style for all. The life style on Malè itself, the capital of Maldives, is hardly sustainable elsewhere on the other islands of Maldives, even assuming that it is sustainable on Malè itself. Education is a process that has to support changes in society whilst harmonizing the evolving contexts with the cultural world-views of the local population. Maldives is a fast changing society with a vibrantly evolving socio-economic context. Education needs to work towards addressing and synchronizing with these changes. The national school curriculum needs to keep pace with the emerging needs through curricular revisions and diversification in order to prepare students both for further education and evolving employment opportunities. The revision and improvement of curriculum and instructional materials can be accomplished by strengthening evaluation and research capacities within the sector of education. Data leading to information on the distribution, use, and appropriateness of learning materials in different classroom settings can contribute significantly toward future decision making. A special emphasis can be given to the review of curriculum with a view to relating to occupational skills more than it does today.

NOTE

The authors would like to acknowledge all the references that have been cited in the bibliography below for the valuable information that contributed toward the completion of this chapter.

BIBLIOGRAPHY

Latheef, M. (1991) *Planning Education in Small Dispersed Island States with Particular Reference to the Maldives* (unpublished) Ph.D. dissertation, University of Wales, Cardiff.

Ministry of Education (1985) *Educational and Human Resource Development Plan 1985–1995*. Ministry of Education, Republic of Maldives.

Ministry of Education (1990) *Development of Island Community Schools*. Ministry of Education, Republic of Maldives.

Ministry of Education (1990) *The Edhuruge*. Ministry of Education, Republic of the Maldives.

The Ministry of Education (1995) *Republic of Maldives Educational Master Plan (1996–2005)*, Vol. I, II, and III. The Ministry of Education, Republic of Maldives.

Ministry of Education (1998) *Educational Statistics 1998*s. Ministry of Education. Republic of Maldives.

Ministry of Education (1998) *Report of Raa Atoll Supervision Trip*. Ministry of Education (unpublished Ministry of Education Internal document).

Ministry of Education (1999) *Maldives: Third Education and Training Project—Sector and Project Economic Anlaysis*. Draft Report.

Ministry of Planning, Human Resources and Environment (1994) *Fourth National Development Plan 1994–1996*. Ministry of Planning, Human Resources and Environment, Republic of Maldives.

Ministry of Planning, Human Resources and Environment (1996) *Analytical Report on the 1985 and 1990 Population and Housing Census of Maldives*. Ministry of Planning, Human Resources and Environment, Republic of Maldives.

Ministry of Planning, Human Resources and Environment (1997) *Fifth National Development Plan 1997–1999*. Ministry of Planning, Human Resources and Environment, Republic of Maldives.

Ministry of Planning, Human Resources and Environment (1998) *Republic of Maldives: Vulnerability & Poverty Assessment*. Ministry of Planning, Human Resources and Environment in cooperation with UNDP (unpublished) Malè, Republic of Maldives.

Ministry of Planning and Environment (1991) *Third National Development Plan 1991–1993*, Vol. I. Ministry of Planning and Environment, Malé, Maldives.

Ministry of Planning and National Development (2006) Maldives Population and Housing Census 2006, Preliminary Results, Ministry of Planning and National Development, Male, Maldives.

Toganivalu, Asilisna Davila (1993) *Report on the Consultancy in the Early Childhood Care and Education of the Republic of the Maldives.* Non-formal Education Centre, Ministry of Education, Male, Republic of the Maldives.

UNICEF (1996) *Maldives Multiple Indicator Survey Report.* UNICEF, Male.

Windham, Douglas M. (1991) *Education Sector Review: Republic of Maldives.* Male, Maldives.

Windham, Douglas M. (1997) *Republic of Maldives: Post-Secondary Education Study,* Vol. 1, Final Report (unpublished).

Chapter 7

SCHOOLING IN NEPAL

Tara Niraula

OVERVIEW OF COUNTRY

Nepal is a landlocked hilly country situated between two of the most populous nations in the world, India and China. With a population of 28.2 million, and covering an area of approximately 147,181 square kilometers, it is one of the least developed countries in the world. Nepal is multi-ethnic and multi-linguistic and enjoys one of the most impressive records of co-existence between various religious and cultural groups. Although Nepal remains predominantly a Hindu state with more than 80 percent of its population being Hindus, other religious groups have grown significantly over the last 15 years or so. Ironically, although Nepal is the birthplace of Lord Buddha, the country's Buddhist population is only about 11 percent. However, the religious composition of Nepalese society is changing quite significantly with growing numbers of Muslims and Christians.

Geo-politically, Nepal has been divided into 5 development regions, 14 zones or provinces, 75 districts and over 4000 villages and municipalities. Ecologically, the mighty Himalayan ranges lie in the north of the country; the hilly region which occupies about 68 percent of the total land area lies in the center; and the *Tarai*, a low lying, tropical/subtropical belt of land, lies in the southern belt of the country occupying about 17 percent of the land. Economically, Nepal is predominantly a subsistent agricultural country in which the livelihood of over 80 percent of the population depends on agriculture.

Nepal, a sovereign nation with rich social and cultural values, has undergone numerous educational experiments over a period of several centuries. Despite the long-standing emphasis on teaching and learning in the Nepali system, the history of a more organized, structured, and modern form of education is little more than a half a century old. Since Nepal has been primarily a subsistent agricultural country, it was not unusual for families to focus on teaching their children about better farming. Education in the ancient times remained a family and community business rather than a nationally organized and structured initiative. Over time, various efforts have been recorded which indicate that education took various forms such as religion-based teaching, and occupational and vocational education.

Any formally structured system of education would have been organized by the state, designed to serve the purpose of the ruling dynasty. Thus, the goals of education were closely aligned with the prevailing political system of the time, designed to support the politics rather than the development of a national human resource capital. Educating the public was perceived to be a threat to the ruling clans, and therefore the system of educating the masses was unavailable and its conception was even denied. However, with the evolving geopolitical and economic changes, advancements in technology and information, and with the diminishing power and control of colonizers in the neighboring countries, the country started to be more open, and as a result, the need for a more organized form of learning became transparent. Even though historically Nepal never directly experienced the colonizing rule of any colonizing power, the indirect influence on Nepal of the British rule in India could not be ignored. However, such influences were often limited to primarily affecting the ruling families.

Today, schools and institutions of higher learning have become an integral part of the national plans for development, but because of the prevailing political instabilities such institutions of learning have become much politicized and highly misused social institutions in the recent times.

HISTORICAL DEVELOPMENT OF EDUCATION AND SCHOOLING IN NEPAL

Although the history of Nepal goes back several centuries, there is not enough reliable documentation of information about the earliest times, particularly concerning the development of an organized and structured form of mass education. Education for the most part remained mostly informal for a very long time, and the early systems of teaching and learning in Nepal ware based on the two major religious philosophies of Hinduism and Buddhism. Over time education was modeled around the existing political realities of the day and remained governed by the decrees and rules of the ruling families. Education was also influenced by the existing caste system in which classification seemed to be based on occupational definitions. The higher the caste group one belonged to, the better were the chances of having access to educational opportunities. In such a caste system, the *brahmins* who enjoyed the highest status in the caste hierarchy were given the tasks of teaching, priesthood, and advisement. Those of the *kshatriya* caste, the second in the hierarchical ladder, seemed to have been trusted with defense and national security issues. Next down in the hierarchy were the *baishyas* who were trusted with commerce, trades, and economic responsibilities. The *sudras*, those of the lowest caste, were often termed as the untouchables and were limited to low level manual occupations such as tailoring, tool making, shoe making, and so forth. In such a systematically organized social structure, education remained the privilege of a few rather than the right of all.

Education in the Ancient Period

The tradition of education in Nepal can be traced back several centuries when teaching knowledge and skills were strictly a "family matter." Educational practices based upon social values were prevalent in the entire Indian sub-continent, and Nepal was no exception. What people learned or were taught was based on the prevailing social and cultural standards and norms. Education was not organized in a formal sense; it was more informal with fathers teaching sons about the work men were expected to do, and mothers teaching their daughters and daughter-in-laws about housework. Mentoring and apprentice-ships were common forms of teaching and learning. Students would spend considerable time with a *guru* (teacher) to learn the skills of a particular vocation. Although it is difficult to give precise accounts of educational development in Nepal due to a lack of reliable documentation, it may be said with quite certainty that, that even as much as 3000 years ago there was a relatively advanced civiliza-tion in various parts of the territory of what is known today as Nepal.

Education in ancient Nepal for the most part was religion-based, and Hindu priests and Buddhist lamas were the teachers. Prior to the origin of Buddhism, the foundation of education was based on the values and standards of the Hindu system, and Vedic education imparted through the medium of Sanskrit was the common practice of the time. The *Veda*, the texts that form the spiritual foundations of Hinduism, are some of the oldest written evidences that reflect the dominance of religion and cultural philosophy over education. Similarly, some of the ancient and perhaps the oldest books of Nepal such as the *Swayambhu Puran* or the story of the Self-Existent one is of Buddhist origin and is an example of the Buddhist influence in teaching and learning at that time in history. The Hindu *pandits* (preachers) and *gurus* (teachers) organized and imparted education in temples, public places, and even in their own homes. Similarly, Buddhist education was also found in *vihars* (schools) and *gompas* (monasteries) in Kathmandu Valley and in the northern areas of Nepal. Such Hindu temples and Buddhist monasteries functioned as schools in preparing Hindu priests and Buddhists lamas in the period around 536 B.C. After about the 3rd to 12th centuries A.D., a great deal of emphasis seemed to have been laid on the development of arts and crafts. Because of the strong influence of the powerful religious philosophies of Hinduism and Buddhism, it might not be unreasonable to state that education in ancient Nepal did not have its own separate identity as is seen in the Nepali educational system today, but was rather a part of the larger South Asian identity.

Since family homes, temples, *vihars*, and *gompas* were the primary sites for teaching and learning, the organization and management of education traditionally remained a family matter among the ruling clans and a few elite families for many centuries. Politically, the Hindu monarchs of Nepal who had absolute power designed education that would best address their needs. In the absence of mass public education, the general public in most part remained uninvolved in national affairs.

Because of long existing inequalities, and the resulting non-participation of the Nepali public in the social and political life of Nepal, education did not become part of the national public policy agenda until the middle of the 20th century. Although not widespread or universal in any sense, this traditional form of education flourished for centuries. With the arrival and subsequent control of India by the British, the Nepali education system was heavily influenced by the then British policies in India.

Education during the Lichchhavi Period

Although not too many reliable sources of educational development are to be found, the Lichchhavi period is considered to be highly influential in defining the Nepali culture and shaping its development. During the Lichchhavi period (about A.D. 300–1200), around the time of Gautam Buddha (the founder of Buddhism), Nepal is said to have taken steps toward overall development in its society. Lichchhavis were known to be efficient rulers, and during their rule Nepali civilization and culture were seen to have expanded over to the neighboring countries principally to Tibet, China, and India. During the Lichchhavi period, often known as the "Golden Age," Nepal seemed to have enjoyed social and cultural harmony and peace as well as great friendly relations with neighboring countries. There seemed to have been a tremendous emphasis to have teachers in the palaces so that the royal children could be educated, but the state had no clear provision for educating the general population. However, around A.D. 1267 the Lichchhavis appear to have developed some interest in public education by donating lands for educational purposes. Teachers' salaries and other expenses, although, were paid by encouraging donations and establishing various funds.

The Lichchhavis had a deep interest in developing arts and culture in addition to promoting education. There is some evidence that even around the 4th century, courses of studies were offered in the arts, *Veda*, law, grammar, philosophies, astrology, and so forth. During the Lichchhavi period, even though local languages were used for the purpose of daily communication, Sanskrit seemed to have been widely used particularly by the monarchs as a court language, and in teaching and learning. All religious events and activities took place in the Sanskrit language, and texts and religious materials were written in Sanskrit. Consequently, it was not unusual to find the dominance of this language among educated groups, teachers, and priests. Education was largely restricted and by choice, and was not widely available to the general public. During the Lichchhavi period, Nepali culture and arts seemed to have been transmitted through education to the neighboring Tibetan societies.

Education under the Malla Dynasty

The Malla dynasty is better known for the advancement of arts and crafts in the Kathmandu Valley. During the Malla rule that prevailed between the 13th century until the 1760s, training centers to impart skills in arts and craft were established. The Malla rulers' love for arts was greater than their desire to provide educational opportunities to the common people, and thus education did not receive too much attention during this period. Like in any other autocratic system, the Malla Palace housed a large number of educated people. Scholars were appointed by the Malla rulers to teach the royal children, the princes and princesses. There was a stronger focus on Buddhist education in the *gompas* and *vihars*. The Mallas had made education compulsory for the *brahmins* who performed the Hindu religious rituals, and for the monks who worked in the *vihars*.

But despite the restrictions and limitations, there is some indication that education during the Malla time did receive some priority in its development and expansion. Around the 14th century, King Jayasthiti Malla formalized various occupational groups and skills education was imparted to individuals within these groups accordingly. For example, those who made utensils and items made of copper were the *tamrakaars* (*tamra* means copper); those who dyed or produced colorful and artistic cloth and materials were called *ranjitkaars*, and so forth; these individuals would be provided with an education that would help them learn the skills of their occupations. King Jhayaysthiti Malla held teachers and scholars in high regard and showed them a deep respect, and under his monarchy both Newari (the language used by one of the ethnic groups known as the Newars) and Sanskrit-based education was developed further. Until about the late 1600s, there was no Christian influence in Nepal. Christianity was introduced in Nepal with the arrival of a Christian missionary named Grover Durbin from Tibet. Durbin presented a telescope to King Pratap Malla of Kathmandu who was so pleased with the gift that he gave permission to promote Christianity in Nepal. Taking advantage of this opportunity, other missionaries followed offering Christian education to children in the Kathmandu Valley. However, the Malla rulers also realized that it was important that there be a focus on Hindu education and advocated the need for translating the Hindu epics *Ramayana* and *Mahabharata* from the Sanskrit into a simpler and more colloquial language.

Education under the Shah Dynasty

The rise of the Shah dynasty and King Prithibi Narayan Shah's victory over Kathmandu in 1769 marked another turning point in the history of Nepal, and led to its unification. King Prithibi Narayan Shah's rule did not mark any significant development in the formal educational system in Nepal, and his primary focus was on warfare that would result in the expansion of his territory. Some might argue that King Prithibi Narayan Shah was an expansionist, others might say that he was an invader, while many in Nepal still believe him to be the unifier of the many discrete kingdoms into the one kingdom of Nepal. Prithibi Narayan Shah certainly emphasized military education and training, and seems to have organized some form of vocational education for the children of military personnel.

The dominance of Sanskrit and Farsi based education in India also seemed to have a noticeable influence on Nepali education. King Prithibi Narayan Shah had a deep understanding of the Mughal rule in India and promoted the use of the Farsi language in Nepal just as it was being used in India during that time. Education historians have noted that Prithibi Narayan Shah sent one of his scholars, Buddhi Man Sing, on a scholarship to study the Farsi language; and at the same time, realizing the need to give more importance to his own culture and language, he sent another scholar Baiyakaran Keshari to study Sanskrit.

Prior to the unification of Nepal, there was no definite plan to provide public education to the kingdom's ordinary citizens, and those who wanted to get an education had to go to the teachers' homes as there were no schools. After Nepal's unification, and due to Prithibi Narayan Shah's interest in nationalism, national unity, and protection of religion and culture, scholarships were made available for those who were sent to study Sanskrit and Farsi. However, despite these efforts, Prithibi Narayan Shah's focus was primarily on the expansion and unification of Nepal rather than on the education of the masses.

After Prithibi Narayan Shah's rule there was a lot of conflict within the ruling dynasty. An outsider, Jang Bahadur Kunwar, took advantage of the situation and captured total power from the Shah dynasty as he introduced the monarchic rule of his own family that lasted for more than one hundred years until 1950.

Education during the Rana Rule

The Rana period, extending from 1847 to 1950, marks another major political period in the history of Nepal. For most of its history, Nepal remained isolated and was closed to the outside world. The Rana family, who reigned in Nepal for over a hundred years, feared that an educated public would one day rise up against the royal family and therefore they continued to deny any educational opportunities to ordinary citizens. Because of the restrictive policies on education, the vast majority of Nepal's population remained illiterate. The educational system under the Ranas served the ruling clan and the few elite families closely associated with them well, but essentially remained inaccessible to the rest of the population. The establishment of the Tri Chandra College in 1918 by Rana Prime Minister Chandra Shamsher marks an important era in the development of public education in Nepal, particularly in the area of higher education. Some would also argue that this led to the ending of the Rana rule in Nepal, and many within his own ruling circle are said to have blamed Chandra Shamsher for the downfall of the Rana family.

With the British presence in India and the subsequent ties with the Ranas in Nepal, Jang Bahadur Rana, the founder of the Rana regime, decided to provide his children an English education rather than the traditional religion based education in Nepal and hired an English teacher to teach his children in the palace in the year 1854. The Rana rulers maintained a good relationship with the British rulers in India, and therefore it was natural that they would arrange to provide an English education for their children and the children of the few elite families who served them well and whose education would have benefited the monarchy. Historians have argued that such educational changes in the Rana Palace marked an important policy modification in favor of English education. Subsequently, the influence of British education became evident and began to transform education policy in Nepal as English education began to establish its supremacy over the traditional Sanskrit-based education. This change was also primarily due to the fact that the British, who were supporters of the Rana regime in Nepal, would recruit only *Gorkhas* (traditional term for the Nepali people who were recruited for the British army). Thus the two examples of educational initiatives undertaken by the Ranas included the establishment of an English school by Jung Bahadur Rana at his palace in 1854 which was known as *Darbar* School (Palace School), which was later moved to its current location near Rani Pokhari (Queen's Pond) by his successor Ranodip, and the establishment of the Tri Chandra College by Rana Chandra Shamsher. This somewhat opened the door to education for some children who did not belong to the ruling clan or elite families.

In the early 1900s, Dev Shamsher announced some significant policy shifts in education and called for universal primary education. He made the Nepali language the medium of instruction and this led to the opening of Nepali language schools known as *Bhasa Pathashala* (vernacular schools). This policy change in education might have caused the downfall of Dev Shamsher who was ultimately deposed. But some of the public schools established during his rule remained operational in various parts of the country. With the opening of some English schools in Kathmandu valley and in other major urban areas of the country, there was an increase in the opportunity for Nepali people to pursue higher educational studies in institutions in India such as Patna University and Banaras Hindu University. With more and more people studying in these and other institutions of higher education including vocational/occupational training centers, the Nepali public started to realize the oppressive nature of the educational system under the Ranas. By the years 1950–1951, the number of primary and middle schools rose to 310, and the high schools through out the country numbered 11. In addition to these schools, 2 colleges and 1 technical school were also established by the time the Rana rule came to an end.

Despite systematic and determined opposition to popular education by the Rana rulers, they were compelled by anti-Rana forces operating in and outside of the country to relax their educational policies. This was a strong indication that education among the common people was beginning to thrive, and some progress in education was definitely being made. However, opportunities for the public were still limited and the condition of educational institutions continued to remain substandard and inadequate. There have been at least seven major educational reform efforts made in the second half of the 20th century in response to the need for improvement in education policy and programs. Nepal's isolation from the rest of the world was partly because of the country's difficult terrain, but also because of the closely guarded authoritarian rule of the Ranas. Because of their restrictive national policies there was no education system designed to serve Nepal's masses. Ranas feared an educated population and their anti-social policies continued until they lost power in 1950. The downfall of the Rana dynasty was also partly due to the fact that the British relinquished control and ended their colonizing rule over neighboring India in 1947. By the end of the Rana rule, an estimated 310 primary schools, 11 high schools, 2 colleges, and about 40 religious schools existed in Nepal.

Education in Modern Nepal: The First Ten Years

On February 18, 1951 King Tribhuwan established a democratic government with a proclamation based on the principles of "liberty, equality, and fraternity." This political change brought about the dawn of freedom in the history of Nepal and interest in education grew along with high expectations for an effective educational system in Nepal. The interest of both the public and the government created a positive atmosphere to nurture educational development in the country. Furthermore, the rapidly changing Nepali society with correspondingly changing needs continued to exert tremendous pressure and influence on Nepal's educational system. Conscious efforts were made to establish a more modernized form of public education system in the country. The formal and systematic planning of education began after recommendations made by the National Board of Education to adopt the establishment of the National Education Planning Commission (NEPC) in 1954, which was charged with making recommendations for national educational policies. In its voluminous report the following year in 1956, the NEPC offered several recommendations concerning the planning, organization, and implementation of educational programs in Nepal. It is worth mentioning that 1956 also marks a turning point in Nepal's national development planning when the first five-year national development plan was introduced. These changes in the 1950s allowed a formal school education system to be introduced and the process of national development began. In 1950 about 98 percent of Nepal's population was illiterate. The immediate provision of providing access to education led to fairly rapid expansion of schools through the country. But because of the political instability in Nepal over the next ten years following the transition to a democratic political system, the education sector did not receive the attention and priority it should have.

The NEPC's report laid down some of the fundamental recommendations to reform public education in Nepal. Some of the major recommendations included establishment of a research department within the Ministry of Education that would focus on comprehensive collection of educational data. The Commission made some other landmark recommendations such as tax supported free public education, five-year primary education curriculum, five-year high school education, and an establishment of a national university system that would comprise colleges of liberal arts and science, agriculture and forestry, teacher education, law, nursing, medicine and dentistry, home science, polytechnics, and other fields as needed. Expansion of adult literacy programs, teacher training facilities, establishment of a firm supervisory and administrative mechanism were some of the other recommendations.

The Commission's report essentially mapped out the long-range educational plans for Nepal. The support of the U.S. government was significant in charting the new educational map of Nepal. Under the U.S. government's technical support scheme, Prof. Hugh B. Wood, a graduate of Teachers College, Columbia University played an instrumental role in the development of the Commission's report that reflected the first ever type of education reform in Nepal. While efforts were made to implement some of the Commission's recommendations that warranted immediate actions, the country continued to experience growing political instability due to the fact that it was an infant democracy struggling to develop. Because of the lack of political will of, and commitment by, the national leaders many of the established educational goals were unattained and the aspirations of the general public for access to education were not realized. Furthermore, the lack of trained and qualified teachers and the lack of well-developed and structured curricula posed severe problems for the implementation of educational initiatives during the1950s and 1960s. At the NEPC's urging, cooperation was established between the Government of Nepal and the University of Oregon in the United States and as a result the first Normal Schools to exclusively train teachers were established in 1954. Two years later, a College of Education was also established primarily to train secondary schoolteachers, inspectors, and other staff of the Normal Schools. Between 1951 and 1961, much progress was made in the technical and vocational education sector.

Growing political instability in the country led to the banning of the multiparty form of political system in 1960 by the late King Mahendra, and he subsequently introduced the undemocratic one-party system, known as the "Partyless Panchayat System." Immediately following the political coup in 1960, the new government sought to address the emerging educational needs of the country by creating a comprehensive education committee whose job was to develop national educational policies. The Ministry of Education, the central educational authority, held the administrative responsibilities for planning and implementation of the national educational system. Even though the NEPC recommended making a more decentralized administration and organization, the system continued to be centrally controlled. The Ministry of Education was the national organizing force, expected to provide some degree of uniformity throughout the educational system. With the introduction of the Panchayat System of polity, efforts to mould the national education system to align its goals with the prevailing political realities were not unusual and uncommon. The education plans, policies, and curricula dealt more about the glory of the Crown and political system it had instituted.

The Early Panchayat Period

The political coup in 1960 by King Mahendra, and the introduction of the single party political system known as the Panchayat system, mark another turning point in the development of educational in Nepal. Instead of designing an education system that would address the social and economic needs of the population and the country, the system was carefully crafted to be more in alignment with the political ideology of the Panchayat system. Even though nobody publicly dared to question the relevance of the public educational policies, small changes were gradually introduced into the organization of schooling over time. After the introduction of the Panchayat system, schooling was organized as primary school which included Grades 1–5; middle school which included Grades 6, 7, and 8; and high school comprising Grades 9 and 10. Similarly, higher education was also structured as two years of the intermediate level; two years at the bachelor's level; and two years at the master level. Although the earlier report of the Commission called for a decentralized education system, the administration and supervision of the schooling in Nepal remained highly centralized. All the programs and policies of schooling, fiscal and regulatory, continued to be imposed by the center. Even the textbooks were prepared centrally and distributed thought the country.

Despite the fact that decentralization was one of the core principles of the newly introduced political system, its practice remained centralized by design and implementation. In spite of increasing pressure from and the commitment of the new government, decentralization had not yet been firmly established. A political tug-of-war between parties and leaders further contributed to the political uncertainties of the1950s. An effort to build a strong democratic political structure was without a stable base, and as a result any attempts to organize and modernize the national educational system remained unsuccessful.

THE NEW EDUCATION SYSTEM PLAN (NESP)

Thus the prevailing educational system continued with the aim of producing an educated mass that was loyal to the absolute monarchy and the Panchayat system of government until another attempt within the existing political framework to reform education was made in 1971. The introduction of the New Education System Plan (NESP) in 1971 was also a significant reform attempt in the history of educational development in Nepal. The NESP, an integral part of the five-year (1970–1975) national development agenda was designed to address emerging individual and community needs in concert with the goals of an all-round national development scheme. To offer vocational educational opportunities with a hope of producing basic-level skilled work force to support national development activities remained one of the primary goals of the new education initiative.

Human resource development was becoming increasingly central to other social, political, and economic developments throughout the country. The shortage of a well-educated and skilled workforce continued to hinder national development. Despite efforts from multiple sectors, Nepal still suffered from many problems: the majority of the population was illiterate; a large section of school-aged children still did not attend schools; school dropout rates remained high; there was a high failure rate (60–70 percent) at the secondary level. The lack of resources; trained educators, teachers, and headmasters; and a lack of national and political commitment were some of the major limitations that the educational sector continued to face. The National Education System Plan (NESP), the most ambitious and comprehensive education plan ever developed in the history of Nepal, was introduced to address these challenges.

One of the main goals of the plan was to vocationalize the educational system, with the objective of addressing the critical shortage of trained middle-level manpower needed for development programs throughout the country. However, as in the previous decades, implicit in the purpose of the plan was an attempt to create popular faith in the Panchayat system. As stated in the national development plans, the development and implementation of educational policies and programs needed to be guided by the goal of broader development objectives, one of the principal objectives being the elimination of poverty. Although the NESP was probably the most ambitious educational plan ever and it called for the eradication of illiteracy—improving equal access to education for all, developing human resources in accordance with national development goals, and making education more relevant to life—it warranted major modifications within a decade of its origin and many of its targets remained unmet. On the positive side the NESP did take some significant steps toward improving educational equity, access, and opportunities for all. A study conducted by the United States Agency for International Development in 1981 indicated that the NESP had articulated a number of changes including increased access to education in rural areas, especially for women; education more fully adapted to Nepalese development needs; and the meeting of more clearly defined workforce requirements. In order to achieve these goals, tuition and textbook charges were progressively eliminated for the primary grades; a new curriculum stressing vocational education was introduced and extended to all secondary schools; and the examination system was reformed. In addition, more creative teaching approaches were fostered and steps were taken to train teachers in innovative techniques. However, the National Education Commission in 1992 reported that the student movement of 1979 put a question mark on the validity of the Panchayat system itself. It was also instrumental in forcing the authorities concerned to reconsider many of the fundamental features of the

NESP and to constitute a Royal Higher Education Commission in 1982, which presented its report in 1983 stating that "The 'panchayatization' of education went ahead full steam, fueling a spirit of revolt in the teaching community. As a result students from primary to higher education grades took to the streets in the historic People's Movement of 1989/1990. They marched shoulder to shoulder with their other compatriots, raising their voice in support of democracy, and many of them laid their down lives" (p. 1). The NESP lasted for approximately ten years, and the system more or less returned to the old approach.

Despite good intentions and effort the severe shortage of trained manpower, lack of adequate physical facilities and financial resources, as well as firm government commitments were obvious contributions to its failure. The Commission's 1992 report further stated, "some of the goals it aimed at were grossly impractical. As years rolled by, it became more and more obvious that its ulterior motive was not to facilitate the good of people, but to frustrate it" (p. 1). Although a significant investment was made in education during the last four decades of the 20th century in Nepal the intended outcomes were not proportionate. Poor management and lack of effective leadership at all levels of the educational structure only created anomalies and incongruities.

Through the 1980s, education remained largely urban based and an unprecedented number of private schools started mushrooming throughout the Kathmandu valley and other urban areas of the country. The inadequacy of public education led parents to look elsewhere for better educational alternatives for their children. There was already a tradition of children from more affluent families attending schools in the bordering states in India. The private schools that offered better quality education to many were unaffordable to many others, particularly to those who came from rural areas and belonged to economically low backgrounds. Thus, sending children to private schools became a very expensive proposition for many families. One can argue that private schools have an important role in schooling and education, but ultimately the country is responsible to provide access to sound educational opportunities for all, and the goal of providing mass public education remained on top of Nepal's public agenda.

Even though Nepal was unsuccessful in providing an ideal education for all of its citizens, some level of success was definitely achieved during the NESP phase. For example, the availability of education was greatly increased, more girls than ever before attended schools, more appropriate curricula were designed, and textbooks were more freely available. Although the overall quality of education left much to be desired it was clearly recognized that the area was significantly growing and improving. Some of the notable and more significant changes introduced by NESP in the organization, structure, and curricula of the national education system were the following:

- Primary education was made available from Grades 1 to 3;
- Vocational education was introduced in all secondary schools;
- Provisions were made to provide special facilities in the more remote areas;

Table 7.1
Growth in Number of Student Enrollment, Teachers, and Schools by 1980

Education Levels	Numbers
Primary Grades 1–3	
Schools	10,136
Enrollment	1,043,332
Teachers	27,384
Lower Secondary Grades 4–7	
Schools	3261
Enrollment	408,907
Teachers	11,294
Secondary Grades 8–10	
Schools	704
Enrollment	120,838
Teachers	4610
Total	
Schools	14,101
Enrollment	1,573,077
Teachers	43,288

- Greater emphasis was given to technical education at the higher education level; and
- Significant changes in the curriculum were made at all levels of schooling and higher education.

However, despite the new emphasis on education further growth and development in education was slow to come and was often limited by poor quality outcomes. Still, there was no denying that by 1980 there was a significant increase in student enrollment, training and recruiting of teachers, and in the total number of schools (see Table 7.1).

The numerical growth alone was not sufficient to sustain and continuously improve the education system for all. The overall goals of education continued to emphasize the need for producing an educated class that was loyal to the Panchayat system and the monarchy. However, with some liberalization in the Panchayat system, there was a significant growth in the number of schools, students, and teachers throughout the country during the 1980s.

EDUCATIONAL DEVELOPMENT IN THE 1990S

The 1990s political movement that brought down the 30-year old Panchayat system and introduced a multiparty democratic system, opened unprecedented opportunities for educational development in the country. Succeeding governments under different political parties came up with their own commission reports. The governments changed frequently and most failed to effectively implement the recommendations of their own commissions. Short sightedness and power struggles between and within parties did not help the school system and instead worked toward making them the most politicized social institutions in the country. The arms struggle launched in 1996 by the Communist Party of Nepal, or the Maoists, and the failure of the national governments to either contain them or bring them to a peaceful settlement further paralyzed the growth of the school system in Nepal and the situation has become worse in the last ten years. Without timely action to stop the political strife in Nepal it is feared that educational development will be set back at least a generation. Emerging local and international demands over time have exerted a great deal of influence on the design of the national educational system in Nepal. Constant pressure has been placed on the system to deliver quality, equitable, and accessible schooling to all. The education system of Nepal has passed through various states of development and reform, particularly during the second half of the 20th century.

Following the restoration of democracy in 1990 and the subsequent establishment of an elected government in 1991, the government took a major step by creating a high-level education commission to study the educational needs of the country and make necessary recommendations for improvement. The High Level National Education Commission of 1992 was charged with the responsibility of reflecting in its report the national aspiration and commitment, international context, and possible educational as well as non-educational trends. After a series of research and consultations, the Commission recommended the following national education goals:

- To bring out the genius inherent in every individual, and to give free play to the chances of personality development;
- To promote the supreme human values, and to inculcate in the individual the national and social norms and beliefs in order to ensure a healthy social growth;
- To strengthen social integrity by socializing the individual;
- To teach the individual to live in harmony with the modern age without losing his identity in the national and international environment;
- To modernize society and develop the human resources in the interest of national construction;
- To conserve the national environment and national wealth; and
- To assimilate the backward sections of the society into the mainstream of national life.

The inter- and intra-party conflicts and the subsequent downfall of the first democratically elected Nepali Congress (NC) government in over thirty years ultimately led to an increase in power for the United Marxist Leninist Party (UML). Within two years after the publication of the High Level National Education Commission's detailed report on the status of the nation's educational system, the UML-led government constituted a second high-level commission to examine the educational needs of the nation in 1994. The UML government was also overthrown in 1995 before the Commission was able to complete its work. However, in 1998 the UML-created Commission, subsequently under NC administration, produced a relatively identical report to that published in 1992.

Table 7.2
School Level Educational Statistics (2004)

		Primary (1–5)	L. Secondary (6–8)	Secondary (9–10)	Total (1–10)
Schools		24,746	7436	4547	36,729
Students	Total	4,030,045	1,444,997	543,764	6,018,806
	Girls	1,865,012	653,159	242,565	2,760,736
	Girls (%)	46.3	45.2	44.6	45.87
	Boys	2,165,033	791,838	301,199	3,258,070
Teachers	Total	101,483	25,962	20,232	147,677
	Total full trained	30,967	7818	9727	48,512
	Total full trained (%)	30.51	30.11	48.07	32.85
	Female	30,542	4238	1732	36,512
	Female (%)	30.1	16.3	8.6	24.7
	Female full trained	8260	1177	731	10,168
	Female full trained (%)	27.04	27.77	42.20	27.85

Source: Ministry of Education and Sports. School Level Educational Statistics: At a Glance 2061. Retrieved on May 9, 2006 from http://www.moe.gov.np/stats/ataglance_2004.php.

Between 1994 and 1998, five different governments took control, and this political instability has continued into the 21st century resulting in the failure to create a secure national direction and a commitment to educational advancement.

Despite all the shortcomings, there have been observable positive developments in the education sector, particularly during the last two decades of the 20th century. During the 1980s and 1990s, there has been remarkable growth in private schooling. Statistically, the growth in the public school sector also remained impressive. However, the growth remained largely quantitative and the quality of education continued to be compromised. The simple statistical comparison of Table 7.1 and Table 7.2 would indicate that in between 1980 and 2004 there has been 46 percent growth in the number of schools, 74 percent growth in student enrollment, and 70 percent increase in the number of teachers employed by the school system nationally. Table 7.2 presents a brief statistical summary of the number of schools, teachers, and students in 2004.

The inability of subsequent governments to deliver on their promises, and the ongoing Maoist movement have not only further plunged the whole nation into a state of chaos and instability, but have made educational institutions including schools dangerously political. In the age of information technology and globalization of trade and transits, knowledge is power and there is a dire need for Nepal to revisit its educational design and make it more relevant to the current and future context. Unfortunately, this process of continuing reform has been stalled because of the ongoing Maoist insurgencies and the current political instability. However, the mass political movement of April 2006 that brought significant political change in the country has given some reason to believe that there may be a way out of the existing crisis, both in terms of restoring full democratic rights of the people and resolving the decade-long Maoist insurgency. Once the dust settles and all parties involved in the situation in Nepal work toward a meaningful conclusion of the conflict and democratic establishment and political instability, educational policies will have to address long neglected issues of Nepali society, primarily social, political, and economic inequities.

IMPACT OF THE MAOIST INSURGENCY ON EDUCATION

Unfortunately, Nepal's education system remains one of the most politicized systems. Political forces have constantly mobilized or used students for political campaigns and movements. Previously, this was limited to occurring in the higher education institutions, but the political changes of 1990 mark an unprecedented influence of political parties on the school system, and as a result teachers, young schoolchildren, and even parents have been forced to advocate for one party over another and participate in political activities. Such overt political engagement has proven to be destructive to the regular operations and functions of educational institutions. To make the situation worse, the Communist Party of Nepal (Maoist) launched an arms struggle, or the People's War, in 1996 with the aim of overthrowing the existing democratic system under a constitutional monarchy and established a people's republic based on the communist ideology of China's Mao Tse Tung. Over 13,000 people have already lost their lives and the number continues to grow everyday. Over 4000 children have been orphaned and hundreds of thousands of people have been displaced. There are reports of young children being recruited by the insurgents into their militia. Examples of national security forces turning schools into their barracks are also often heard. Most of Nepal's rural areas are under the severe influence of the Maoists. There are plenty of stories of Maoists abducting schoolchildren and teachers, taking them to isolated areas, and orienting them about the Maoists philosophies and immediate goals of their arms struggle. Because of the unprecedented violent situation through out the country, many schools have been shut down and young children's futures have been severely compromised.

In summary, without proper investment in development of human capital nations fall behind in progress. As John F. Kennedy said in his message to Congress on February 20, 1961, "Our progress as a nation can be no swifter than our progress in education.... The human mind is our fundamental resource." If Nepal as an emerging new democracy fails to make education a priority in its national agenda, it will fall behind in its quest for progress and prosperity in the local, national, and international spheres. Although resolving the ongoing conflict and political instability that continue to plague the nation remains the first priority of the parties involved, an overhaul or even redesign of the entire education system to one that provides equal quality educational opportunities for all must also be an urgent goal. With emerging positive political change, the new government of new Nepal faces the challenge to deliver on the promises that have been made to the people. The emerging democratic process provides Nepali people a reason to believe that there lie ahead unique opportunities to restructure their nation and address its deep-rooted social, political, and economic inequalities.

BIBLIOGRAPHY

Educational Efficiency Clearinghouse (May 1988) *Nepal, Education and Human Resources Sector Assessment.* Tallahassee, FL: Florida State University.

Harsha Narayan Dhaubhadel and Gaja S. Pradhan (Eds) (1990) *Education and Development 1989–90.* Kathmandu, Nepal: Research Center for Educational Innovation and Development.

High Level National Education Commission (1992) *The Report of the High Level Education Commission.* Kathmandu, Nepal: Keshar Mahal.

High Level National Education Commission (1998) *The Report of the High Level Education Commission.* Kathmandu, Nepal: Keshar Mahal.

Horace B. Reed and Mary J. Reed (1968) *Nepal in Transition, Educational Innovation.* Pittsburg, PA: University of Pittsburg Press.

Hugh B. Hood (1965) *The Development of Education in Nepal.* Washington, D.C.: U.S. Department of Health, Education, and Welfare, Office of Education.

Hugh B. Wood (1987) *Nepal Diary 1953–1962.* Tillamook, O.R.: American Nepal Education Foundation.

Kedar Nath Shrestha (1980) *Educational Management in Nepal.* Kathmandu: Tribhuwan University, Institute of Education.

Kedar Nath Shrestha (1982) *Educational Experiments in Nepal.* Kathmandu: Thibhuwan University.

Krishna Raj Aryal (1970) *Education for the Development of Nepal.* Kathmandu: Shanti Prakashan.

National Education Committee (1977) *National Inventory of Educational Innovations.* Kathmandu: Center for Educational Research, Innovation and Development.

Nepal National Education Planning Commission (1956) *Education in Nepal, Report of the Nepal National Education Planning Commission.* Kathmandu: Bureau of Publications, College of Education.

Chapter 8

SCHOOLING IN PAKISTAN

Sajid Ali and Iffat Farah

OVERVIEW OF COUNTRY

Pakistan is a relatively young country that came into existence only in 1947 as a result of the end of the colonized rule and subsequent departure of the British from the Indian subcontinent. The British arrived in India in the 18th century as traders under the banner of the British East India Company and gradually took political and administrative control of the geographic region that comprised present-day India, Pakistan, and Bangladesh. India was formally declared as a British Colony after 1857 and remained so until 1947. World War II and the indigenous freedom movements in India weakened the control of the British who eventually decided to leave India and declare the nation independent of their rule. There were a large number of Muslims in India who believed that their interests would be compromised in a united independent India and demanded a separate country for themselves. As a consequence, British India was divided into two countries, India and Pakistan, in August 1947 when the British ended their colonial rule in India. Subsequently, most areas with a Hindu majority stayed with India and most areas with a predominantly Muslim population formed Pakistan. For the first 33 years after independence Pakistan existed as a country with two distinct parts, East and West Pakistan. East Pakistan separated in 1971 to form a new country now known as Bangladesh while West Pakistan became what is now known as Pakistan.

Present-day Pakistan is comprised of the four provinces of Sindh, Punjab, Baluchistan and North West Frontier Province (NWFP), along with the Federally Administered Tribal Areas (FATA) and the Federally Administered Northern Areas (FANA). It shares borders with India in the south and east, China in the northeast, Afghanistan in the northwest, and Iran in the west. The Arabian Sea in the southwest separates it from the Gulf States but also provides a channel and easy access to the Middle East and beyond. The population of Pakistan is approximately 165 million of which the majority of 64 percent lives in rural areas. Islam is the state religion and 97 percent of the population is Muslim. The remainder of the religious minority of 3 percent includes Hindus, Christians, and Parsis. Urdu is the national language while English is used as an official language in most governmental written transactions. In addition, there are four major languages spoken in each of the provinces along with many other local languages and dialects. Islamabad is the federal capital while Karachi, Lahore, Peshawar, and Quetta are the major cities as well as the provincial capitals. Pakistan has a bicameral parliamentary democratic form of government, in which the prime minister is the head of government while the president is the head of state. Unfortunately since its inception Pakistan has not had a steady history of parliamentary democracy. There have been large periods of military rule and many changes in the elected governments. These changes have had a negative effect on consistency in priorities and policy implementation in all sectors.

Although Pakistan is a new country politically, the history of this geographical region can be traced back to the ancient times where some of the greatest civilizations like those of Indus and Gandhara evolved and flourished. Throughout history, this region served as a passageway for warriors and merchants. Alexander the Great of Macedonia, the Greeks and the Afghans came here from the northwest; the Mongols came from the northeast; and the Arabs came from the south. Each of these groups left their influence on the socio-cultural milieu of Pakistan which is now a rich blend of various racial and cultural stocks. These social, political, and cultural elements also influenced the educational systems in the region, and this will be more apparent when the different time periods in history are discussed in detail.

HISTORICAL DEVELOPMENT OF EDUCATION

The chapter is divided into sections based on historical periods, mainly the ancient times before A.D. 700s, the pre-colonial Muslim rule between A.D. 700 and the 1700s, the British colonial period between the 1800s and 1947, and the present time from after 1947. These timelines are unique to the history of this region and will be clarified when discussing a particular period in detail. The education systems under each of these time periods will be discussed separately. It is important to note that the historical time lines are loosely defined, which means that one era does not exactly end or begin at a particular point of history but develops gradually over time before becoming distinct from the preceding period. Further, as the region has remained under the influence of different political and cultural forces which sometimes existed side-by-side, one can find several strands of educational systems existing simultaneously.

Ancient Education Systems (until A.D. 700s)

The archaeological remnants discovered from various regions in Pakistan point to a history beginning during the Stone Age. The sites near the Soan Valley near Rawalpindi, Seria Khola, and Mehergarh (NWFP) date back from 50,000 to 10,000 B.C. River Indus, which flows down from the Himalayan ranges and passes through the center of present day Pakistan, has remained the site of great civilizations such as Kot Diji around 3500 B.C. and gave rise to the Indus civilization around 2500 B.C. Remnants of this civilization have been discovered in Moen-jo-Daro, Harappa, and Taxila located in present day Pakistan. These sites show evidence of the existence of monasteries that educated and supported scholars. According to one perspective, around 1700 B.C. the Aryans invaded this region from the northwest, destroyed the Indus civilization and decided to stay here and founded a civilization called the Vedic civilization.

Knowledge of the educational system as practiced in those times is limited. Historians have mostly relied on archaeological evidences to ascertain any information about the earliest educational system. The excavations at Moen-jo-Daro and Taxila have revealed a highly evolved form of urban life and the presence of language scripts on seals, which suggests an educated society capable of reading, writing, and basic vocational skills. The findings further suggest that the educational system evolved mainly to satisfy religious and economic needs of the society and was initially limited to particular classes of society. The two great religions of the ancient times in this region were Hinduism and Buddhism, which also influenced the systems of education. Although both of these systems existed side-by-side over a large period in history, they will be discussed separately here in order to elaborate their distinctive features.

Brahmanic or Hindu System

The Brahmanic system of education was based on Vedic and Upanishadic texts. The *Veda* were the ancient religious texts which were initially transferred via the oral tradition and later captured in writing somewhere around 2000 B.C. The *Veda* comprised four books written in Sanskrit and contained hymns, chants, and mantras based on ancient mythology representing godly figures. The *Upanishad* were composed at a later stage sometime during 800–500 B.C. and mainly contained philosophical treatises. In the very beginning of the Vedic civilization, there was no discrimination on the basis of sex or class; both women and men and people belonging to all social classes were equally free to get education. Later, however, the caste system started to emerge and education became more restrictive and was categorized according to social classes. The castes were divided into four categories: *brahman* (priests), *kshatriya* (noble-men and warriors), *vaishya* (traders and agriculturists), and *shudra* (artisans and sanitation workers). The study of the *Veda* was common to all castes mentioned earlier except the *shudra* caste. The purpose and system of education was different for the higher and lower castes. The purpose of educating the *brahmans* was to maintain a class of priests who would guide people in their religious affairs. The *brahman* students were educated in the hymns and their meanings in a structured and organized manner and were required to learn long hymns by heart, which needed long hours of practice. The purpose of educating the *kshatriya* and *vaishya* castes was to prepare professionals and so it was more like vocational training mainly through practice and participation in the occupational activities. No educational provision was available for the *shudra* caste except training in menial jobs. The formal education system in Hinduism consisted of two kinds of institutions, *tol* (places for *brahman* students to learn Sanskrit and to gain knowledge in religious affairs) and *patshala* (schools for *vaishya* students who would learn about trade and agriculture and for *kshatriya* students who would learn basic arithmetic and commerce.

For the upper caste *brahman* the education system was quite extensive. An initial phase of basic religious education for a period of 5–6 years (roughly between the ages of 5 and 12 years) was offered at the *tols*. Students were required to learn *mantras* (hymns) from the *Veda* and master the *Upanishad* (philosophical debates about God, man and soul) along with subjects of general nature, such as grammar, science, logic, and metaphysics. This was followed by a phase equivalent to secondary education which required students to live and sojourn with a teacher to learn about nature and the realities of life. According to Brahmanic or Hindu beliefs there were four stages in adult education: *brahmachari* (student life), *grahasti* (domestic and practical life), *sanyasi* (ascetic life), and *vanapasti* (recluse). Only the bright students were allowed into the higher stages or the post-secondary stage of learning. The teachers for post-secondary levels were referred to as *guru* and the students were known as *chella*. The *gurus* were independent scholars, having gained high religious morals, and were firm believers in simple living and high thinking. Prospective students who wanted to pursue higher education and learning beyond the secondary levels would request to study with the scholar-teachers, or *gurus*. Upon admission the *chellas* had to live and travel with the *guru* on a full-time basis to gain both religious and worldly wisdom.

The curriculum at the *patshalas* comprised of general physics, chemistry, medicine, astronomy, geometry, and civics depending on the expertise of the teachers. This initial introduction to different fields was later followed by apprenticeship and on the job learning. Usually students joined their family business and gained mastery in a particular field. The curriculum for the *kshatriyas* focused on learning war games and affairs of governance. Initially, before the advent of script, all the education was imparted verbally and thus all education, particularly that based on Vedic and Upanishadic texts, involved a great deal of rote memorization.

Buddhist System

As indicated earlier, education system in ancient times was mainly constructed around religion. Buddhism as a religion evolved from Hinduism in the Indian subcontinent during the period between 500 and 300 B.C. Around the year 300 B.C. the first consolidated government of the subcontinent emerged under the leadership of King Ashoka, who formed the Maurya dynasty. Later Ashoka embraced Buddhism giving it immense strength.

Buddhism marked the beginning of popular education in this region. Like the Hindu system, the Buddhist education system was also constructed along religious lines and on the basis of the teachings of its founder Gautam Budhha. The embracing of Buddhism by King Ashoka provided state support to the Buddhist education system and it is believed that Ashoka built several monasteries and nunneries throughout his kingdom. Monasteries were built to cater to the education of boys and nunneries were dedicated to the education of girls. Buddhist monasteries and nunneries served as centers for learning and were open to students from all classes of society. They were like residential schools and housed dormitories for students. The archaeological sites discovered in Taxila show dormitories attached to the monasteries. According to Huan Chwang an ancient Chinese traveler, there were several hundred monasteries in Sindh at the time of his travel. Schooling in the monasteries generally lasted for ten years during which students were asked to wear a particular robe; the design and color of the robes changed with each passing stage indicating the level of studentship. Education in the monasteries and nunneries was designed to build students' moral character, develop their speech capacities, and increase their philosophical maturation. They were also trained to debate about and preach religion. This education mainly served a religious function by creating devout followers who, upon graduation, were able to preach the religion.

Influenced by Hindu education, Buddhists also included several secular subjects in their curriculum such as logic, philosophy, oratory, arithmetic, grammar, interpretation of dreams, dramas, prosody, sculpture, and shipbuilding. The basic learning outcomes of Buddhist education were expected to be the achievement of self-actualization and the attainment of knowledge and wisdom. This required both meditation as well as the acquisition of subject matter knowledge in various disciplines. The students/disciples were required to engage in the (1) contemplation of body; (2) contemplation of feelings; (3) contemplation of thought; and (4) contemplation of ideas. The development and progress of all the students throughout the different stages of schooling was closely monitored by the monks who also served as the teachers and who used strict punishment to discipline the students. After graduation the brighter students who performed better would become monks and teachers at their own monasteries or take up positions in other monasteries.

Other Influences during Ancient Times

Persians invaded this region in about 500 B.C. and remained here for quite sometimes, followed by the Greeks who invaded in 327 B.C. under the command of Alexander the Great. These invasions must have brought traces of Greek and

Persian thoughts in the cultural fabric of this region although documentary evidences to identify these traces are not available.

Education Systems in the Pre-Colonial Muslim Rule (A.D. 700–1700s)

The Muslims reached the Indian subcontinent initially from Arabia and later from Persia and central Asia. In A.D. 711 Muhammad Bin Qasim, an Arab general, first conquered Sindh but did not establish any central government. By A.D. 872 there were independent Arab states such as the Emirate of Al-Mansurah and Emirate of Multan in this region. By the turn of the century in A.D. 1001, Mahmud of Gazan (Persia) started attacking India and annexed the areas of Punjab and Peshawar to his rule. The first Muslim Sultanate in the subcontinent was established by Muhammad of Ghur with the support of his general Qutubuddin Aibak, who became the king of Delhi in A.D. 1206 and who founded the so-called Slave Dynasty. From that time the Indian subcontinent remained under different Muslim dynasties, with central governments of different strengths, until the 19th century when it gave way to total British rule.

With the advent of Islam in the northwest of the region, the influence of Hinduism and Buddhism moved away from what is modern day Pakistan and more toward the northeast. Hinduism became concentrated mainly in the area which now comprises India, while Buddhism became concentrated in several countries to the east such as Tibet, China, Sri Lanka, and so forth. Islam arrived as a major influence in the subcontinent and established its own system of education, popularly known as the *madressa* system, which began in a similar manner as other earlier systems (Hindu and Buddhism) in terms of the purpose of education, that is, to impart religious education and to prepare religious scholars and preachers who can also advance in worldly education. Hindu and Buddhist systems continued to exist along with the Muslim education, each influencing the other. Another tradition of Muslim education can be referred to as *Sufi* (mystic) education. *Sufis* were the people who devoted their lives in search of the truth with deep love for the Creator. The *mureed* (disciples) who used to choose this path remained attached to their teacher who was known as *murshid*. This tradition was based on philosophical orientations, meditations, and deep reflections on the Quran and on nature. It is important to note that other approaches to learning, such as apprenticeship where a disciple joined the expert teacher to develop expertise in becoming an artisan, a blacksmith, a goldsmith, or even a medical practitioner, also existed alongside with *madressa* and *Sufi* education.

Madressa Education System

Before discussing the *madressa* educational system it will be useful to briefly review its origins. In the Islamic faith, education is considered to be a religious duty. Both the holy Quran and the traditions of the holy Prophet placed repeated emphasis on seeking knowledge. Hence education in Islam is considered a life long process without any discrimination of gender or class. Non-formal adult education is equally emphasized and was reflected in the formation of *halqas* (literary gatherings) of adult learners in mosques around particular scholars for discussion. The basic aim of Islamic education is to create faith in God's supremacy, train pupils morally, develop scientific understanding, create self-consciousness, and help establish a just society. The early Islamic traditions did not distinguish between education for this world and education for the hereafter, and therefore both religious and earthly knowledge were pursued, which resulted in significant advancement in the fields of science, astronomy, chemistry, mathematics, and medicine.

The formal education system of Islam, which is now known as the *madressa* system, evolved gradually from the time of Prophet Muhammad in Arabia in about A.D. 500. Initially, mosques were the centers of all educational activities. During the times of the Prophet, the people of Suffah were attached to the mosque of the Prophet in Medina and devoted their entire lives to learning. At a later stage, as the number of people engaged in educational activities within the mosque grew, separate rooms for learning and teaching were attached to the mosques to avoid distractions for worshippers. Increasingly, *maktabs* (primary schools) and libraries were built attached to the mosques. At a later stage, *madressas* were built to engage in scholarly work at a more advanced level. The system evolved in Arabia and spread to the rest of the Muslim world, and with the arrival of Arabs in the Indian subcontinent it reached the area of present day Pakistan through Sindh.

Before the formal *madressa* system, the education system in Muslim societies was composed of: (1) *maktabs*, for developing Arabic literacy and recitation; (2) private education delivered in the homes of the students; (3) *kutub khana* (libraries or reading rooms); (4) houses of *aalim* (scholars); (5) special literary seminars organized by caliphs; and (6) education in the mosques. The first known formal *madressa* in Muslim history is said to have been established in A.D. 1005 by the Fatimid caliphs in Egypt. However, the first organized system of *madressa* was established by a Seljuk *vizier* (minister) by the name of Nizam-ul-Mulk Hassan Bin Al-Tusi, in A.D. 1067. It is important to note that the *madressas* did not grow out of *maktabs* but were established separately as centers of higher learning. The *maktabs* provided primary education while *madressas* provided secondary and post-secondary education. In the Sindh region of Pakistan, the early form of education system was introduced through mosques that were established by Muhammad Bin Qasim. Later, Caliph Umer bin Abdul Aziz (A.D. 717–720) ordered the establishment of *maktabs* attached with mosques throughout his Caliphate and also arranged for paying stipends to the students. In Sindh, both *maktabs* and *madressas* were established due to which many of the cities of Sindh like Sehwan, Bakhar, and Debal flourished as centers of learning by the years A.D. 700s. Around the same time, Mansurah, a small town in present day Punjab province, was also recognized as a place of learning that produced several notable scholars. Despite these advances, the Muslim rulers in India did not take on education as a state responsibility but they did provide opportunities, endowments, and free land for establishing *madressas*. All the Muslim dynasties, for example the Slaves, Khiljis, Tughlaqs, Sayyids, Lodhis, and the Mughals took a keen interest in the establishment of *madressas* where both religious and non-religious subjects were taught. This keen interest spurred an era of mass literacy at the primary level, followed by ample opportunities to pursue advanced studies privately or through state support. *Madressas* were highly dependant on endowments and so a *madressa* would begin to decline due to a lack of resources with the death of its founder or patron.

The earliest education of Muslim children used to be organized at home where some early lessons in Arabic reading and religious knowledge were given. Many parents also enrolled their children at an early age in *maktabs* for primary education, and sometimes children themselves took the initiative to join some *halqas* (literary circles) even at a young age. *Madressas* admitted relatively mature students who wanted to develop an expertise in a particular area of knowledge. Many of these *madressas* were full-time residential schools and provided boarding and lodging facilities and a few also gave stipends as scholarships to needy students. Thus *madressa* education was accessible to the poor and the rich alike and became popular among the masses. This tradition of providing lodging and board continues even today.

The Islamic Teachers

There were three kinds of teachers within the Muslim education system. First, the *maktab* teachers who were responsible for the basic level of children's learning; second, the *ataleeq* (private tutors) who were the teachers for the children of noblemen; and third, the *ulemas* (religious scholars) who were responsible for specialized and advanced level learning in the *madressas*. The *maktab* teachers possessed basic qualifications to read and recite the Quran and a basic level of understanding of religious knowledge; some of them were also *hafiz*,[1] that is, they had memorized the complete Quran. Both *ulemas* and *ataleeqs* usually possessed the highest level of qualification with distinction in their fields. The *ataleeqs* were highly respected and treated as family members of their students. They used to reside with the student or were given special accommodation facilities. There was no formal certification during the early days of Islam but with gradual institutionalization of the *madressa* system, certificates were awarded to recognize a specific level of mastery in various disciplines. The graduates of the *madressas* occupied different places in society: some preferred to become teachers and preachers, while others joined government service to work as *sadr-i-jahan* (chief justice), *shaikh-ul-Islam* (person in charge of ecclesiastical affairs), *qazi* (judge), *mufti* (jurist), *muhtasib* (accountability judge), *imam* (prayers leader), *khatib* (preacher), and teachers in state maintained schools.

The Curriculum

Knowledge is classified in two forms within the Islamic tradition: revealed knowledge which is taught by God through the prophets, and earthly knowledge which is discovered by humans. This became the basis of an Islamic education curriculum. The early Muslims excelled in both fields and this growth of knowledge reached its zenith in Spain where Muslims ruled for 800 years. However, with the gradual social and political decline of the Muslims, their education system also deteriorated and became confined to the study of religious affairs only.

The curriculum taught by the *maktabs* was quite basic and included reading and reciting of the holy Quran, basic religious knowledge, and, depending on the expertise of the teacher, Arabic and Persian languages, basic arithmetic, and some poetry. The curriculum taught in the *madressas* was first developed in Baghdad in A.D. 1067 by a Seljuk minister named Nizam-ul-Mulk, and included the teaching of both religious and earthly knowledge. It aimed to prepare religious scholars who were also well acquainted in dealing with governance issues. The early history of *madressa* curriculum in the Indian subcontinent is not very well documented. The earliest information refers to the curriculum followed by the Firuz Shahi Madressa founded by King Firuz Tughluq (A.D. 1355–1388). The main subjects taught at this madressa were *tafsir* (interpretation of Quran), *hadith* (Prophet's sayings and traditions), and *fiqh* (Islamic jurisprudence). The main textbook for *hadith* was *Mashariq-ul-Anwar* and for *fiqh* was *Hidaya*.

The heavy emphasis on religious knowledge in the *madressa* curriculum was maintained to ensure religious conformity through uniform teachings of Islam for all, and to prepare people who can run affairs of the state according to the Islamic principles. In the subcontinent, *madressa* curriculum gradually confined itself to religious knowledge paying little attention to the teaching of earthly knowledge. However, other scholars argue that many *madressas* in the subcontinent modified their curriculum according to need and available expertise and included subjects like literature, history, mysticism, ethics, and more advanced scientific subjects like botany, medicine, geometry, logic, astronomy, and mathematics. Several important curricular reforms were introduced during the Mughal period. The most significant changes were made by Mulla Nizam-ud-Din during the rule of King Aurangzeb Alamgir (A.D. 1658–1707) who devised a curriculum later known as Dars-e-Nizamiya.[2] This curriculum is still being practiced in current *madressa* systems in Pakistan. Dars-i-Nizamia consists of two parts—*manqoolat* and *maqoolat*. *Manqoolat* emphasizes the understanding of religious texts, and the knowledge of Quran, *fiqh*, and *hadith*; while *maqoolat* includes subjects like languages, philosophy, psychiatry, medicine, mathematics, geometry, algebra, and engineering. Gradually, the *madressas* limited their teachings to *manqoolat* and dropped *maqoolat* from their curriculum.

The teaching methods used in the *maktab* and *madressa* were different from each other. Teachings in the *maktab* emphasized repetition, rote memorization, and reproduction of religious text. Teachers used strict measures to make sure that students acquired desirable competency in reading and memorizing the Quran and other recommended texts. On the other hand, the *madressa* teachers were usually scholars with high moral respect for individuals and their learning. Because of the residential nature of *madressas*, teachers focused on the holistic development of individuals which included their academic as well as moral well being. Students considered their teachers as role models and many of them went on to become scholars, continuing and extending the work of their teachers. Although the dominant method of teaching was the lecture followed by question and answers, discussions based on logical reasoning and reflections requiring higher order thinking skills were also common. Private tutors who taught nobles also used the lecture method. However, since they taught many non-religious subjects too their methods differed as well. An *ataleeq* hired for teaching physical fitness and sports engaged more in the practical methods and approaches of teaching as compared to someone who would teach philosophy.

Education Systems during British Colonial Times (A.D. 1700s–1947)

The Mughal Empire started disintegrating after about A.D. 1707 and the British took control of the Indian subcontinent thereafter. The British came to the subcontinent as traders under the banner of the East India Company and gradually took complete political and administrative control of India. The provinces that comprise present day Pakistan were annexed under the British crown one after the other with Baluchistan being annexed in 1840, Sindh in 1843, Punjab in 1849, and North West Frontier Province (NWFP) in 1849. The British stayed as merchants of the East India Company until the Indian uprising of 1857, after which, the British government took direct control of the Indian subcontinent and remained there until 1947. The colonial period under the East India Company and that under direct British government rule had distinct educational features and will be discussed separately.

Education under the East India Company

Initially, the Company had no specific plans for educational provisions in India. However, gradually having consolidated their rule and becoming masters of the conquered land, they started recognizing the need for their officers to learn about local religions, culture, and languages. This would allow the officers to better understand the local context in order to help improve their governance structures. Thus some secondary and post-secondary institutions called colleges were established by different military generals of the East India Company in their respective jurisdictions in what is present day India.

Some more systematic thoughts on education in general started emerging in the 1830s. Two major issues that became the focus of discussion among British policy makers were related to the systems of education (local versus western) and the language of education (local languages versus English). William Adam, a former Baptist missionary turned journalist, submitted a report to the British government in 1835 on vernacular Education in Bengal and Bihar (two of the states in what is now eastern India). He urged developing an educational system based upon the already established local system of education of *patshalas* and *madressas* in almost every village. This suggestion was vehemently opposed by Lord T. B. Macaulay, member of the Supreme Council of India, who insisted upon establishing a fresh system of education offered in the English language and demanded abandoning official support for the local academic languages like Persian, Arabic, and Sanskrit. In addition, he emphasized the introduction of a western form of education possible through English only. Through such reforms he wanted to create a class of local Englishmen. In his own words,

We must at present do our best to form a class who may be interpreters between us and the millions whom we govern; a class of persons, Indian in blood and color [*sic*], but English in taste, in opinions, in morals, and in intellect. (Macaulay's minutes on Education, 2nd February, 1835)

These Minutes were approved by Governor General William Bentinck in the same year. The minutes introduced a new era of education in the Indian subcontinent, marked by a continuous struggle over language issues which continue to this day in Pakistan. In 1854, following Macaulay's footsteps, Sir Charles Wood drafted the future design of spreading western education system throughout British India which is commonly known as Woods Despatch. A major aim of this education was to prepare a class of professionals mainly for government services.

Education under the British Administrative Government

In 1857, the local population revolted against the British East India Company in an attempt to regain local governance. Although the British suffered heavy losses they managed to regain control. These political upheavals resulted in direct control of the Indian subcontinent by the British Crown. The British government appointed a Secretary for India in the British Parliament, and a Viceroy in India to represent the British Crown. These two offices were also responsible to formulate an education policy for India. In 1859, Lord Stanley's Dispatch reaffirmed the propositions made in the Woods' Dispatch to aim education at spreading western knowledge and thoughts and preparing public service professionals. Hence, British education policy in the subcontinent focused mainly on providing secondary education and producing matriculates to satisfy minimum qualification for government service.

The British did not intend to establish a mass education system, and therefore, largely ignored both primary and tertiary levels of education, particularly the latter. For example, Sindh did not have a university even until 1921. The British government encouraged the locals, particularly the elites, to establish and maintain their own schools which would be assisted by the government through grants-in-aid. Despite the fact that the government did not take sole responsibility for providing education across the board, it did establish and maintain certain schools mainly for urban population. There appear to have been three kinds of schools during the British rule: (1) Chief's Colleges for hereditary aristocracy; (2) European or English schools for professional elites; and (3) the vernacular school or Anglo-vernacular schools for the general public mainly in urban areas.

The Chief's Colleges were funded mainly through the private pockets of the chiefs and supported by grants from the British government. Apart from education, the main purpose of these schools was to anglicize young princes and to create affection amongst them for the British way of living. This was done to ensure loyalty of the princely states and preclude events such as those of the revolt in 1857. One such college was established in 1886 in Lahore (in present day Pakistan) for the Chiefs of Punjab and was named Aitchison College. The college still exists as an elite school and while now the admission is primarily merit based, it still mainly educates children from socially and politically influential families. The European schools were highly sought after by emerging elite classes such as high level professionals and the government servants. Apart from being expensive the admission to these schools was also tough as they allocated only 15 percent seats for the Indians. The head-masters and senior teachers for these schools, as well as those for the Chief's Colleges, were mainly British. English remained the medium of instruction of these schools. They aimed to prepare their students for the Cambridge School Certificate Examination for enabling them to pursue higher education in England. The vernacular schools which offered instruction in the local languages, and the Anglo-vernacular schools which offered instruction in English, were viewed as the schools for the general public. One of the major aims for such schools was to prepare clerks for public services institutions. The system was not intended to prepare students for higher education. Compared to the elite schools, these schools offered lower quality education, were staffed by local teachers, and were supervised by the provincial education departments through their field inspectors.

Thus the new system of British education created and reinforced a class division based on educational achievements. The role of English language proficiency rather than subject area expertise became the defining factor for success in the lives of young people in the subcontinent. Those who could speak the language could join the elite club and those who could not remained at clerical levels. This division still exists in present day Pakistan. The British policies also proved detrimental to the role and status of teachers, particularly those in the general public schools, as compared to their role and status in the older systems of *madrassas* and *patshalas*. In the earlier indigenous educational systems the teacher had the responsibility of setting the curriculum that he/she deemed harmonious with the students' cultural lives. In contrast, the new system emphasized the role of standardized textbooks, hence limiting the role of the teacher in curriculum development. In addition, unlike the teachers of elite schools, the vernacular school teachers were paid lower salaries and slotted near the bottom of the hierarchy of governmental bureaucracy.

Muslim Reaction to English Education

As described in the last section, Muslims had a history of an independent education system considered to be closely associated with forming the Muslim identity and meeting the community's spiritual and material needs. The British Policy of education in India created three responses among the Muslim community. The first response came from conservatives who preferred to stick to the system of *maktabs* and *madressas* and wanted no contact with the English system of education which they considered to be a threat to their religion and culture. The proponents of this view founded a *madressa* in Deoband (in present day India) in A.D. 1866 which used an adapted version of the Darse Nizami, following the tradition of focusing on subjects related to religion (*manqulaat*) like *hadith*, *fiqh*, and *sunnah*. Scholars graduating from this *madressa* established a particular school of thought and an educational movement under which new *madressas* were established and affiliated with Deoband. Several *madressas* in current day Pakistan are affiliated with the Deoband movement but offer their own certification.

The second response to British initiatives came from those Muslims who looked favorably toward the English system of education but believed that since Muslims had lagged behind other Indians in modern education, they needed a form of affirmative action and special institutions to be educated in worldly and modern knowledge. This view took on the form of a movement called the Aligarh Movement that was initiated by Syed Ahmad Khan. Under his leadership, some Muslims of India established the Muhammadan Anglo-Oriental College at Aligarh (in present day in India) in A.D. 1875. This college later became a university where Muslims of India acquired English education without fear of losing or tarnishing their identity, religion, or culture. With the passage of time, and the evidence of college education leading to economic gains, secular education became popular amongst Muslims, particularly those from the middle or upper classes. *Madressa* education came to cater only to the children of the economically weak who could not afford secular education. This trend has continued in present day Pakistan.

The third reaction to British Policies sought to seek a balance between religious and secular education and came mainly from religious scholars who wanted reform in the *madressa* system. As a result, Nudwatul Ulema (Association of Religious Scholars) was formed in A.D. 1893. This association suggested curriculum reform in the age-old *madressa* curriculum, and suggested the addition of astronomy, philosophy, arithmetic, geography, and English language to the religious subjects already offered. This suggestion was rejected by the mainstream *madressas*, following which a model *madressa* with the name of Darululum Nudwatul Ulema was established under the leadership of Maulana Shibli Naumani in A.D. 1898 at Lucknow (in present day India). This institution however faced opposition both from mainstream *madressas* and the British government and could not achieve popular success.

Education Systems in the Present Times (Post 1947)

In 1947, Pakistan became an independent country. In the early years of independence, it had a weak physical and administrative infrastructure and poor financial resources. As seen above, the British had not provided education to the masses and a relatively small number of elite English schools had been established in the larger cities. At the time of independence in 1947, Pakistan had a very small number of educational institutions and a very low participation rate.[3,4] In order to strategize for the future education system of Pakistan, the first educational conference was held in 1947 and is often regarded as the first initiative in setting up education policy guidelines for the new country. It recommended the introduction of free and compulsory education by the state. Over 20 years later in 1971, the constitution of Pakistan also asserted the right of all citizens to obtain education and the responsibility of the government to provide at least 10 years of education. Since then large gains have been made in the provision of schooling in both rural and urban population in Pakistan. However, considerable gaps still exist mainly in terms of the quantity and quality of schools in rural and urban areas, for boys and girls, and for different socio-economic classes.

There are four stages of schooling in Pakistan: (1) primary schools which include Grades 1–5; (2) middle schools with Grades 6–8; (3) high schools with Grades 9–10;[5] and (4) beyond this stage students can spend two years in college and reach what is called the intermediate level. Then they may continue another two years in college to get a Bachelor of arts or Bachelor of science degree (B.A./B.Sc.) or go on to professional colleges in the medical, engineering, or business fields. After a Bachelor's degree, students can go on to enroll in a two-year masters' program (M.A. or M.Sc.). Students may also join the university after their intermediate certificate to enroll in a Bachelors' (honors) three-year degree program. Most universities in Pakistan also offer Ph.D. degrees in several fields.

TYPES OF SCHOOLS IN PAKISTAN

At present there are several types of schools in Pakistan. This typology is based on the management structure, source of income, location, medium of instruction, and the socio-economic class of students and teachers. Several other distinctions are discussed below.

Government Schools

These schools are fully supported by the government which constructs and maintains the school building, appoints and pays the teachers, prescribes the text books for all levels, and determines rules and regulations. They charge a nominal fee of a few rupees but parents must pay for other school costs such as uniform, books, and other learning materials. The medium of instruction in these schools is Urdu which is the national language of Pakistan but which is not necessarily the first language of the students. The Sindh province has both Sindhi medium and Urdu medium primary and secondary government schools. Sindhi is also taught as a subject, or content area, in these schools. The NWFP has government primary schools with both Urdu and Pushto (the provincial language) as the medium of instruction, but all secondary government schools use Urdu as the instructional medium. In all four provinces, Urdu and English are taught as compulsory or mandatory subjects. Both children and teachers in these schools belong to low-income groups. Teachers should have undergraduate or graduate teaching qualifications as an appointment precondition to teach in primary or secondary government schools. Generally, government schools have limited resources. Typically rural schools face a shortage of teachers and basic facilities such as classrooms, toilets, and drinking water. One or two teachers must teach several classes and multigrade classes are common. In urban schools, there is a shortage of teachers in some subjects such as science and math, and a shortage of space so that each class has a large number of students sometimes over a hundred. The following vignette provides a glimpse into the day of the life of a rural school child.

Ali's Story: A Day in the Life of a Rural School Child

Ali is ten years old and studies in class three. There was no school in his village till about five years ago when the government primary school was established. His sister attends class two in a community-based school for girls run by a community-based organization (CBO). This school was opened only two years back. His older sister does not go to school because there was no school in the village when she was little and now she is 12 years old. His parents say she is too old to be running around the village alone and go to school.

Ali gets up early to go to the mosque to learn to read the Quran. He spends about half an hour there and returns to get ready for school. School begins at 8 A.M. and he can walk there in five minutes. His school has two rooms and open grounds with a few trees. They rarely have classes in the rooms and most times the teacher pulls his chair outside under a tree and the boys sit on the ground in front of him because there is no electricity in the school and it gets very hot in the small rooms. Besides, the rooms are too small to accommodate all the children. The school has two teachers and five classes so students from Grades 3–5 all sit together and are taught by the teacher at the same time. The other teacher teaches the students of Grades 1–2. Grade 4 boys are often asked to help Grade 3 boys. Most of the time the teacher asks the boys to stand up and read from the text books of Urdu and Social Studies, or to copy the answers to the questions at the end of the lessons. He either tells them where the answers are in the book or writes them on the board. They hardly ever read from their English book. The teacher explains math questions on the board and they all copy them in their notebooks.

They have a short break at 11 A.M. and sometimes Ali runs to his house to drink water or use the toilet. Sometimes the teachers ask him and the other boys to bring tea from the tea-shop near the school and then he can't go home or play with his friends. School is over at 1 P.M. and he walks back home with his friends. Sometimes they stop and play in the lane. He can rest in the afternoon or go out and wander around. But most days he goes to help his father in the field, gather fodder for the cattle, and do other odd jobs. His other friends have to do the same chores in helping their fathers in the shop or in the field. In the evening often he goes to the neighbors to watch TV. When there is homework he does that before going to bed and sometimes he forgets to do it. His mother can't read or write; his father can a little bit but doesn't ask if homework is done. Everyone in his family goes to bed early around 9 or 10 P.M. This year his father seems to have more money because he has bought him all the school books. Last year he could not buy all of them and Ali was scolded all the time for not having all his school books and even stopped going to school for a while. He also missed school this year because one time the family had to go to a relative's wedding in a nearby village and another time when there were floods in the village and Ali's family moved to a relative's house in another village.

Private Schools

There are a large and growing number of private schools in Pakistan. These schools are owned and managed by private individuals, trusts, or community boards. A decade back most of these schools existed in large cities and catered to children from the upper socio-economic class. During 1971 all private schools were nationalized and in 1979, with a change in government, they were denationalized regaining their status as private schools. In the past decade government policy has promoted public-private partnership in many sectors including education. This has resulted in tremendous increase in the number and variety of private schools. The large private schools in the urban areas have a high fee structure charging between Rs. 1500 and Rs. 5000 (One USD is equivalent to about 60 Pakistani Rupees) per month. They have well equipped classrooms, most have large school buildings, and the students and teachers are generally drawn from upper and upper-middle income groups. The medium of instruction in these schools is English and both students and teachers use English for most interactions in and out of school. Urdu is taught as a compulsory subject. Schools are affiliated with the national/provincial examination boards or with the British examination boards at Oxford and Cambridge and follow the national curriculum or British O'Level and A'Level curriculum respectively. Another type of private schools are located in both urban and rural areas and charge a much lower fee of Rs. 200 to 600. These types of schools are often housed in small residential buildings and have very basic facilities. Many of them are officially English medium schools and use text books written in English but most classroom interaction is in Urdu or a local language since both teachers and children have very low proficiency in English. These schools follow the national curriculum but self prescribe textbooks for their own school until Grade 8. In Grades 9–10, all schools affiliated with government examination boards must use books prescribed by the government Text Book Boards. Private school teachers are appointed on the basis of their general educational background and no training is required at the time of appointment. However, an increasing number of private schools are either developing professional development facilities in their own schools or sending their teachers for in-service training to other private institutions. The following vignette illustrates a typical day in the life of an urban girl who attends private school.

Sana's Story: A Day in the Life of an Urban School Child

Sana is a 14 year old girl studying in an English medium private school in Grade 8. She lives in an apartment with her younger siblings Anwer and Amna, and her parents and grand mother. Her siblings go to the same school with her in the morning. Her father works in a private firm in the accounts department.

Sana wakes up at 7 A.M. and quickly gets ready for school while also helping both Anwer and Amna. She then moves to the kitchen to help her mother prepare breakfast. They eat a quick breakfast while watching television and then rush outside to catch the school van which arrives at 7:30 A.M. Her school is housed in a bungalow which is converted into a school and is located on a busy street along with other schools in the vicinity. The school has Grades 1–10. Each grade level has three sections. Each section sits in a separate room with benches and tables arranged in rows close together. In the front of the class is a teacher's table and chair. The school has separate buildings for primary and secondary sections. It has combined classes for boys and girls until Grade 5, but since Sana is in Grade 8 she is in a separate classroom for girls. The school holds a morning assembly, where the school day begins with the recitation of some verses from the Holy Quran, singing of the national anthem, and doing light stretching exercises. They have different teachers for different subjects and each subject period lasts for half an hour. They have a half hour break at 10:30 A.M. Sana usually eats the snacks she brings from home along with her brother and sister, and sometimes they buy candies from the school canteen. After having a quick snack Anwer and Amna go to play with their friends, while Sana walks along and talks with other girls. The recess ends at 11 A.M., and then they have classes until 1 P.M. The school van drops them home at around 2 P.M.

Sana changes her school uniform and takes a quick shower. Her mother arranges lunch for the family and they all eat together. Her brother Anwer is fond of cartoons and never misses a chance to watch television during the day at home specially during meals. They take a short nap after lunch and wake up at 4 P.M. A *qari* (teacher of Quran) comes to teach them to read the Quran for half an hour. After that both Anwer and Amna rush down to join their friends for play. Anwer usually plays cricket with other boys but nowadays they play bay-blade (a game of spinning tops after a cartoon program shown on Cartoon Network). Amna plays with other girls and they usually play hide and seek and badminton. As Sana has grown older she remains with her mother to help in household chores and preparation of dinner. At 6 P.M. all three of them go for tuition classes for two hours to a tutor who lives in their apartment. At tuition Sana does her school work and takes additional help in understanding the work done at school. Her tutor takes regular tests to check her learning. She is working harder this time because she has to get higher marks in order to choose the science strand for her secondary school certification. They return home at 8 P.M. and by that time her father has also arrived. Sana likes to see her favorite television play along with other family members. Dinner is served at 9 P.M. and they eat while watching different programs on television. After dinner Sana helps her mother in doing the dishes. Afterwards, she does any additional school work or lesson revision. Sometimes she goes down to play with other girls and they usually stroll and have a lively chat. Girls of her age make sure to keep a distance from boys and not to go outside the boundaries of the apartment. She has to go to bed early around 10:30 P.M. to wake up in time for school.

On weekends Sana's father takes them for some entertainment and outing. Alternately, they go to their relatives or sometimes they come to their home for dinner. This time her father is concerned as the school has again raised the school fee and he is feeling the additional burden. However, he is committed to bear it in the hope of a prosperous future that is more likely if his children get better education.

Community-based Schools

In Pakistan there is now a category of schools known as the community-based schools. These schools are normally meant for poor and rural communities where neither the government nor the private sector has provided any schools. They are established by the local community in collaboration with non-government organizations (NGOs), and with or without support from the government or an international donor agency. The community provides accommodation for the school and identifies a teacher who is paid either through a government or donor grant, or from community resources. Students are charged a small tuition fee and they also have to pay for their own books and uniforms. A committee of community members is often supported by the NGO to manage the school, offer some teacher training, and monitor or supervise teaching. Most community-based schools are at the primary level and are meant for girls in rural areas. They mostly use Urdu as the medium of instruction although there are examples of English medium community schools as well where both boys and girls are enrolled.

Madressas

According to data from the Ministry of Religious Affairs and Education, Pakistan had 247 *madressas* at the time of independence in 1947, which increased to 6761 by the year 2000. These *madressas* are affiliated with four different boards associated with different sects of Islam. In 2001, the government set up the

Pakistan *madressa* Education Board and some *madressas* are now affiliated with this board. These *madressas* offer education from primary to post-graduate levels comprising a total of 17 years of schooling. The *madressas* are usually attached to a mosque, have minimum government funding support, and are usually sponsored and financed by national or international Muslim groups or individual donors.[6] They typically do not charge fees from the students and often provide residential facilities. Most of the students and teachers in the *madressas* belong to low-income groups and the very poor who cannot otherwise provide any education to their children or meet their basic needs.

CURRICULUM AND EXAMINATIONS

School curriculum was a provincial subject until 1973 when the constitution of Pakistan placed it in the Concurrent Legislative List of the federal government. Since then school curriculum in Pakistan is centrally controlled through the Federal Curriculum Wing in the Ministry of Education. This Curriculum Wing liaises with the Provincial Bureaus of Curriculum and Textbook Boards that are responsible for adopting and implementing the federally approved curriculum mainly through producing and prescribing textbooks.

Schools conduct their own annual examinations and promote students from one grade to the next up to the Grade 8 level. After this students must appear for external examinations in Grades 9–10 that are conducted by the provincial or federal Examination Board. These Boards not only conduct the examinations but also award certificates to successful students. Likewise, the Boards of Intermediate Education conduct external examinations for Grades 11–12 and award the corresponding certificates. All graduate degrees are awarded by public or private universities which are regulated by the government through the Higher Education Commission.

All of the primary schools teach six compulsory subjects including English, Urdu, math, science, social studies, and Islamic studies. New subjects such as environment and health have been introduced in some private and community-based schools. In the secondary schools students are placed into one of three streams: science, arts, or commerce. This streaming is not totally dependent on students' choice but largely on their school performance in the earlier years. The students with high performance in the Grade 8 annual examinations are encouraged to join the science stream and those with lower grades to join the arts and commerce streams. Streaming at this stage also determines future directions. For example, within the science stream, students who take biology in secondary school usually move toward a medical profession whereas those who take math usually go for an engineering profession.

The curriculum in *madressas* varies but mainly focuses on religious subjects like *fiqh, hadith,* Quran, Arabic language, and literature. Some *madressas* have introduced a few secular subjects particularly those *madressas* that are affiliated with the Pakistan *Madressa* Education Board, and these are obliged to teach

English, computer science, math, science, and Pakistan studies. However, most *madressas* are affiliated with their own examination boards which award certificates and degrees and there are government attempts to affiliate them with the central *Madressa* Examination Board.

Teaching methods in the majority of the schools employ teacher-centered approaches with an emphasis on rote learning. This approach is dominant in government schools and in the *madressas*, and is encouraged by the public examinations that test knowledge and memory rather than understanding and application of knowledge. Some primarily elite private schools have begun to use more student-centered approaches to teaching which focus on understanding and engaging in learning activities.

MANAGEMENT OF SCHOOLS

The education policies and programs of the government of Pakistan are implemented through the federal Ministry of Education and the provincial Education Departments each headed by a minister of education at the federal and provincial level respectively. The federal government, through the Ministry of Education, has overall policy making, advisory, and coordinating authority and controls a development budget. The provincial education departments, with their head quarters in the provincial center, are responsible for provincial policy making as well as the implementation of national and provincial policies in all schools in the provinces and disbursement of the provincial education budget. In 2000, the government decentralized and devolved management of all sectors from the provincial to the district level. Much of the management of public schools is now based in the district where the Executive District Officer of Education (EDOE) is also responsible for planning, budgeting, and managing education in his/her district. The EDOE is supported by the District Officers of Education (DOE) and the Deputy District Officers of Education (DDOE), and each is responsible for a different portfolio such as teacher training, primary education, or literacy. Each district is composed of several *tehsils* (a subunit of the district) and an Assistant District Officer is responsible for managing education at this level. This officer is helped by supervisors, learning coordinators, and other resource persons whose main responsibilities include inspection and supervision of schools.

POLICY AND PROGRAMS FOR EDUCATIONAL REFORM

National educational policies in Pakistan are formulated by the Ministry of Education at the center in cooperation with the provincial education departments. Feedback and input is obtained at different stages from various groups such as teachers, NGOs, and individual experts. Moreover, the influence of donors and international development agencies on educational policies in Pakistan, as in other developing countries, is very significant. The education polices are expected to be translated into the plans prepared by the planning commission at the center and the planning departments in the provinces. The plan documents are expected to identify priorities and plans and allocate necessary funds for their implementation.

Over the years a number of education policies have been introduced in Pakistan,[7] usually in conjunction with a change in government. There have been significant policy changes with regard to the level of schooling, the place of religion in curricula, the medium of instruction, and the role of private organizations. For example, in the early years of Pakistan's educational history, secondary and vocational education was the focus of policy interventions. However, since the 1980s the emphasis on policy and financial resources has shifted to the provision of primary schooling, and more recently has included introduction of early childhood education and higher education and a return to vocational education. During 1970, government policy discouraged private schooling and all schools were nationalized, but education policies since 1992 have recognized and asserted a growing emphasis on public-private partnership for the provision of education. Although during the 1980s a policy of making Urdu as the medium of instruction in all schools was introduced, with the change in government this policy was abandoned and English and Urdu medium schools became common. Moreover, provincial ministries of education have also vacillated on the language policy wavering between introducing English as a subject at the primary level, and using it as the medium of instruction.

There has been a consistent policy focus on increasing female participation in education which has so far typically been lower than male participation. A number of reform initiatives have been taken including relaxation in criteria for the appointment of female teachers in rural primary schools; the inclusion of community and parents in the management of schools; provision of scholarship; and free books, uniforms, and school meals for girls in government schools who continue studies beyond the primary level. Studies conducted on the effectiveness of these initiatives have shown some positive outcomes but also note that participation and non-participation in schools is a result of many factors particularly the level of family poverty, traditional beliefs about women's role in society, and parents' perceptions about quality of schooling and outcomes of schooling.

ROLE OF NON-GOVERNMENT ORGANIZATIONS (NGOs) IN EDUCATIONAL DEVELOPMENT

NGOs have been active in Pakistan since the time of its independence and often supplemented government efforts to improve educational access and quality. However, since the 1990s the numbers of such NGOs have grown considerably. One of the reasons for their growth is an increased interest by the donor agencies to fund the educational programmers for primary school age children, disadvantaged communities, and adults. The NGOs have primarily focused their presence in disadvantaged areas, both in urban and rural settings. In the education sector their contribution is manifold. The main form of NGO participation in the education sector is through non-formal schools. These include literacy centers and home schools with flexible learning hours and community support. Some NGOs are also involved in teacher training for formal and non-formal schools, while others are working to produce stimulating learning materials to improve active learning through attractive and affordable materials. Most of the NGOs are supported by international, and some national, donor agencies. One of the biggest challenges for such initiatives has been short-term and inconsistent flow of funds which are generally available only for a limited period, which seriously challenges the sustainability of these initiatives.

CONCLUSION

Schooling in Pakistan has been shaped by a long history of the integration and tensions between many different social and political forces. The first institutions of education in the Indian subcontinent, of which Pakistan was a part, were mainly religious and aimed to prepare individuals who would propagate particular religious beliefs and a way of life and perform religious functions. These kinds of institutions and aims of education have remained part of the present day education system in Pakistan in the form of *madressas*. During the British occupation of the subcontinent, schooling took on a more secular purpose but also contributed to class distinctions through differences in the purpose and quality of education offered to different socio-economic groups. Thus education became more a tool of creating and maintaining distinctions rather than removing them. The context and system of schooling in present day Pakistan reflects many of these distinctions mainly through the difference between public and private schooling and the medium of instruction. New initiatives, such as enhanced provision of schools, stronger and devolved infrastructure, and the participation of non-government sectors positively contribute to strengthening schools in Pakistan. However, some of the initiatives such as increase in private provision may also increase differential provision.

NOTES

1. Those people who have learnt the holy Quran by heart are referred as *Hafiz* and the process of learning is called *Hifz*.

2. Often, people confuse between the two Nizams. The first Nizam was the Saljuk minister in Baghdad who initiated the *Madressa* system as an institution. The second Nizam who is referred to here was the minister of Mughal emperor Aurangzeb and who made major curriculum reforms in the *Madressa* curriculum of the subcontinent. His devised curriculum is called *Dars-i-Nizamiya* or *Dars-i-Nizami*.

3. In 1947–1948, it was estimated that there were 10,000 primary/middle schools (1700 for girls), 408 secondary schools (64 for girls), 46 secondary vocational institutions

(18 for girls), 40 arts and science colleges (5 for women), and only 2 universities. There were no professional colleges (Jalil, 1998).

4. Participation rate at primary level (Grades 1–5) was 15.8 percent and at the secondary level (Grades 6–10) it was only 9.4 percent.

5. In the past few years, there have been efforts to introduce three levels of school, the elementary (1–8) secondary (9 & 10) and higher secondary (11 & 12).

6. Government and voluntary groups in Muslim countries such as Saudi Arabia, Arab Emirates and so on fund some other madressas.

7. Education policies of 1970, 1972, 1979, 1992, 1998; in addition there have been several plans most recently the Education Sector Reform Action Plan and the EFA plan of Action.

BIBLIOGRAPHY

Ali, M., Farah, I., Ostberg, S., Penny, A., and Smith R. (1998) *NORAD Support to Primary Education in Pakistan: Lessons from Experience.* Karachi: AKU-IED.

Amin, M. (2000) *Perspectives of Education and Contemporary Social Issues.* Mardan and Peshawar: Mardan College of Education and Institute of Education & Research University of Peshawar.

Anzar, U. (2003) Islamic Education: A Brief History of Madrassas with Comments on Curricula and Current Pedagogical Practices (Draft paper). International Workshop on Curricula, Textbooks, and Pedagogical Practice, and the Promotion of Peace and Respect for Diversity. Washington, D.C. 2005.

Awan, M. T. (1991a) *History of India and Pakistan.* Lahore: Ferozsons Pvt. Ltd.

Awan, M. T. (1991b) *History of India and Pakistan: Great Mughals.* Lahore: Ferozsons Pvt. Ltd.

Aziz, Q. (1990) *The Prophet and the Islamic State.* Karachi: Islamic Media Corporation.

Bajwa, F. (2002) *Pakistan: A Historical and Contemporary Look.* Karachi: Oxford University Press.

Baloch, N. A. (2003) *A National System of Education and Education of Teachers.* Larkana: Sindh Institute of Policy Studies Larkana.

Baqir, F. (1998) *The Role of NGOs in Education. Education and the State Fifty Years of Pakistan.* Karachi, Oxford: P. Hoodbhoy.

Bray, M., Clark, P., and Stephens, D. (1998) *Islamic Education: Continuity and Change. Education and Development in Africa: A Contemporary Survey.* J. Nwomonoh. London: International Scholars Publications, pp. 41–67.

Cohn, B. S. (1996) *Colonialism and its Forms of Knowledge: The British in India.* Princeton, NJ: Princeton University Press.

Cousens, H. (1929) *The Antiquities of Sind.* Karachi: Department of Culture, Government of Sindh, Pakistan.

Damohi, M. U. (1996) *Karachi: Tareekh ke aaine main.* Karachi: Indus Publications.

Farah, I. (1996) *Roads to Success: Self-Sustaining Primary School Change in Rural Pakistan.* Oslo and Karachi: IMTEC and AKU-IED.

Farah, I. and Shera, S. (In press) "Female Education in Pakistan: A Review." In Rarieya, J. and Qureshi, R. (Eds) *Gender and Education in Pakistan.* Karachi: Oxford University Press.

Farooq, R. A. (1993) *Education System in Pakistan: Issues and Problems.* Islamabad: Asia Society for Promotion of Innovation and Reform in Education.

Gupta, A. (2006) *Early Childhood Education, Post Colonial Theory, and Teaching Practices in India: Balancing Vygotsky and the Veda*. New York: Palgrave Macmillan.

Hussain, J. (1981) *An Illustrated History of Pakistan* (Book 1). Karachi: Oxford University Press.

Jalil, N. (1998). "Pakistan's Education: The First Decade." In Hoodbhoy, P. (Ed.) (1981) *Education and the State: Fifty Years of Pakistan*. Oxford University Press, Karachi: Pakistan.

Jin Technologies Private Limited. Political History of Pakistan. http://www.storyofpakistan.com, accessed September 15, 2005.

Khalid, S. M. (2002) *Deeni Madaris main taleem: kaifiyat, masail, imkaanat*. Islamabad: Institute of Policy Studies and Aalmi Idara Fikr-e-Islami.

Lelyveld, D. (1996) *Aligarh's First Generation: Muslim Solidarity in British India*. Oxford: Oxford University Press.

Qureshi, I. H. (1999) *Education in Pakistan*. Karachi: Bureau of Composition, Compilation and Translation, University of Karachi.

Rahman, T. (2004) *Denizens of Alien Worlds: A Study of Education, Inequality and Polarization in Pakistan*. Karachi: Oxford University Press.

Shalabi, A. (2004) *Musalmanoon ka Nizam-e-Taleem*. Lahore: Book Home.

Siddiqui, H. (1987) *Education in Sindh: Past and Present*. Jamshoro: Institute of Sindhology, University of Sindh.

Singh, R. P. (1989) *Educating the Indian Elite*. New Delhi: Sterling Publishers.

Social Policy and Development Centre (SPDC) (2003) *Social Development in Pakistan: The State of Education 2002–2003*. Karachi: SPDC.

Stein, B. (1998) *A History of India*. Oxford: Blackwell Publishers.

Whitehead, C. (2003) *Colonial Educators: The British Indian and Colonial Education Service 1858–1983*. London: I.B. Tauris.

Chapter 9

SCHOOLING IN SRI LANKA

Swarna Jayaweera

OVERVIEW OF COUNTRY

The Republic of Sri Lanka is a tropical island located in the Indian Ocean, about 800 kilometers north of the equator and about 30 kilometers away from the southern tip of India. The island of Sri Lanka measures 435 kilometers from north to south and 225 kilometers from east to west. The Dry Zone and Wet Zone lowlands have a uniformly moderate temperature throughout the year with high levels of humidity. The Central Hills in the Wet Zone have the coolest weather. The island is subject to two monsoons, one from the southwest in May and the other from the northeast in November. The Dry Zone receives rainfall between 125 and 190 centimeters and the Wet Zone between 250 and 500 centimeters a year.

The population today is estimated to be around 20.2 million. The 2001 Census was held in 18 districts only as the northern and eastern regions could not be covered fully due to intense ethnic conflict. In these 18 districts, the population comprised 81 percent Sinhalese, 4.3 percent Tamils, 5.1 percent descendents of Indian immigrant plantation labor workers, 8 percent Moors who arrived first as Arab traders in the 13th century and Malays who were brought in later by the colonial powers, and 0.2 percent Burghers who are the descendants of the Eurasian population of the Portuguese, Dutch, and British colonial periods from the 15th century. A small number of families of the indigenous population, the Veddahs, have survived in the interior regions while other families have been absorbed by the majority population. A few Parsee and Borah families who have recently migrated from India live chiefly in Colombo. With regard to their religious background, the majority of the population in Sri Lanka are Buddhists (76.7 percent), and the rest are Hindus (7.9 percent), Muslims (8.5 percent), Roman Catholic Christians (6.1 percent), and other Christians (0.8 percent).

The female population is more than the male population; the average annual population growth rate is 1.2 percent; 32.9 percent of the population is under the age of 18 years; and the majority of thee population in Sri Lanka lives in the rural sector.

Sri Lanka has had universal franchise since 1931. The country has a democratic governance structure with an Executive President elected by the people every six years, a Parliament that is determined at the time of general elections on the basis of proportional representation, a Prime Minister, and a Cabinet of Ministers. Two major political parties and several small parties contest during elections. In 1972 the country became a republic within the British Commonwealth and its name was changed from Ceylon to Sri Lanka.

HISTORICAL DEVELOPMENT OF EDUCATION

Sri Lanka's long recorded history of at least 3000 years had very clear phases of political, social, and economic changes that cannot be divided into the conventional ancient, medieval, and modern periods in any review of the history of education in the country. The pre-historical years are being explored afresh under the Cultural Triangle Project led by the United Nations Educational, Social and Cultural Organization (UNESCO) and because of the scant information available this period is still included in the Ancient Period. There were no significant changes in the educational traditions and system in the medieval period in history. Hence the first section discussed will cover around 2000 years of educational history, until the end of the 15th century in what is known as the period of Sri Lanka's traditional society.

The 16th century saw the arrival of the Portuguese as the first European colonial power, followed by the Dutch in the 17th century. Both these colonial powers conquered only the coastal areas of the country, and the period between the 16th and 18th centuries saw the country transitioning toward British control which was completely achieved by 1815. The foundations of the modern system of education were laid in the 19th century by the British colonial administration which continued to wield power till the mid-20th century. The history of education in post-independent Sri Lanka is a continuation from the end of the direct British control of the country in 1930, extending from the transition years from 1931 to independence in 1948, and to the present.

The Ancient and Medieval Period

It is difficult to determine the beginnings of history in Sri Lanka but records on ola leaf and stone exist from the first millennium before Christ. In pre-historic times, the lives of people, young or old, differed very little from that of those in societies in a similar stage of development. The cave dwellers, for instance, learnt the use of tools and acquired skills for living informally and orally transmitting religious rituals and ceremonies within their families and communities.

The Socio-political Context

Formal institutions developed only when society needed special agencies to perform the tasks of socialization and education. In the first millennium before Christ, the highly developed Vedic culture and new methods of agriculture, irrigation, and local industry were transferred from India to its southern neighbor Sri Lanka, or Ceylon as it was called then. The ancient and medieval periods in Sri Lanka's history were rooted in its agrarian economy based on irrigation agriculture, its semi-feudal social order, and the strong religious foundations of Buddhism and Hinduism, the former following the latter in its advent in Sri Lanka. The ancient kingdoms of the Rajarata, Anuradhapura, and Polonnaruwa, held sway till the 11th century A.D. despite invasions at different times from India. From the 12th century to the British conquest of Sri Lanka, the kingdoms of power were moved from center to center in the southwest, and finally to the Kandyan kingdom in the central hills. In addition, a kingdom was established in Jaffna in the north during this period. There were, therefore, long periods of political stability as well as intervals of instability and war.

The hydraulic civilization, based on large tanks for agriculture in the Rajarata, flourished before the 11th century and fell into disuse with the movement of population to the southwest and the jungle grew over the ancient cities and their art and architecture virtually till the twentieth century. Society was organized around feudal service and on an occupational basis that was reinforced as a caste system, which was however, less rigid in its social consequences than the caste system in India. Patriarchal social relations based on customs and norms and relatively liberal laws determined the role of women within the family and in society.

Educational Traditions

Religion was an important facet of life, and education developed as having a strong religious base. Elementary education in reading and writing such as forming letters on sand, and religious instruction was imparted to only boys in the local temple or in the households of *brahmin* teachers. More advanced education, both at secondary and higher levels, was given by the Brahmin gurus in their households or in *pirivenas* (Buddhist monastic centers). According to the ancient chronicle, the *Mahavamsa*, *brahmin* tutors in their role of *purohitas* (advisors) also educated royal princes and the sons of the elite. As Brahmin education in Sri Lanka was organized on a caste basis, only members of the upper castes, the *brahmins* and *kshatriyas*, received an education which included the study of the four books comprising the *Veda*, grammar, the science of numbers, astronomy, logic, law, and ethics. Royal persons were taught the duties of a king, the science of politics, logic, and the military arts. Buddhist education in *pirivenas* evolved from the need to educate novices for religious life as *bhikkus* (monks) but very soon the *pirivena* became the center of superior or post-elementary education to higher education as they catered to the needs of lay scholars and the professions. Buddhist philosophy occupied a dominant place but other subjects were taught including literature; prosody; languages such as Sinhalese, Pali, Sanskrit, and Tamil; history; political science; law; economics; mathematics; astronomy; and even medicine, to meet the needs of lay professionals and potential leaders. Both the Buddhist and Brahmin formal educational institutions strengthened the academic tradition and trained individuals for high level occupations and were therefore for the elite.[1]

Parallel to this system of education but non-formal in its organization was the apprenticeship system under guilds that trained persons for technical and vocational education. The master instructors and craftsmen trained apprentices on the job within a range of occupations. It is this training system that made possible the complex construction of the large tanks for irrigation and agriculture in the north central and southern areas of the Dry Zone, and also the architectural splendors of the ancient and medieval periods. In addition to the training of craftsmen who built the tanks and created the stone palaces and religious places of worship, and the religious and secular sculpture that have survived and are the objects of admiration even today, the system of apprenticeship also trained musicians and dancers who were an integral part of the lifestyle of the elite, in palace ceremonies and religious rituals. These training guilds were caste based and reinforced the divisions of society into caste groups. There were also shorter periods of training by *brahmins* for cultivators and traders based on their actual experiences, and for traders in particular on aspects such as salesmanship and the value of gems.

Informal learning occurred extensively in the home and the community, and focused on social norms and ethical values. All children therefore were nurtured within this culture, but boys went to temple schools and a limited number went on to *pirivenas* and to *brahmin gurus* (teachers) to acquire an advanced education in religion, academic scholarship, and in professional training.

Girls and women in Sri Lanka at that time had no access to formal educational institutions such as the *pirivenas*, or the households of *brahmin gurus*. But women of all classes and castes were allowed to join the *Sangha* (the Buddhist religious order) to become *bhikkunis* and receive religious instruction at the highest levels. There is evidence that women from royal and aristocratic families received instruction from private tutors and became reputed for their learning and their accomplishments in literature, art, and music. While the majority of women had no opportunity to be literate, historians have demonstrated verses found inscribed on the mirrored walls of the historic 8th century rock fortress at Sigiriya to have been composed by women. Some of the religious songs such as the *Theri Gatha* too are said to have been written by women. Women in non-affluent families worked in the fields and engaged in domestic industries such as weaving, spinning, sewing, and pottery. Girls and women were also among the apprentices in the music and dancing guilds. Finally, girls from all economic levels received an informal education in their homes in their ascribed familial roles as daughters, women, and mothers.

This ancient education system was elite and caste based and therefore prevented upward social mobility. The system survived not only the 2000 years of the ancient and medieval periods but the *pirivenas* continued to meet the needs of Buddhist novices and scholars through the modern period. They were neglected under the colonial rulers and were not able to change to meet new needs. With the revival of Buddhism and Hinduism in the second half of the 19th century they became important centers of education once again although they were unable to compete with emerging modern educational institutions.

The Early Modern Period

The first western colonial powers to reach Sri Lanka, or Ceylon as it was then called, were the Portuguese. In the attempt to seeking the spices and riches of the east, especially in India, Portuguese sailors followed the sea route discovered by Vasco Da Gama which lay around the Cape of Good Hope. In 1505, the Portuguese ships were driven off their course to India and reached Sri Lanka almost by chance. Their commander established contact with the king of the Kotte Kingdom near modern-day Colombo, and after more than 50 years of bloodshed and pillage, gained control over the coastal areas of the country including the Kotte Kingdom and the Jaffna kingdom in the north. Throughout their 150 years of colonial rule till the mid-17th century, the Kandy Kingdom in the interior of the Sri Lanka maintained its independence.

Impact of Portuguese Rule

The first impact of Western culture on Sri Lanka was seen as the Portuguese reached and occupied the country and was limited to the coastal areas. The Portuguese established fortresses along the coast and made it their main mission to convert their subjects to their religion of Roman Catholicism. Although they succeeded in converting the king of the Kotte Kingdom, only a minority of the public changed their religion from Buddhism and Hinduism despite the fact that some of their temples and places of worship were destroyed. However, members of royalty and the elite classes did adopt the dress and some customs of the colonizers, and Portuguese words entered the language of even the masses. When the Portuguese were defeated by the Dutch and had to abandon control of the coastal belt in 1658, they left behind their impact on language, dress, religion, and also in the form of a group of people of mixed Portuguese and Sinhalese/Tamil descent.

Education was used as an instrument for religious conversion and as a political and social agency that would strengthen the Portuguese rule in Sri Lanka. The agencies which undertook education, mainly the missionary orders of the Jesuits, Dominicans, Augustinians, and Capuchins, subordinated educational goals to religion. They appointed teachers who were instructed to assemble children in parish schools near churches, the boys in the morning and the girls during the afternoons, and teach them Roman Catholicism, prayers, and the elements of reading. According to available records, the numbers of children who attended these schools, especially girls, were very limited. The Portuguese rulers also provided an advanced education for the sons of royalty and elite families in Seminaries. By 1605, the Jesuit Seminary or College was established in Colombo and another college was opened later in Jaffna. The Fransiscans also had three colleges for the boys of the upper classes. The Jesuit College in Colombo had three departments: the elementary school which undertook the teaching of reading, writing, and Roman Catholicism; the secondary department which focused on the teaching of Latin and the humanities; and the higher department which specialized in the teaching of moral theology. Instruction was in Portuguese and the curriculum was the same as taught in the schools in Portugal. Records indicate that only a handful of students attended these institutions. Some of the royal princes were sent to the university in Lisbon to ensure that they absorbed the Portuguese culture.[2] Handicrafts and other useful skills were viewed as manual labor and considered to be degrading, and were thus confined to slaves. In the interior of the country the old educational institutions continued to function, and even in the coastal areas they struggled to survive despite hostile action.

Developments under the Dutch Administration

The second Western power to invade Sri Lanka was the Dutch colonizers from Holland, or Netherlands as it is now called. The Dutch East India Company, which was the Dutch agent of colonial expansion in Asia came to India, to the Dutch East Indies which is now called Indonesia, and to Sri Lanka in the 17th century. The Dutch drove the Portuguese away from the coastal areas of Sri Lanka in 1658, thus establishing their rule in these areas for 150 years, until they were replaced by the British colonizers at the end of the 18th century. The Dutch, too, were unable to capture the Kandy Kingdom which continued to control the interior of the country and maintained its independence.

The Dutch introduced additional economic and social changes in the areas they controlled. They encouraged the growth of the cinnamon industry and took over and strengthened the forts built by the Portuguese along the coast. Like the Portuguese, their mission was to convert the people to their religion, and this time it was Protestant (Calvinst) Christianity. They attempted to achieve this through the churches and schools they established and by honoring and awarding titles to Christians and other elites who converted to Christianity. They were more organized than the Portuguese in their educational activities.[3] They established an official organization called the Scholarchal Commission which was to be responsible for the spread and control of education and had inspectors to enforce their policy of compulsory education. The Dutch parish schools were intended to teach Christianity, and reading and writing was taught to promote this objective. Parents were asked to send their children, both sons and daughters, to these co-educational parish schools. School years extended to eight years and the School Visitor, or inspector from the Commission, examined students in religion, reading, and writing and then discharged them from school with a certificate that indicated their levels of accomplishment. The school *thombos* (records) gave the names of the parents and the children; their date of admission to school, and their discharge; dates of baptism, marriage, death; and the date they left the village. These comprehensive records such as the Land *Thombos* and School *Thombos* are available in archives in Sri Lanka and Holland and have been used by historians to study living conditions in Sri Lanka at the time. The report of the Matara School in 1760, for instance, stated that they provided only elementary instruction in the local languages as they could not get sufficient Dutch teachers. Parents were reported to have withdrawn children, especially girls, from schools after a few years. These schools were the first formal provision of education in the country for girls, but the girls were taught chiefly to repeat prayers without which they could not get married under the Dutch laws.

Advanced education was provided in the Dutch Seminary in Colombo and later in a Seminary in Jaffna which was closed down in 1723. Even at the best of times the Colombo Seminary did not have more than 40 male students, all from elite families including young men who were trained to become preachers or to teach in the parish schools. They also educated at one time 12 Sinhalese and 12 Tamil boys free of cost and promised to give them employment in the Dutch East India Company. The main objective of the Seminary was to educate and create a Christian local elite group, including *mudliyars* (headmen) to assimilate the Dutch way of life, and to train personnel to assist in the Dutch administration as local officials and interpreters as well as assist in the schools. The Colombo Seminary provided a Western education and was modeled on the institutions in Holland. Three courses were offered: a preliminary course teaching Dutch grammar and composition, and translations from the local languages; a second course in which Dutch, Latin, Greek, and Hebrew were taught; a final course in higher theology taught in the Latin medium, and Logic. Careful attention was focused on the teaching of religion and Western classical languages. The Dutch Governor himself came to the examination and Ribeyro, a Dutch historian, reported on Governor Van Imhoff's statement that it was "astonishing to hear little black fellows chatter in Latin and construct Greek when they hardly knew Dutch."

Although the Dutch were more organized than the Portuguese and had more schools, their impact was limited as it was restricted primarily to teaching a new religion, and was geographically confined to the coastal areas. Some of the questions at the Seminary examinations were intended to qualify students to argue with "heathen" fellow Sinhalese and Tamils. While the Dutch encouraged minor industries like carpentry and established cinnamon plantations, the education they imported was confined to memory work and was academic in nature. Their chief impact was in their influence on the language which contains many words of Dutch origin; the spread of Dutch dress, food, furniture, and customs among the upper classes, which also seeped down to the local masses to some extent.

Both the Portuguese and Dutch used education to spread their religious beliefs and to influence the local elite to adopt their way of life so that their influence could be extended to the larger population. However, the parish schools were not extensive and the Seminaries, which educated only boys, had such a small number of students that they changed the lives of only a few families. Within the Kandyan Kingdom and in much of the coastal areas, children grew up in their local cultural context and the earlier educational institutions based on local religions continued to function with minimum support in the coastal areas.

British Colonial Administration: Late 18th Century to 1930

The British East India Company took control of the coastal areas of Sri Lanka from the Dutch in 1796 as part of their military strategy in the Eastern hemisphere during the French Revolutionary Wars. In 1802, Sri Lanka became a Crown Colony under the direct administration of the British Colonial Office, and with the conquest of the Kandyan kingdom in 1815 British imperial rule was extended over the entire island. The penetration of British political, economic, and social influence transformed the development of the country over the next 150 years.

Colonial Policy

British colonial policy was directed to consolidating political power, meeting economic demands created largely by the Industrial Revolution in Britain, nurturing a loyal colonial elite, and disseminating Christianity and the social norms of the European world. The centralized colonial administration of the country under the British Governor wielded authority. The minimal local representation in the Legislative Council had little influence on colonial policy until 1930 when direct colonial rule ended and a transitional political structure, the State Council, was introduced to prepare for independence.

The British abolished the country's feudal service in 1833 and the colonial economy was restructured to meet Britain's need for raw materials, markets, and opportunities for investment of British capital. Consequently, the hill country was opened up for coffee plantations from the third decade of the 19th century; when the coffee plantations were destroyed by pests they were converted into tea plantations, and rubber plantations were opened at the end of the 19th century. The owners and managers of the coffee, tea, and rubber estates were British, and South Indian immigrant labor was imported to work on the plantations. British business interests and the monetization of the economy resulted in the emergence of a small class of local capitalists who supplied the needs of the expanding plantation economy and invested their profits in acquiring plantations and also developing coconut estates.

The spread of Western education in urban centers resulted in the rise of a new middle and professional class, consisting initially of Burghers (the Eurasians of the Dutch period who had adopted English as their mother tongue) and the Sinhalese and Tamil families who could afford to attend English schools. Roads and railways were constructed to meet the needs of the plantations, and a modern administrative infrastructure developed during the 19th century. The failure to develop any industries during the entire colonial period meant that government services as well as the legal and medical professions were the main avenues of employment for those who benefited from English education. The neglect of domestic agriculture and the absorption of village land into plantations resulted in increasing landlessness and the perpetuation of poverty and deprivation among the masses of the population.

Transition to Modern Education

The first British Governor, Lord North, laid down the primary objectives of colonial educational policy: to train local persons to assist in the administration; to educate a local elite to absorb British social norms and values and inculcate loyalty to the Empire; and to support the spread of Christianity as colonial officials were at this time greatly influenced by the Christian Evangelical Movement in England in the first half of the 19th century. At the same time, education was not a state priority in contemporary England and had been largely left to Christian religious denominations. Consequently, in Sri Lanka too, education in the early decades of the 19th century was left to the missionary societies despite North's efforts. North attempted to revive the Dutch parish schools which taught reading, writing, and Christianity in the local languages. He also established the first English school in Colombo in 1800 for the sons of the local elite and the Burghers, and for the training of interpreters to assist colonial officials. As a result of the lack of financial support from the Colonial Office the parish schools were reduced from 170 to 90 by 1830 and the 4 English schools barely survived.

Meanwhile, some of the Governors of the time encouraged the missionaries to establish schools. The London Missionary Society sent a few ministers in 1805. In the second decade of the 19th century, the large missionary societies such as the Baptist Missionary Society (1812), the Wesleyan Methodist Missionary Society (1814), the American Mission (1816) which worked only in Jaffna in the north, and the Church Missionary Society (1818) established themselves in the country. They built different types of schools including vernacular schools that offered instruction in the local languages such as Sinhalese and Tamil, in villages to spread Christianity among the rural population; elementary English schools in urban centers; and boarding schools and high schools in central towns which numbered about 235 in 1832. Batticotta Seminary opened in Jaffna by the American Mission in 1823 was considered to be equal to any secondary school of the time. The Mission's Uduvil Girls School was one of the earliest major girls schools and was established to provide future Christian wives for those educated in the Batticotta

Seminary. Other Missions established similar schools in the south of the country, and the practice of opening boys' schools and girls' schools for the elite in the same neighborhood was followed through colonial rule.

During the 19th century colonial education policy underwent several changes with regard to schooling. In 1833, the Colebrook Commission recommended the appointment of a School Commission (later the Central School Commission), consisting of officials, Christian clergy, and missionary representatives who would be responsible for education. The Commission also recommended that English should be the only medium of instruction. A private boys school was taken over by the colonial government and converted into the Colombo Academy for the sons of the elite. This school was renamed Royal College in 1881 and continues to be the leading state school for boys even today. Over 30 Elementary English schools were opened also in the 1930s. In 1843 three Central Schools were opened for boys in major towns, namely Colombo, Kandy, and Galle. Between 1843 and 1862 four Female Superior Schools were opened in the same towns. Principals were recruited from England and in the case of the girls schools some of the Principals were sent by the Society for Promoting Female Education in England. These English schools levied fees and their students were the children of Eurasian and Burgher families and a small number from affluent Sinhalese and Tamil families. In fact, it was noted in 1868 that 87 percent of the students in the Female Superior Schools were Eurasians and Burghers. These girls schools taught chiefly English, Western music, and art as accomplishments for girls belonging to elite families. Most conservative Sinhalese and Tamil families had governesses, chiefly Burgher ladies to instruct their daughters in their homes.

Vernacular state schools were not permitted for some years but when the colonial government realized that they could not reach the majority of the population through a small number of English schools, they established a Normal School (training school) for teachers in the local languages in 1845 and opened 30 vernacular schools in 1847. There was no consistent policy regarding state education in the local languages at this time, and the Normal School was closed in 1858 and the vernacular schools, which were limited to teaching the three R's, were neglected. Mixed schools that were started to teach first in the local languages and then in English became English schools very soon. To meet the demand for higher education the Colombo Academy had an upper section called Queen's College, from 1859 for about ten years to prepare for the first examinations of the University of Calcutta.

Establishment of the Colonial Educational System

These uncertain years in colonial education policy came to an end in 1867 when the Morgan Report recommended a department with a Director and officials from England to administer educational institutions, and to oversee the expansion of vernacular schools for boys and girls in all villages and the restriction of English education to a limited number of students.[4] The state withdrew from

English education, closing down its English schools with the exception of Royal College, and leaving English education in the hands of the missionaries. In 1895, a petition from parents to start a secondary school of the same level as Royal College for girls was refused as it was felt that missionary girls schools could meet this need. A system of grants was introduced to support non-state schools. Hence for the rest of colonial rule, the main features of the education system were a centralized educational administration under a British Director and a department, a denominational system of grant aided schools organized by religious societies, and a dual structure of schools which included fee levying English schools for those who could afford to enroll in them, and free, inferior vernacular schools for the masses.

The education system in England at this time also was based on the social class structure but the situation was worse in Sri Lanka because the division was additionally based on language as well so that the English educated had access to avenues of remunerative employment and those educated in the local languages were not only drawn from the poor but also received a very limited education that offered few prospects for employment except as teachers in vernacular schools or notaries and village headmen. Children in these two types of schools almost lived in two different worlds. The few Anglo-vernacular schools that were expected to teach initially in the local languages and later in English did not attract children because the demand was higher for English education. Although the number of vernacular schools did increase, they also, however, continued to receive little attention with regard to facilities and curriculum. On the other hand, the policy of restricting English education could not be implemented as the greater demand was for English education which became almost the monopoly of missionary organizations.

In the second half of the 19th century, the revival of Buddhism in the south and Hinduism in the north of Sri Lanka resulted in increasing resistance to missionary schools, and to the establishment of Buddhist and Hindu village schools and a small number of English schools. These schools were started chiefly by the Buddhist Theosophical Society and the Saiva Paripalana Sabha which was a Hindu society. As the missionaries were part of the power structure in education, Buddhist and Hindu schools had to overcome many barriers imposed through regulations regarding the distance of new schools from existing schools although most missionary village schools had students from other religions. The Buddhist and Hindu schools in the English medium had to conform to the curriculum in other English schools in order to compete with them. The curriculum offered to students differed according to the type of school. In the upper classes of the Colombo Academy and the missionary schools for the elite, the typical curriculum included subjects such as Christianity, English, mathematics, history, geography, and Latin and sometimes even Greek. In the upper classes, subjects taught included logic, elements of English law, principles of natural philosophy, astronomy, Latin, Greek, and Hebrew as these students were likely to join the service of the colonial government, or become lawyers or members of the Christian clergy.

The Superior Girls schools had a more restricted academic curriculum at this time and focused more on skills accomplished in music and needlework.

A significant change occurred after 1880 when the Cambridge School Certificate Examinations that were conducted in England were also introduced in Sri Lanka. They became the goal of all secondary schools for boys and girls because they were the avenue to employment and higher studies and also reflected social prestige. These examinations transplanted the British curriculum of schools in England into the Sri Lankan schools, and included the teaching of English history, English geography, botany which was limited to the study of species of English plants, and so forth. The only difference between the curriculum of the girls' schools and the boys' schools was the teaching of needlework and domestic science in the former. New subjects were added over the years through the Cambridge examinations such as physics, chemistry, botany, and French. The popularity of the Cambridge School Certificate Examinations is reflected in the fact that the number of boys appearing for the Senior Cambridge Examination increased from four in 1880 to 1176 in 1925, and the number appearing for the Junior Cambridge Examination increased from 17 to 820. The first girl took the Junior Cambridge Examination in 1881, and the Senior Cambridge Examination in 1885. But by 1925, 154 and 150 girls appeared for these two examinations respectively. Importance was attached to Western classical languages. It took many years to teach Sinhalese and Tamil even as optional languages, and practical subjects were never in demand as they did not lead to many jobs in a country in which industrialization had never been promoted. School activities, or extra curricular programs, were modeled along the lines of the Public Schools in England, and sports such as cricket, football and tennis became an important feature of the Colombo Academy and other prestigious missionary schools.

Throughout the years of British rule, about 85 percent of the school-going children were in vernacular schools and were confined by the educational policy expressed clearly in the Morgan Report in 1867 to the study of reading, writing, the four rules of arithmetic, and the basic outlines of history and geography. Grants were paid on a lower scale than for English schools and no superior or secondary level subjects were to be taught. It was only toward the end of the colonial rule in the second decade of the 20th century that the Vernacular School Leaving Certificate Examination was introduced, including the addition of needlework, drawing, agriculture, and sanitation to enable students in these schools to qualify for teaching positions or for village level positions.

The colonial school curriculum reflected the same British cultural imperialism and elitist social values and social class-based differentiation as seen in the wide gulf between English schools and the schools in the local languages. They also sought to inculcate the gender related social norms of 19th century England, particularly through English Girls High Schools and boarding schools. Information in the Morgan Report indicated that the education of girls was promoted as they were expected to occupy a central role in the family in imparting Christian morality, and domestic virtues and roles. In the early 20th century, the objectives of girls education continued to be to equip them for marriage and their domestic duties but the well-known English girls schools concentrated now on nurturing social values and skills to be successful "helpmates" to educated men, and the Cambridge examinations were seen to contribute to the achievement of this objective. By this time, educated women were working as teachers and nurses and even those who encouraged a career for girls desired them to be employed only in what they saw to be "feminine" occupations such as teachers, doctors, nurses, clerical assistants, telephone operators, and dressmakers. It was found that the vocational aspirations of boys in English schools were to be doctors, lawyers, administrators, engineers, and clerks.

Higher education developed more slowly than it did in neighboring India, as colonial policy makers delayed establishing university level institutions. The upper level of the Colombo Academy that functioned from 1859 to 1869 was established to prepare students for entrance to Calcutta University. A few medical and Christian theology students were also sent to India for training. With the expansion of the colonial administration there was a need for doctors and lawyers, and the colonial government was compelled to meet this need by establishing a Medical College in Colombo in 1870; a private institution for legal education known later as the Law College was opened in 1876 to train lawyers to be familiar with the new laws introduced by the colonial administration. The first woman student entered Medical College in 1892 but during the next ten yeas the only women students were from the Burgher community.

Instead of establishing a university, two scholarships were awarded each year to British universities. Sri Lanka became a center for the University of London examinations by the end of the 19th century. After much lobbying by educated local leaders, the University College was established in 1921 in Colombo to prepare for the degree examinations of the University of London. In 1929, by the end of direct colonial rule, there were 339 students in the University College of whom 22 were women.

An Agriculture School was opened in 1884 in Colombo for the sons of landowners but it had to be closed down in 1901 as there were no students. The sons of the landed elite aspired more to enter British universities rather than enroll in an agriculture school that did not lead to prestigious jobs. In 1917, the School of Agriculture was opened to train for mid-level agricultural offices. The Technical School opened in Colombo in 1893 had also to be converted to a Technical school to train for technician level employment in government departments. There were no women in the agricultural or technical education institutions. The state and the missionaries opened training institutions for male and female vernacular school teachers in the 1880s, and the only English teacher training institution was opened in Colombo at the beginning of the 20th century. The few industrial schools were only charitable institutions for orphans and other destitute children. Clearly, post-secondary education was only successful when there were job opportunities for the products of these institutions.

British colonial policy did manage to work toward introducing modern education in Sri Lanka, cut across the caste structure, help to create an educated middle class who entered the professions and middle level employment, and improve the living conditions of those who benefited from English education. In fact, English education was the chief agent of upward social and economic mobility, simultaneously creating a new class structure based on education, language, and income. Christian influence continued to dominate education in Sri Lanka till the end of the colonial rule. The slow rise in literacy rates between the first Census of Population in 1881 (29.8% male literacy and 3.1% female literacy) and the 1921 Census (56.4% male literacy and 21.2% female literacy) indicates that the pace of expansion of education was limited, particularly in the case of women. No Census was held in 1931, at the end of direct colonial rule.

Despite the influence of Indian nationalism, and the impact of the defeat of Russia by Japan, the process of social and cultural de-nationalization in colonial and missionary schools prevented the development of a strong national move-ment; even so Buddhist and Hindu schools endeavored to impart a national ethos, and the Ceylon National Congress was formed in 1917 to agitate for political reforms. The majority of the population had access only to vernacular schools without modern facilities, and the traditional pattern of life continued in villages throughout the country. There was no improvement in their living conditions and the neglect of agriculture resulted in the loss of self-sufficiency in rice production, the staple food; the import of rice from other countries; the jungle still covered much of the old agricultural tanks and fields; and the villagers continued to be governed in an alien language.

From Eve of Independence to Post-independent Sri Lanka

The end of direct colonial rule in 1930 was followed by the introduction of a semi-representative government during the period of transition to political inde-pendence in 1948. The colonial Governor and his chief officials retained financial and overall administrative control. A local assembly called the State Council was elected on the basis of the universal franchise introduced in 1931. The State Council along with a Board of Ministers of whom the majority were Sri Lankans, became responsible for formulating and implementing policies in areas such as agriculture, education, health, and industry. Most members of the State Council had been very critical of the colonial administration and were sensitive to needs and aspirations at the local level. In agriculture, for instance, colonization or settlement schemes were organized in the Dry Zone in the former centers of irrigation-based agriculture to achieve self-sufficiency in the staple food, rice, and to improve the living conditions in the villages that had been overrun by jungle.

Educational Initiatives in the Immediate Post-colonial Years

This transitional period was seminal in the field of education in Sri Lanka as the policies that were introduced shaped educational development in the post-independence decades and changed the lives of the majority of the Sri Lankan population. These policies emerged as a reaction to the colonial educational policies that had limited modern education within an elite group, created a dual system of schools based on language that disadvantaged the majority of children in the so-called vernacular schools, and had established Christian control on education. The Sri Lankan Minister of Education and the Executive Committee on Education of the State Council worked to get the control of education transferred to the State Council by the Education Ordinance of 1939. During the 1940s, before political independence, they introduced radical changes in educational policy and practice.[5]

Central Schools were established in rural locations. Secondary education in the English medium that had been so far confined to urban centers was thus extended to the rural sector. The primary schools in the area in which the Central Schools were located were to be the "feeder schools" and the brightest children in these village primary schools were given scholarships to the Central Schools and to higher education if they qualified for admission. Eleven schools were opened in 1940, the number increasing to 54 by 1947, with at least 1 school in each electorate. The Junior Cambridge Examination was not held in Sri Lanka after 1937 and the Senior Cambridge Examination was replaced by the local Senior School Certificate Examination in 1943 partly as a result of difficulties in sending answer scripts to England during World War II. In 1942 the Medical College and the University College were amalgamated to form the first local university, the independent University of Ceylon, which was established on the model of universities in England. These developments led to the adoption of local curricula in the university and in the secondary school system. Local history, geography, natural sciences, and languages such as Sinhala and Tamil became important subjects in the school curriculum.

On the basis of the recommendations of a special committee, the Special Committee, appointed by the State Council to propose reforms in education, free education in state or state assisted primary, secondary, and tertiary education institutions including universities was introduced in 1945 and the medium of instruction was changed in all English primary grades to the mother tongue. In implementing these changes, local policy makers believed that every child had the right to education and that education should be free in a democratic society. Their vision was that education should reduce socio-economic inequalities and enable every child to reach the highest positions in society. This was a vision that went far beyond the international basic needs goal in the 1970s, the narrow limits of the "education for all" concept of the 1990s, and the Millennium Development Goal of only universal primary education in the year 2000.

The Committee also proposed a school structure that was borrowed from the selective system of secondary education in England at that time. A test taken at 11 years of age was to determine selection and entry into three types of unequal secondary schools: secondary schools, senior schools, and practical schools. The State Council rejected this impractical scheme and suggested two types of secondary schools, senior secondary schools and senior practical schools, after a selection test taken at 14 years. Little progress was made in its implementation as only four practical schools had been opened by 1947. Another significant development was the introduction of a conscience clause in 1939 for children of other religions in denominational schools, and the compulsory teaching of the child's religion in state schools from 1947. The report of the Committee also spoke of creating national harmony among the different ethnic groups in the country and promoting character development through schools.[6]

Political developments such as the country's Independence in 1948, and the change to the status of the Democratic, Socialist Republic of Sri Lanka in 1972, did not bring about any immediate policy changes. The implementation of the policies of the 1940s led to an enormous expansion of educational opportunities which were accelerated by the change in the medium of instruction in secondary grades to the mother tongue, grade by grade from 1953 to 1959. This change occurred in the Arts Faculties (Departments) of the universities in 1960. Criticism of the denominational schools over the years led to the State taking over most of these schools in 1961 while a few large schools became private schools. The percentage of the GDP spent on education increased from 2.7 percent in 1950 to 4.6–5 percent in the late 1960s. Consequently, the number of schools increased from 4537 in 1945 to 8937 in 1963, and the number of students from 933,358 in 1946 to1.5 million in 1953 and 2.5 million in 1963. The percentage of co-educational schools was 77.6 percent in 1945 and 89.2 percent in 1963. The education participation rates of the age group 5–14 years rose from 57.3 percent in 1946 to 71.7 percent in 1953 and 76.7 percent for boys and 72.0 percent for girls in 1963. In fact, from 1946 to 1953 there was an increase of 12.8 percent in the population and of 40.1 percent in school enrolment. The most rapid increase took place in senior secondary grades where the number of students in Grades 9–10 increased fourfold from 69,233 in 1952 to 284,253 in 1965, and those in Grades 11–12 increased six fold from 5000 to 7000 in 1957 to 46,353 in 1965. By the end of the 1960s there were more girls than boys in Grades 9–12. While around 1500 students had appeared for the Senior Cambridge examination at the end of direct colonial rule, the numbers appearing for the local Senior School Certificate increased from 52,982 in 1952 to 222,532 in 1965. The number of candidates for the Higher School Certificate/Advanced Level Examination in Grade 12 increased from 2026 to 31,188 over the same period of time. The rapid expansion in educational opportunities within a relatively short period of time in a low-income country such as Sri Lanka was a very significant development.

Gender inequalities declined and were almost eliminated as a consequence of free education as there was no longer the need for parents to invest their resources only in the education of their sons. The percentage of girls of the total enrolment increased from 36 percent in 1931 to 46 percent in 1963. Similarly, enrolment in the universities increased from 902 at the time of the establishment of the university in 1942 to 14,210 in 1965, and the percentage of women students increased from 10.1 percent in 1942 to 40.3 percent in 1967. Research studies on the backgrounds of university students indicated that socio-economic inequalities also declined. The findings showed that the percentage of students from urban professional families had been 80 percent in 1950, but that by the end of the 1960s 70 percent of the university students were from the rural sector. The expansion of secondary schools was, however, uneven as only arts subjects were taught in Grades 11–12 in the newly upgraded secondary schools. As a result the percentage of arts students in universities also increased from 40 percent in 1942 to 70 percent by the end of the 1960s.[7] Attempts were made during these years to change the structure of the school system and the curriculum on the lines of the then social class-based selective secondary school system in England. In 1950–1951, plans to select and enroll students after a test at 14 years into either an academic secondary school or a practical secondary school were not successful. Again in 1966, the proposal to allocate students after a test at 14 years to four types of unequal secondary schools was rejected by Parliament as it was likely that poor students would find themselves in the last type of school, the local practical school. The curriculum continued to be textbook centered and examination oriented, and practical subjects were not popular as they did not help to get employment. The Central Schools offered practical subjects in the 1940s but parents wanted these schools to teach the same subjects as the larger English schools. Efforts were made to teach crafts in the 1950s and agriculture in the 1960s in as many schools as possible, but few students wanted to study these subjects in school.

Educational Policy and Practice in the Late 20th Century

From the late 1960s less attention was given to extending educational opportunities as unemployment had become a problem and "experts" from developed countries urged that education was an investment in people and should therefore be reorganized to meet employment needs, that is, it should meet the demands of the labor market. Until the mid-1960s education had assisted occupational advancement or upward mobility by increasing access to jobs in the expanding state administration and in the professions. However, from the late 1950s the prices of Sri Lanka's exports chiefly tea, rubber, and coconut, fell in the world market and economic growth slowed down, making it difficult to provide employment. Free health services had reduced the number of deaths since the mid-1940s, the population had increased rapidly in the 1950s and 1960s, and consequently, students coming out of schools and universities in the late 1960s were unsuccessful in getting jobs. Male and female unemployment rates that were 7.3 percent and 8.9 percent in 1963 rose to 14.3 percent for male unemployment and 31.1 percent for female unemployment in 1971. Ever since, unemployment has remained a major problem in Sri Lanka. The unemployment rates of women have been double those of men for around 35 years because although girls and women have equal access to education, they do not have equal opportunities in employment as do the boys and men. The highest unemployment rates have been among youth and among secondary school and university graduates so that education no longer provides easy access to employment. The state introduced two pre-vocational subjects in secondary schools in 1972 to help students get jobs when they left school but the scheme failed because there were not enough jobs. Vocational training programs in technical schools, training centers, and apprenticeship programs were not sufficient for school graduates and further, did not assist those who trained to get jobs.[8]

In the 1970s mathematics and general science were made compulsory subjects in secondary schools in addition to the study of the mother tongue, English, religion, social studies, art/music, and pre-vocational or technical subjects. A common curriculum, syllabi, and state textbooks were introduced but methods of teaching continued to encourage rote learning for examinations. As the placements in universities were limited and there were few other higher education institutions except in law, teacher education, and accountancy, an environment of steep competition was created at the General Certificate of Education/Advanced Level (GCE/AL) examination in Grade 12 for admission to universities and there was an increasing demand for private tuition. The Central Schools had been neglected after the 1960s, and as there were wide differences in the standards of schools, district quotas based on population were introduced in the 1970s to assist students from poorer districts to enter universities. However, little was done to extend schools with senior secondary grades and science streams. The new macro economic policies introduced at the end of the 1970s were market oriented and were less concerned with extending educational opportunities. The cost of living rose; income inequalities and poverty increased; and the expenditure on education declined to 2.2–2.5 percent in the 1980s and 1990s making it difficult to expand educational programs or to improve standards. The number of schools increased from around 9000 in the 1960s to only 9550 in the mid-1980s and has been nearly 10,000 since then.

The education participation rates of children in the 5–14 years age group increased to 83.7 percent for boys and 83.6 percent for girls in 1981, and to 88.3 percent and 87.9 percent respectively in 1991. In spite of the policy direction in the 1978 Constitution that everyone should have access to education, and in spite of free education for over 50 years and the provision of free textbooks since 1980, all children did not attend even primary schools as poor families could not afford the cost of items such as school stationery and shoes. Participation rates of the youth in the 15–19 years age group had increased from 11 percent in 1953 to 43 percent for boys and 36.6 percent for girls in 1963. But in 1981, participation rates had only increased to 41.2 percent for boys and 42.7 percent for girls. Non-formal literacy centers that had opened in 1980 for out-of-school children, did not receive much official support. In 1995, of the 132,582 students who appeared for the GCE/Advanced Level examination, 55,535 qualified for admission to universities but only 10,000 could find places, which resulted in much frustration.

From the beginning of the 1990s there was again an interest in extending educational opportunities partly because there was also international concern. Sri Lanka ratified the U.N. Convention on the Rights of the Child in 1990 and accepted the goal of Education for All promoted by the U.N. in 1990. A National Plan of Action for Children was developed in 1991. Materials were distributed for school uniforms from 1993 and midday meals were provided to children in need. A National Education Commission was appointed in 1991 and education reforms are being implemented to extend educational opportunity by enforcing compulsory education regulations for the 5–14 years age group from 1998, revive the policy of Central Schools by attempting to develop at least one well equipped school in each Division, introduce curricular reforms in primary and secondary grades, as well as in teacher education institutions and universities, improve management in schools, and meet employment needs.[9]

The impact of educational developments in the post-colonial years is seen in the rise in literacy rates and the increase in the educational levels of the population. Literacy rates rose from 76.5 percent male literacy and 46.2 percent female literacy in 1946 to 85.6 percent and 67.1 percent in 1963; to 90.5 percent and 82.8 percent in 1981; and to 90.2 percent and 83.1 percent in 1991. The percentage of the population that never went to school declined from 41.6 percent in 1953 to 13.3 percent males and 29.2 percent females in 1963; to 8.7 percent and 17.5 percent in 1981; and to 6.1 percent and 11.3 percent in 1991. The percentage of the population who had GCE/OL qualifications were 5.5 percent men and 4.5 percent women in 1963, and 14.3 percent men and 14.9 percent women in 1994. Those with GCE/AL qualifications had increased from 0.9 percent men and 0.7 percent women to 4.9 percent men and 5.8 percent women from 1963 to 1994.

Educational developments suffered not only because of a lack of resources and the poverty levels of a section of the population, but also as a result of the youth unrest of 1971 and 1987–1989 that was the result of the lack of jobs and the frustration of youth, as well as the ethnic conflict between the Sinhalese and the Tamils which increased after Sinhala was made the official language in 1956. In the late 1980s, both Sinhala and Tamil were accepted as official languages and English as a compulsory second language. But the ethnic conflict developed into a war from 1983, and although a ceasefire was declared in 2002 the ethnic problem has yet to be resolved. The areas affected by the armed conflict in the northern and eastern Provinces of Sri Lanka, and in the neighboring North Central, Uva and North Western Provinces have resulted in loss of life, displacement of families, damage to schools, and loss of schooling for children. Subsequently, rehabilitation programs have been organized to restore school buildings, bring children back into schools, and to support families that have been affected by armed conflict.

THE PRESENT

Schooling in Sri Lanka today is a different experience from that of even a century ago in the country's long history. More children go to school even from disadvantaged families than in many other economically developing countries, even though there are differences in the quality of the schooling available to them. Many Sri Lankan children are beginning to have access to the ever-widening horizons of information technology. With an average economic growth rate of around only 5 percent in the 1990s and at the commencement of the new millennium; with at least 25 percent of the population living in poverty; with an on-going ethnic conflict that has yet to be resolved; and most importantly, with an educational expenditure of only around 3 percent of GDP and 8–10 percent of the national budget; there are several short-comings and challenges that current educational reforms face and are expected to address.

Provision of Education

A little less than four million children currently attend about 10,000 schools teaching in Sinhalese or Tamil, according to the ethnic proportions of the local populations. Among these schools 96.6 percent are co-educational schools and the small number of single sex schools are generally situated in the larger towns. Many of these schools are the well-known schools that had been established during the colonial period. Private schools number less than 3 percent of the total number of schools and are in the major towns. A number of *pirivenas*, a legacy of the ancient period, hold regular classes for older students. Plantation schools began to offer better educational facilities after they were absorbed into the national system two decades ago. The few schools for children with dis-abilities are not sufficient to provide education for children who cannot attend regular schools. Since the 1980s, international schools in the English medium have increased in number but are registered as companies because the Educa-tion Ordinance prohibits the opening of new private schools for the 5–14 years age group.

The state school system has four types of schools: (1) Type I AB schools (6.4 percent in 2004) have Grades 1–13, and offer science education in Grades 12–13 (GCE/AL grades); (2) Type I C schools (18.1 percent) also have Grades 1–13 but do not have a science stream in Grades 12–13; (3) Type II schools (43.8 percent) have only Grades 1–11 up to the General Certificate in Education/Ordinary Level (GCE/OL); (4) Type III schools (31.7 percent) are primary schools with a few schools having Grades 1–8/9. Hence, only around 6 percent of the schools (the Type I AB Schools) offer a comprehensive secondary school curriculum that includes senior secondary science educa-tion which is an avenue to remunerative employment in a technologically advancing global environment. These schools are found mainly in towns and their distribution across the island of Sri Lanka is unequal as 36.8 percent of the schools in the Western Province in which the capital Colombo is located are the IAB schools, whereas only 3.3 percent of the schools in the North Central Province and 4.7 percent of the schools in the Uva Province belong to this category of schools. Many of the Type III schools are small and ill-equipped, often in poor or remote communities. Moreover, 29.4 percent of all schools have a hundred or less students while 0.4 percent of the schools which are the most prestigious and popular in the country, have 3500 to over 5000 students.[10]

There were 187,338 teachers in 2004 of whom over 90 percent have received some professional training and 69.3 percent are women. The distribution of teachers is also unequal as schools in difficult or remote areas and small schools do not have well qualified teachers. Despite the provision of free education and many other incentives such as free textbooks in Grade 11, scholarships particularly at Grade 5 level on the basis of a competitive examination, uniforms, midday meals to needy children, and subsidized transport, the relationship between the socio-economic background of students, the quality of the school facilities, and the educational attainment of students is a predictable relationship as that seen in many other countries.

Participation in Education

It is estimated that around 5 percent of the school age population does not enter the school system and that the educational participation rates of the 5–14 years age group are now 95 percent for both girls and boys. Participation rates of the 15–19 years age group are between 55 percent for boys and 60 percent for girls. In 2001, retention rates at the end of primary education were 96.9 percent for boys and 98.3 percent for girls, and retention rates at the end of junior secondary education were 79.1 percent for boys and 86.3 percent for girls. Further, in 2004 the percentage of girls in the total enrolment of Grades 1–5 was 49.1 percent; in Grades 6–9 the enrolment of girls was 50.2 percent; in Grades 9–11 the enrolment was 50.7 percent; in Grades 12–13 the enrol-ment was 56.5 percent. This pattern of more girls in secondary grades has continued for 40 years. More girls than boys are enrolled in secondary grades because boys tend to drop out more readily from schools as they have a better chance of employment than girls during school years. In 2000 dropout rates in primary grades were 0.8 percent for boys and 0.5 percent for girls, and in Grades 1–10, the dropout rates were 3.1 percent for boys and 2.2 percent for girls. Dropping out from schools in Sri Lanka is concentrated chiefly in low-income urban neighborhoods, remote and/or very poor villages, plantations, and areas that have been affected by armed violence. Non-formal centers for out-of-school children presently meet the needs of only around 5 percent of such children. If the compulsory education regulations were to be implemented effectively it would be possible to bring children belonging to vulnerable groups such as working children, children with disabilities, and children living on the streets in major towns, into schools and toward achieving at least universal primary education, a goal which has been envisioned but has yet to be realized. Children living in areas affected by armed ethnic conflict for over two decades, and in the coastal areas in the east, south, and north devastated by the tsunami in December 2004, have suffered from lack of access to education as schools have been destroyed and teachers and the families of the children have been displaced. Education facilities need to be improved further in these areas for all children to be able to benefit from education. Pre-school education has never received the attention it deserves but the percentage of children in the 3–5 years age group in pre-schools has increased from 20 percent in the 1980s to 60 percent. The quality of care and education offered in many of these pre-schools has been found to be in need of considerable improvement.

Schools have a common curriculum in Grades 1–9 and the primary school curriculum at least is activity based. In addition to the core curriculum in Grades 10–11 which consists of the mother tongue; English, mathematics, science, social sciences, and religion, there are options in aesthetic and technical subjects for the GCE/OL examination. Information Technology (IT) is now a subject that is offered at the GCE/AL examination level, and a large number of schools have been provided with computers. Students opt for three subjects in the GCE/AL examination and appear for a Common General Test for university admission. The GCE/AL qualification is necessary also to enter all tertiary education institutions such as Law College, Teacher Education institutions, Advanced Technical Institutes, Accountancy, Management, and IT courses.

Achievement levels in schools vary according to the quality of schooling and according to district based socio-economic differences as seen in the wide gap in performance levels between Colombo district and the most disadvantaged district, Moneragala. The curriculum and teaching methods in schools have still to change sufficiently to promote creative learning, personality development, ethical values, and national harmony in a multi-ethnic country.

There are hardly any gender differences in achievement between girls and boysfrom Grade 1 to university level. However, as a result of stereotypes or images of socially acceptable gender roles, girls tend to choose "feminine" practical subjects and arts as seen in the fact that two-thirds of those enrolled in Grades 12–13 are girls, and more boys than girls opt for science and technical subjects in schools, universities, and vocational training institutions. Schools and universities have made no efforts to promote the idea of gender equality in the minds and attitudes of boys and girls or to question social practices that discriminate against women. Post-secondary educational opportunities are insufficient to meet the needs of secondary school graduates. There are 15 universities including the Open University. In 2004–2005 there were nearly 75,000 students of whom 54 percent were women. Women students totaled about

70 percent in the faculties of Arts, Law, and Architecture, but were limited in number in the Engineering and Applied Science faculties. Networks of technical and vocational educational institutions are found throughout the island: technical colleges, centers of the Vocational Training Authority, the National Apprenticeship and Industrial Training Authority, and the National Youth Services Council. But these have not been much of a help for school graduates to find jobs. Very few agricultural institutions/centers exist in this country considering the large number of people still employed in the agricultural sector. The majority of female students are enrolled in traditional women's courses such as dressmaking and secretarial work while the majority of trainees in technical programs are men.[11]

Education and Society

While unemployment has declined in recent years to under 10 percent after 2000, female unemployment rates are still double those of men as girls and women have acquired few vocational skills that are in demand by employers. Education is required for high level employment but does not necessarily assure jobs as the highest unemployment is among those with secondary and post-secondary educational qualifications, and the lowest unemployment is among those with very little formal education as in the plantations. In 2004, the unemployment rates of those with GCE/OL qualifications were 9.4 percent for men and 23 percent for women, and those with GCE/AL qualifications and higher education were 11.9 percent for men and 23.8 percent for women.

The extension of educational opportunities over the post-colonial years has resulted in relatively high literacy rates with 92.3 percent for males and 89.2 percent for females in 2001, and 94.5 percent male literacy and 90.6 percent female literacy in 2003–2004. Urban/rural and gender differences hardly exist except among the population of over 50 years of age which was the school-going generation before free education was introduced. The percentage of those who never went to school declined to 5.8 percent of the men and 9.7 percent of the women in 2003.

Some of the benefits of the spread of schooling and literacy have been the wide use by families of health services resulting in the decline in death rates of infants, children, and adults; increased longevity; and decline in the size of families and in the population growth rate to 1.2 percent. Although schooling has extended the horizons of knowledge; improved living conditions, and reduced social, ethnic, and gender inequalities, it has not been able to eliminate poverty or to substantially change negative social attitudes. Educational policies have been successful in providing access to education for the majority of the population. The failure of economic policies has prevented many products of the schools and other educational institutions from getting the maximum benefits from education.

VOICES AND VIGNETTES: A DAY IN THE LIFE OF ...

Harshini's Story

Harshini is a relatively affluent Colombo-based child with a wide range of opportunities and sophisticated interests.

On the days that I have activities in school in the morning I wake up at around 5:30 A.M. I wake up this early as I travel to school by bus. On Monday, Wednesday, and Friday I have tennis from 6:45 A.M. to 8:00 A.M. On Tuesday and sometimes on Thursday I have choir practices. It is held from 7:00 to 8:00 A.M. If I don't have any activities in the morning I sleep till about 6.00 A.M. On most days I have extra curricular activities after school. On Monday I have tennis from 2:15 to 4:15 P.M. at school. After that I go home and go for swimming from 5:45 to 6:30 P.M. On Tuesday I have guiding from 2:30 to 4:30 P.M. and elocution from 5:00 to 6:00 P.M. On Wednesday I have tennis from 2:15 to 4:15 P.M. and ballet from 6:15 till about 8:00 P.M. This is a long lesson but I really enjoy it. On Thursday I come home straight after school and do my school work. I then go for tennis from 6:00 to 7:00 P.M. If possible, on Friday I go for swimming from 3:15 to 4:15 P.M. and then for ballet at 6:15 P.M. On Saturday I get up at 7:00 A.M. and go for a computer lesson from 8:30 to 9:30 A.M. On two Saturdays of the month I have choir practices from 10:30 A.M. to 12:30 P.M. and on the other two Saturdays ballet and modern dance lessons from 11:15 A.M. to 2:30 P.M. On Sundays I am free to do as I please. On weekdays I go to bed around 10:30 P.M. after doing my homework.

Malinga's Story

Malinga is a child whose parents commute to Colombo for work from the adjoining district so that child care arrangements need to be made for after school hours till the parents return in the evening. This is a commonly seen situation:

I live in Dodamgoda. I have an older sister and a baby sister. I am studying at Mathugama Ananda Shastralaya, in Grade 6. My class teacher, Leela, is very kind and she loves us. My elder sister is studying at the C.W.W. Kannangara M.M.V. and she is in Grade 7. My father is working in a Colombo Office and my mother, Ayanthi, too is working in a Colombo office as a draftsman. After school from 2:00 P.M. till my parents return from work in the evening we stay with our grandmother. I like to play cricket and to play with my little sister when I am free. At home I also help my mother to hang clothes on the line when she washes them and bring back the dried clothes into the house. I help her in household chores. While my mother is cooking I look after my little sister.

Kaushalya's Story

Kaushalya is a bright child from a low-income rural family with a father who is temporarily employed. Based on her high academic performance, she has won a scholarship to a big school but she lives in a relatively economically disadvantaged home. She is an example of the beneficiaries of the free education policy:

I am studying in Grade 9 in a leading school in Colombo. At the scholarship examination in 2001, I was able to score 165 marks. I am continuing my studies with great difficulty as my father does not have permanent employment. I travel to school from Kalutara. My mother wakes up around 3:00 A.M. in the morning, prepares breakfast and lunch, and attends to other household chores. She accompanies me to school to protect me from harm. After school I help my mother in household tasks like cleaning the garden and house, and scraping coconut. I am compelled to do school homework in the evening since we do not have electricity and I cannot work at night. My ambition is to be a doctor

Table 9.1
Timeline of Educational Milestones in Sri Lanka's History

Date	Event	Period
3rd century B.C.	Establishment of the first *Pirivena*	Ancient & Medieval Sri Lanka
17th century A.D.	Dutch Scholarchal Commission	Early Modern Years
A.D. 1800	First English School	British Colonial Administration
1812–1818	First Christian missionary schools	
1832	First School Commission	
1835	Establishment of Colombo Academy (Royal College)	
1843	State Central and Female Superior Schools	
1850s–1890s	Revival of Buddhist and Hindu systems	
1867	Department of Public Instruction Later Department of Education	
1870	Colombo Medical College	
1876	Law College	
1881	Introduction of Cambridge School Certificate Examinations	
1881–1902	Establishment of teacher training institutions	
1921	University College, Colombo	
1931	Universal franchise	State Council Administration
1939	Education Ordinance	
1940–1947	Establishment of Central Schools	
1942	First Local University	
1943	Local Secondary School Examinations	
1945	Free Education: Grade 5 scholarships Mother tongue medium-primary grades	
1947	Religion compulsory in state schools	
1948	Ministry of Education	Independence
1953–1959	Mother tongue medium: Secondary grades	
1960	Mother tongue medium: university arts courses	
1961	State take-over of denominational schools	
1972	Education reforms	

(continued)

Table 9.1 Continued

Date	Event	Period
1980	Free textbooks for Grades 1–11	
1990	Ratification of the UN Convention on the Rights of the Child: Education for All	
1993	Free uniform materials	
1997	Education reforms introduced: Primary–University	
1998	Compulsory education regulations: 5–14 years	
2003	Proposals for education reforms	
2004–2005	On-going education reforms	

NOTES

1. Paranavitane, S. and Ray, H. (1959) *The University History of Ceylon to 1500. Parts I and II.* Colombo: Ceylon University Press.

2. Perera, S. G. (1916–1917) "The Jesuits in Ceylon in the 16th and 17th Centuries." *The Ceylon Antiquary and Literary Register*, 1(4): 217–226.

3. Palm, J. D. (1846–1847) "The Educational Establishments of the Dutch." *Journal of the Royal Asiatic Society (Ceylon Branch)*, 1(2): 105–137.

4. Jayaweera, Swarna (1969) "British Educational Policy in Ceylon." *Pedagogica Historica. International Journal of the History of Education*, IX(1): 68–90. Gent, Blandijnberg.

5. Jayasuriya, J. E. (1969) *Education in Ceylon Before and After Independence.* Colombo: Associated Educational Publishers.

6. Jayaweera, Swarna (1998) "Education in Sri Lanka—Fifty Years since Independence." In A.D.V. de S. Indraratne (Ed.) *Fifty Years of Independence: A Socio-economic Review.* Colombo: Sri Lanka Association of Social and Economic Studies, 311–341.

7. Ibid.

8. Asian Development Bank (1989) *Education and Training in Sri Lanka.* Vol. 1. New Delhi: Educational Consultants India Limited.

9. See note 6.

10. Alailima, Patricia J. (1992) "Education–Employment Linkages." *Sri Lanka Journal of the Social Sciences*, 15: 1–46.

11. See note 6.

BIBLIOGRAPHY

Ancient and Medieval Periods

Ariyapala, M. B. (1956) *Society in Mediaeval Ceylon.* Colombo: Department of Cultural Affairs, pp. 269–280.

Geiger, William (1950) *Mahavamsa* Chapters X and XVII, Translation. Colombo: Government Information Department.

Rahula,Walpola (1974) *The Heritage of the Bhikkhu: A Short History of the Bhikkhu in Educational, Cultural, Social and Political Life*. New York: Grove Press.

Wijesekera, N. de S. (1949) *The People of Ceylon*. Colombo: M.D. Gunasena.

The Early Modern Years

Anthonisz, R. G. (1907) *Report on the Dutch Records in the Government Archives*. Colombo: Government Press.

Peries, P. E. (1914) *The Portuguese Era*. Vol. II Ch. VI. Colombo: Apothecaries Ltd.

Queyros, F. D. (1971) *The Temporal and Spiritual Conquest of Ceylon*. Translated by Perera, S. G. New York: AMS Press.

Reimers, E. (1927) *Translations of Selections from the Dutch Records of the Ceylon Government*. Colombo: Government Press.

Ribeyro, J. (1846) *History of Ceylon, 1685*. Translation from the French Edition by Lee, George. Colombo: Government Press.

British Colonial Administration

American Ceylon Mission (1849) *Brief Sketch of the American Ceylon Mission*. Jaffna: American mission Press.

Gratiaen, L. J. (1926) *The Founding of the Mission Schools*. Colombo: Ceylon Historical Association. Paper No. 9.

Gratiaen, L. J. (1927) *The Story of Our Schools, The First School Commission, 1832–1841*, Colombo: Ceylon Historical Association. Paper No. 11.

Gratiaen, L. J. (1931) *The Colombo Academy under Marsh and Boake*. Colombo: Ceylon Historical Association. Paper No. 17.

Gratiaen, L. J. (1922) "The First English School in Ceylon." *Ceylon Antiquary and Literary Register*. VII: 141–147.

Jayaweera, Swarna (1990) "Colonial Educational Policy and Gender Ideology under the British Colonial Administration." in K. M. de Silva, Sirima, Kiribamune, and C. R. de Silva (Eds) *Asian Panorama*. New Delhi: Vikas Publishing House, 210–227.

Jayaweera, Swarna (2001) "Education of Girls and Women in Sri Lanka—Past and Present." In *Education and Empowerment, Women in South Asia*. Calcutta: Bethune School Prakatni Samiti, 8–28.

Selkirk, J. (1844) *Recollections of Ceylon*. London.

Wyndham, H. A. (1933) *Native Education*. London: O.U.P.

Post-colonial Years, Independence to the Present

Alailima, Patricia. J. (1997) "Social Policy in Sri Lanka." In W. D. Lakshman (Ed.) *Dilemmas of Development*. Colombo: Sri Lanka Association of Economists, 127–170.

Gunawardene, Chandra and Jayaweera, Swarna (2004) *National Survey on Schooling and Absenteeism*. Colombo: UK Save the Children.

Jayaweera, Swarna (1984) "Access to University Education—The Social Composition of University Entrants." *University of Colombo Review*, 1(4): 6–40.

Jayaweera, Swarna (1988) *Educational Policies and Change from the Mid Twentieth Century to 1977*. Occasional Papers No. 2. Maharagama: National Institute of Education.

Jayaweera, Swarna (1993) "Education and Socialisation." In *Shadows and Vistas*. Colombo: Centre for Women's Research, 148–182.

Jayaweera, Swarna (2002) "Women in Education and Employment—Fifty Years in Retrospect." In Jayaweera, Swarna (Ed.) *Women in Post Independence Sri Lanka*. New Delhi: Sage Publications, 91–142.

Jayaweera, Swarna (2004) "Education and Human Development." In A.D.V. de S. Indraratne (Ed.) *Human Development in a Knowledge Based Society: Sri Lankan Scene*. Colombo: Sri Lanka Economics Association, 93–122.

Lakshman, W. D. (1997) "Introduction." In *Dilemmas of Development*. Colombo: Sri Lanka Association of Economists, 1–27.

Little, Angela. W. (ed.) (2000) *Primary Education Reforms in Sri Lanka*. Colombo: Ministry of Education.

Ministry of Education (1997) General Education Reforms.

National Education Commission (2003) Envisioning Education for Human Development.

Nystrom, K. (1985) *Schooling and Disparities. A Study of Regional Differences*. Stockholm, Sweden: University of Stockholm.

Report of the Central School Commission (1842).

Strauss, Murray (1951) "Family Characteristics and Occupational Choice of University Entrants." *University of Ceylon Review*, 9(2): 125–135.

Uswatte Arachchi, G. (1974) "University Admissions in Ceylon. Their Economic and Social Background and Employment Expectations." *Modern Asian Studies*, 8 (4): 6–40.

Wijetunge, Swarna and Wickramaratne, Vineetha (2003) *National Study on Child Care Provision in Pre Schools in Sri Lanka*. Colombo: UNICEF.

World Bank (2004) *Treasures of the Education System in Sri Lanka: Restoring Performance, Expanding Opportunities, Enhancing Prospects*. Colombo: World Bank Office.

BIBLIOGRAPHY

BOOKS

Altbach, P. G., Saldanha, D., and Weiler, J. (1987). *Education in South Asia*. New Delhi, India: Vistaar Publications.

Bose, S. and Jalal, A. (1998). *Modern South Asia: History, Culture, Political Economy*. U.K.: Routledge.

Breton, R. (1997). *Atlas of the Languages and Ethnic Communities of South Asia*. Walnut Creek, CA: AltaMira Press.

Chandra, R. (2003). *Encyclopaedia of Education in South Asia*. India: Kalpaz Publications.

Crook, N. (1996). *The Transmission of Knowledge in South Asia: Essays on Education, Religion, History, and Politics*. Delhi, India: Oxford University Press.

Kabeer, N., Nambissan, G.B., and Subrahmanian, R. (Eds) (2003). *Child Labour and the Right to Education in South Asia: Needs versus Rights?* New Delhi, India: Sage Publications.

Kohli, A. (Ed) (2001). *The Success of India's Democracy*. Cambridge, U.K.: Cambridge University Press.

Mahbub ul Haq (2002). *Human Development in South Asia 2001: Globalization and Human Development*. New York: Oxford University Press.

Mujtaba, S. A. (2005). *Soundings on South Asia*. New Delhi, India: New Dawn Press.

Robinson, F. (2000). *Islam and Muslim History in South Asia*. New Delhi, India: Oxford University Press.

Shapiro, M. and Schiffman, H. (1981). *Language and Society in South Asia*. Delhi, India: Motilal Banarsidass.

OTHER RESOURCES

Human Rights Education in Asian Schools, Vol. 2 available at http://www.hrea.org/erc/Library/curriculum_methodology/HRE-in-Asia2/chapter2-3.html.

One World South Asia available at   http://southasia.oneworld.net/article/
frontpage/158/1792.

South Asia available at www.aasianst.org.

South Asia Documents available at http://indowindow.virtualstack.com/sad/.

South Asia Network South Asia Network is a Directory of Science and Technology,
Environment and Livelihood Education Organizations/Experts in Five South
Asian Countries (Bangladesh, Bhutan, India, Nepal, and Sri Lanka).

South Asia Research Institute for Development available at www.sarid.net.

The South Asian available at http://www.thesouthasian.org/archives/2004/
education_in_south_asia.html.

South Asian Books found at: www.easternbookcorporation.com and www.
southasiabooks.com.

South Asian Women's organization listed at www.sawnet.org.

2005 and Beyond: Accelerating Girls' Education in South Asia (UNICEF) available at
American Forum for Global Education available at http://www.teachingsouthasia.
org/Eldis available at http://www.eldis.org/southasia/index.htm.

UNICEF Report of a conference, http://www.ungei.org/resources/files/
unicef_rosareport_28_03_full.pdf.

The World Bank Report on Child Labor in South Asia available at http://lnweb18.
worldbank.org/sar/sa.nsf.

Also look up centers and institutes for South Asian Studies at various universities such
as Columbia University, Harvard University, University of Pennsylvania, Berkeley,
University of Toronto, and so forth.

INDEX

ABOUT THE EDITOR AND CONTRIBUTORS

EDITOR

Dr. Amita Gupta is currently Assistant Professor of Education in the School of Education at The City College of New York. She is a native of New Delhi, India, and has earned her Doctorate from Teachers College, Columbia University. The early education of children and the preparation of their teachers has been at the core of her inquiry both in her field-based professional experience as well as in her academic research over the last 18 years. Amita Gupta has extensive cross-cultural experience in classroom teaching, school administration, and teacher development in both India and the United States. She continues to offer professional development workshops for teachers and school administrators in both countries. Her research interests include cross-cultural and culturally relevant pedagogy; international and comparative education; postcolonial theory; socio-cultural-historical constructivism in teaching and learning; and the place of implicit beliefs and practical knowledge in the pedagogical practices of teachers from "non-western" backgrounds. Amita Gupta has published several articles in journals of education, and is the sole author of a book published by Palgrave Macmillan in 2006. This book is based on her doctoral research which won the National Association of Early Childhood Teacher Educators/Merril Prentice Hall Award for Outstanding Doctoral Dissertation in 2003. Currently, Dr. Gupta is also serving as Vice-President of the New York State Association of Early Childhood Teacher Educators (NYS-AECTE).

CONTRIBUTORS

Sajid Ali is currently a Senior Instructor at the Aga Khan University, Institute for Educational Development (AKU-IED). His responsibilities include teaching

Pedagogical Leadership, Effective Leadership and Management course in the Master's program. He also coordinates the Education Sector Reform Assistance (ESRA) research program at AKU-IED. The program includes four research studies on different themes related to current education reform and decentralization in Pakistan. Sajid has extensive experience of doing research in the areas of community education, impact evaluation, educational change, and citizenship and human rights education. Prior to joining AKU-IED, Sajid was a lecturer at Hamdard Institute of Management Sciences, Hamdard University. Sajid has also been a visiting faculty member at the Department of Sociology, University of Karachi. In 2003 he was honored with the Commonwealth Youth Leadership Award for Pakistan. Sajid has an M.Ed. in Leadership, Policy, and Change from Monash University, Australia. His current research interests include education policy studies particularly issues related to policy implementation, problems of planning, and role of values in policy; educational leadership, management and governance; educational change and reform; globalization and education policy; individual and organizational learning; and knowledge creation and management.

Dr. Sajeda Amin is a Senior Associate in the Policy Research Division of the Population Council. She works on a range of issues related to gender, work, poverty, and family in the developing world. She is currently involved in a multi-country study on adolescent livelihoods with a particular focus on emerging opportunities for young women in the formal sector. She has collaborated on a project on cultural theories of fertility decline in Bengal and has worked on population processes in the context of poverty. Prior to her current position at the Population Council, Sajeda Amin was a Research Fellow at the Bangladesh Institute of Development Studies in Dhaka, Bangladesh. She received her Doctorate in Demography and Sociology from Princeton University in 1988. She has published a number of articles and papers in her field.

Tenzin Chhoeda has a Masters degree in Education from the University of London. He has worked in the Education Ministry in Bhutan from 1984 to 2003 in educational planning. He is currently the Director of the Department of Information Technology under the Ministry of Information and Communications in Thimphu.

Dr. Iffat Farah is a Professor at the Aga Khan University, Institute for Educational Development (AKU-IED), Karachi, Pakistan. She obtained a Masters degree in Applied Linguistics from the University of Kent in the United Kingdom and a Doctorate in Education from the University of Pennsylvania in the United States. She has 20 years experience of teaching at various universities. Dr. Farah has conducted large-scale national studies in the area of school improvement and reform, community management and finance of schools in Pakistan, girls' schooling in Pakistan, and literacy policy and practices in Pakistan. She teaches courses in school improvement and educational reform in developing countries, and education and development. She has been a consultant on educational research with several international organizations including UNESCO and the World Bank. In addition to publishing several papers, book chapters and research reports, Dr. Farah has co-edited two books.

Dr. Swarna Jayaweera has a Masters and Doctorate from the University of London and was a post-doctoral Fellow at Columbia University, New York. She also has a Hon. D.Litt degree from the University of Colombo and the Open University of Sri Lanka. She taught in the Universities of Peradeniya and Colombo and was Professor of Education and Head of the Department of Social Science Education of the University of Colombo. She was also UNESCO Advisor and UNICEF Consultant on the Access of Women to Education in Nepal and has been a consultant to U.N. agencies and bilateral agencies in Sri Lanka and in the Asian Region, on Education and on Women's Issues. She is one of the founders and Joint Coordinators of the Centre for Women's Research (CENWOR), Sri Lanka. She has contributed extensively to books and to local and to international journals on women and on education. Currently, she is Emeritus Professor of Education, University of Colombo and a Fellow of the National Academy of Science and is a Research Fellow of the Faculty of Graduate Studies of the University of Colombo.

Dr. Mohamed Latheef is currently the Maldives Representative to U.N. in New York, and Ambassador to the Unites States. Previously he held the post of Minister of Education in Maldives, in addition to several other key public governmental positions such as Deputy Minister of Atolls Administration, Director General of Maldives Centre for Management and Administration, National Director of UNDP/ILO project for Public Administration Reform, and Director of Educational Development Centre. Dr. Latheef has a Masters in Education and a Doctorate in Educational Planning from the University of Wales.

Dr. Tara Niraula is an educator with over 20 years of experience in education research and policy development. He has served in a number of positions such as Administrator of the Save the Children Fund, Education Program Officer of the Swiss development Cooperation/Nepal, Director of Newcomer Education Policy with the New York Immigration Coalition, Education Researcher and consultant with Fordham University, and adjunct graduate faculty at Teachers College, Columbia University. He has also served twice as a member of the Nepal's National delegation to the UNICEF's Annual Executive Board meetings. As a student leader, he also served on the Board of the Trustees of the Teachers College as well as on the Columbia University Senate. Dr. Niraula holds a Masters and a Doctorate in Educational Administration from Teachers College, Columbia University. His particular interests are focused on teaching and research in international education development, educational administration, policy and reform, and leadership development. Until recently, Dr. Niraula served as Senior Research Scholar and Director of Education Schools Research Project at Teachers College, Columbia University. Currently, Dr. Niraula works as an education consultant to national and international groups. He is also the President of the America–Nepal Friendship Society, Inc.

Roozbeh Shirazi received a B.A. degree from the University of Wisconsin-Madison and his M.A. from Teachers College, Columbia University. During his M.A. program, Roozbeh won the distinguished 2004–2005 Elihu Rose Fellowship for his work on the Teachers College, Columbia University Afghanistan Project. Roozbeh is currently a Ph.D. student in Comparative International Education at Teachers College, Columbia University. His area of interest is education in the Middle East focusing on discourses of democratization and political identity among secondary students in Egypt and Jordon.